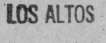

HORSES DON'T FLY

HORSES DON'T FLY

★

FREDERICK LIBBY

Introduction and Notes by
Winston Groom

Afterword by
Sally Ann Marsh

ARCADE PUBLISHING ★ NEW YORK

FIRST EDITION

Library of Congress Cataloging-in-Publication Data

Libby, Frederick, 1892–1970.
   Horses don't fly / by Frederick Libby ; introduction and notes by Winston Groom ; afterword by Sally Ann Marsh.
      p. cm.
   ISBN 1-55970-526-4
   1. World War, 1914–1918 — Personal narratives, American. 2. Fighter pilots — United States — Biography. 3. World War, 1914–1918 — Aerial operations, British. 4. Libby, Frederick, 1892–1970. 5. Great Britian. Royal Flying Corps — History. 6. World War, 1914–1918 — Aerial operations, American. 7. World War, 1914-1918 — Campaigns — France. I. Title.

D606.L53   2000
940.4'4'092—dc21
[B]   00-26659

Published in the United States by Arcade Publishing, Inc., New York
Distributed by Time Warner Trade Publishing

Visit our Web site at www.arcadepub.com

10 9 8 7 6 5 4 3 2 1

Designed by API

EB

PRINTED IN THE UNITED STATES OF AMERICA

In Flanders Fields

In Flanders fields the poppies blow
Between the crosses, row on row,
That mark our place; and in the sky
The larks, still bravely singing, fly
Scarce heard amid the guns below.

We are the Dead. Short days ago
We lived, felt dawn, saw sunset glow,
Loved and were loved, and now we lie
In Flanders fields.

Take up our quarrel with the foe:
To you from failing hands we throw
The torch; be yours to hold it high.
If ye break faith with us who die
We shall not sleep, though poppies grow
In Flanders fields.

John McCrae

CONTENTS·

Introduction

E VERY SO OFTEN AN UNDISCOVERED MANUSCRIPT WILL TURN UP that gives delight to the reader-historian. Such is certainly the case with *Horses Don't Fly*, Frederick Libby's fascinating memoir of his early life, growing up on a western ranch, turning into a first-rate cowboy, and finally becoming an ace aviator in World War I with the Royal Flying Corps.

In self-effacing, utterly charming prose, Libby tells a straight-forward story of being raised by his father and relatives after the death of his mother when he was four. He was born in 1892 in a small town on the Platte River in the Platte Valley of Colorado. Those were the last years of the Old West, and Libby's vivid descriptions of it evoke the tones of Mark Twain's *Huckleberry Finn*. He got into the usual boyhood "trouble," fights, pranks, screw-ups, but from the time he was able to sit in the saddle it was apparent Frederick Libby was going to be one of the finest horsemen in the country. As a teenager his travels took him on the ranges, from Mexico to Arizona to the plains of Colorado where he spent an entire winter trapped alone in a tiny sod hut while one of the great blizzards in weather history killed thousands of cattle around him.

After that experience it was his passionate dream to go to Tahiti, but he never made it. He and a friend traveled to the Pacific Coast and worked their way northward until they found themselves in Calgary, Alberta, just as the First World War broke out. At the age of twenty-two he enlisted in the Canadian army, and was trained as a truck driver before shipping out to France and the pitiless fighting on the Western Front. Soon he discovered that the British Royal Flying Corps was looking for "observers" to fly in their primitive two-seater fighter planes. An observer, in their parlance, was actually a machine gunner, and, his first day in the air and second time firing a machine gun, Libby downed a German plane. He was soon commissioned an officer and not long afterward was made a pilot. Captain Libby quickly distinguished himself and was ultimately decorated with the Military Cross by the king of England at Buckingham Palace, a rare honor indeed, especially for an American. With delightful insight, Libby captures the panorama of the war years, the battles in the air, life in London on leave, the loss of friends, and his triumphant return to America where his tattered American flag streamers were auctioned off at Carnegie Hall before a crowd of thousands for a staggering sum at a Liberty Loan drive.

What is so striking about this story is that, despite Libby's persistent understatement of his own achievements, he was the real thing; every piece of the tale squares with the record, including his being officially credited with shooting down fourteen German airplanes, and by some accounts twenty-four, ten as an observer and fourteen as a pilot. *Horses Don't Fly* is not only an important piece of previously unpublished history, it is a gripping and uplifting story to read.

Winston Groom

Preface

A<small>FTER MUCH PERSUASION</small> by my friends, I have written this book, covering the first twenty-six years of my life. *Horses Don't Fly* is in no way fiction. The things recorded here are events that happened during that period of time and are noted down from memory in the sequence in which they occurred. The book is written from my heart. All events are true and described to the best of my ability and memory as to time and place. My sincere wish is that those who read these pages will enjoy them as much as I did in the writing.

Captain Frederick Libby, M. C.

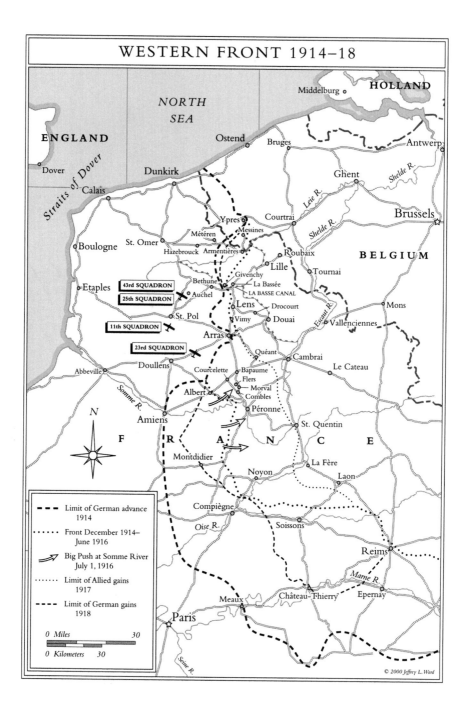

WESTERN FRONT 1914–18

HOLLAND

Middelburg

NORTH
SEA

ENGLAND

Dover

Straits of Dover

Ostend

Bruges

Ghent

Shelde R.

Antwerp

Dunkirk

Calais

Brussels

Boulogne

St. Omer

Ypres

Météren

Messines

Courtrai

Leie R.

Shelde R.

BELGIUM

Hazebrouck

Armentières

Roubaix

Lille

Tournai

43rd SQUADRON

Bethune

Givenchy

La Bassée

LA BASSE CANAL

Mons

25th SQUADRON

Auchel

Etaples

St. Pol

Lens

Drocourt

Escaut R.

Vallenciennes

11th SQUADRON

Vimy

Douai

Arras

23rd SQUADRON

Abbeville

Doullens

Courcelette

Quéant

Cambrai

Le Cateau

Somme R.

Albert

Bapaume

Flers

Morval

Combles

Péronne

Amiens

St. Quentin

N

F   R   A   N   C   E

Montdidier

Noyon

La Fère

Laon

Compiègne

Oise R.

Soissons

Reims

Marne R.

Château-Thierry

Epernay

Meaux

Paris

Seine R.

- - - Limit of German advance
1914

· · · · Front December 1914–
June 1916

⇗ Big Push at Somme River
July 1, 1916

· · · · · Limit of Allied gains
1917

- - - Limit of German gains
1918

0 Miles   30

0 Kilometers   30

© 2000 Jeffrey L. Ward

HORSES DON'T FLY

1

Sunrise

I BEGAN LIFE WITH AN AWFUL TRAGEDY. Mother left us shortly before my fourth birthday. Where she had gone or for how long, no one told me and I didn't know. There was a house full of people, some patting me on the head saying "What a big man." But I wasn't. This was in 1896. I was only a little boy.

There were strange women trying to hold me on their laps with no success. I was conscious of something wrong. Just what, I was too young to understand.

The fact that Mother had died of quick consumption came to me in the days that followed, sort of piecemeal. Someone seeing me for the first time would remark, "Why, he looks just like his mother." Then I remember hearing Father say, "When a boy loses his mother he has lost everything, because it is the mother that keeps a family together and makes a home." It finally dawned on me that Mama was gone forever. While this was terrible for me, it must have been doubly hard for Father. Mother's death left only four of us, Father, my sister Minnie, Brother Bud and myself. Minnie, who was thirteen years older than I, was sent east to live with an aunt, leaving the three of us together.

Thank God for Father. He turned down all the aunts and uncles who were bent on taking me to raise, saying we would fight it out together, and when they insisted that I needed a woman to look after me, I was so young, Father replied, "I will take care of that." And he did. Coming to live with us and take care of everyone was Sally, a colored lady. To me, she was an angel. She looked after me, baked cookies, cakes, fresh bread, and right or wrong was always on my side. This Father pretended was wrong, but he liked it very much, because he was keeping the three of us together and could give the back of his hand to all the doubting aunts and uncles.

Two events awakened me to life after the death of Mother. On my sixth birthday when I started to school, Father gave me a pony, saddle, bridle and the whole works. My riding before had always been on the back of one of Bud's horses, with him leading and me hanging on. This pony was my first of my very own, and with this little monster, named Slowpoke, I started my career with horses.

Slowpoke and I were about the same age, but there the similarity ended. For this little guy had forgotten more about boys than I would ever know. There were times when he humored me by doing everything perfect. He would let me ride him everywhere like we were real pals. Then all of a sudden he would decide the ground was the best place for me. With a few well placed jumps, there I would be, walking home, with him just ahead dragging the reins — so far and yet so near. Boy, I could kill him.

Our home was on the edge of a small cowtown in Colorado, named Sterling, near the Platte River in the Platte Valley. Here no one could be a stranger for long. Everyone spoke to each other whether they had met before or not. Here I learned that cowmen are the kindest and friendliest people on earth.

On both sides of the river for miles and miles in every direction cattle and horses grazed without interference, except immediately along the river where there were many farms raising hay and grain. It was a real cow country for real cowmen. A place to be happy about.

Father and Brother had cattle and horses. At the home ranch some thirty miles from town there was a large pasture for horses, while the cattle roamed the range. Here I liked to spend my vacation, or any time I could, watching Brother Bud break horses to ride. I looked forward to the time I could do the things he was doing, only I was growing too slowly and time was passing slower. Every time I returned to our house in town after watching Bud front-foot some horses, I would try this on my pony, Slowpoke. He was a total loss.

He would run about twice then stand still with his little rump facing me. To rope him was impossible.

We had our final battle just before I was eight years old. He stepped on my foot and walked over me, knocking me flat. To say that I was wild would be putting it mildly. Looking for something to work him over with, I found my ball bat in the back yard. With the small bat in one hand, limping and crying tears of anger, I chased him around the corral, trying to get close enough to conk him back of the ear, calling him a ——— so and so, when my brother showed on the scene. "My God, Pard. Such language! Your Sunday school teacher wouldn't like that. And what do you think would happen if Father could hear that kind of talk? What did you do to Slowpoke or what were you trying to do?" I explained I was only trying to play elephant like they do in the circus — you know, where the elephant throws the man up on his back with his trunk. "I was only trying to teach him to throw me up with his head, but he is so dumb he walked all over me and stepped on my foot."

"Pard, by now you know an elephant he is not, even if he does act like one at times. I am going to give you two Indian ponies I just bought, and you'll need a new saddle as you've outgrown Slowpoke *and* your saddle. I think we should give Slowpoke and your saddle to our banker's little girl. You need something with more life if you are to learn to be a rider. These new ponies are fast and tough and will stand no foolishness. If you learn to ride them, you'll be plenty good. By the time you're ten, I may have a real cowboy for a brother."

With these two characters, a sorrel named Kid and a dark bay named Shoefly, life really became interesting. Where Slowpoke was short and squatty, these beautiful babies were slim and sleek and moved with the ease of a cat on a hot stove. Along with my two close pals, the King brothers, Willard and Earl, I roamed the prairies near our house, where we roped wild burros and were always busy. We were in the same class at school and wore the same kind of clothes — cowboy boots and long pants. The others, sissies, wore knee pants and shoes. The King boys' daddy was in the cattle business. As we were all going to be cowpunchers, we were always together. Where there was trouble, we would go down together.

One day our grocery boy was making a delivery. He drove a horse and wagon which had a canvas top to keep the groceries dry. All Father or Bud had to do was leave orders at the store and they would be delivered, a convenience that left Sally no worries. The horse was a nice gentle plug that was used to the route. He would simply pull up in front of the house and then stand still like he was dead, while the man ran around back with the groceries.

This day the three of us were just getting home from school. Coming to the front where the half asleep horse was standing, Earl said, "Let's have some fun. I'm going to wake Old Dobbin up." With that, he extracted a small vial from his pocket and quickly dashed a few drops on the plug's hind end. What was in the vial, I didn't know. It looked like water, but water it was not, for the old boy threw up his head, surprised like, then began to wiggle his behind like he had the itch, then gave one hell of a jump and hit for the prairie, with the wagon bouncing every which way, and groceries going in every direction. About this time the most excited man in our town came around the corner of our house to see his grocery wagon upset and his horse traveling like a wild bull in fly time. Me, I was as surprised as the groceryman, as this was my first experience with Hoky Pokie. The liquid, applied properly, will bring the deadest creature that has hair to life with a bang for a short time, but has no lasting effect on the animal, only makes him wonder what in the world happened.

Had I known what it was all about, I would have had Earl sprinkle some on the guy's tail so he could catch his horse, but I was dumb and just stood there while the King boys, all of a sudden, had to go home.

Had Sally not come to my rescue, the guy probably would have scalped me — he was mad enough. But he accepted Sally's explanation that his old horse was stung by a bee, and I made my escape to the back of the house.

The next day Earl's father paid the store for its loss in groceries and repair of the wagon. But the horse was never the same. At our house, he would never stand and wait but always had to be tied, even for a minute. Earl and Willard were a couple of swell guys. They could have left me holding the sack, but they told their mother, who could handle their father, and that made everything dandy.

Alone or with this pair, there was never a dull moment. We were all trying to grow up too fast and do the things that men did, like the day I climbed on a chair and helped myself to a fair portion of Father's tonic, which was in a decanter high on the cupboard. It had a horrible smell, but Father seemed to enjoy it so much before supper, I knew I needed some. I only poured about half the amount Father usually poured into a water glass. If I didn't like it, there wouldn't be much loss. Settling down in his big chair, I took a gulp and swallowed real quick. Then the smell, the burn, the choke. I could hardly breathe when Sally came in. "Boy, what did you do?" She didn't need to ask. The smell was enough. With my "Oh Sally, I think I am going to be sick," she promptly gave me her apron. I didn't quite die, but almost. It was many a year before I could stand the smell of whiskey.

Once my Uncle Sam came to visit us for a few weeks. He was my mother's brother and my favorite uncle. In fact, my favorite over everyone except Father and Brother Bud. He always enjoyed life so much. After each meal, he would take a plug of chewing tobacco out of his pocket and bite off a big chew. This didn't smell bad like whiskey but was pretty and brown like the crust of Sally's pies. Boy, did I want to try this! Whether by accident or on purpose, Uncle Sam left the plug on the dining room table. This was all that was needed. Grabbing myself a large mouthful, chewing fast and furious, I got a mouthful of juice, which I swallowed. Down went the chew with the next swallow and up came everything I had ever eaten, plus my stomach. I broke out in a terrible sweat and was so dizzy I couldn't walk. If chewing tobacco makes a man, I knew that I would never make it. And chew tobacco I never have.

2

An Antelope, a Rope
and a Small Boy

SUNDAY MORNING. We have just had breakfast. One week from to-morrow school will be out, so I can go to our home ranch for the summer. With me there is always something different. Father has promised a new saddle for my tenth birthday, in July, only a short time away. Brother Bud has ordered me a new custom-made pair of cowboy boots, just like he wears, black and tan with the small heel. My measurements and order have been sent to Mr. Hier in Kansas City. With my big Stetson hat, long pants stuck down in the boots and a special belt with a silver buckle to hold my pants up, I'll look just like my brother, only he is twelve years my senior. To be just like him, to rope and ride as he does, will be something. I practice hard with the rope. I can spin and do fancy tricks now, but Bud says that is only for show. To front-foot and rope from your horse is what makes a good cowhand. He is the best.

The new saddle is not going to be a boy's saddle. It will be a full-sized man's, the kind bronco riders use.

This morning at breakfast I lost my final battle with Father. It wasn't much of a battle, with what I have coming up soon, a birth-day and summer vacation. I know when to quit and did.

Last week one of my aunts in the East sent me a waist which she made. Father thinks it is very beautiful, but it makes me sick to look at the thing. It is white with a great big collar with lace all around the edge and sleeves with lace cuffs that fold back over the end of your coat sleeves. Up the front are two rows of lace. The bottom of the waist ties around your middle, and it doesn't stick down in your britches like a man's shirt. This affair you wear over the suspenders that keep your pants up. It is horrible looking, and I am much too old for this kind of junk. Today I am to wear it to Sunday school and then church. I have a new blue suit with knee pants. This I wouldn't mind so much if I could wear a real shirt with a tail to tuck in my pants. With me in black shoes, black stockings, my new blue suit and the damn waist with a ribbon bow tie, the kids are going to make it plenty tough. But Father won't understand. He is the finest father I know and usually easy to handle, but after my attempt at breakfast, I know I'm sunk. He says I will look just like little Lord Fauntleroy, whoever he is, and all the little girls will be after me. Them I can do without. They smell terrible, all perfume and stuff. Horses smell better. Bud says girls will smell better as I get older, but he is always kidding. There is one thing I know: I'll never let my ponies see me. I wouldn't be caught dead in the stable in this outfit, and if some kid pulls the lace I won't even sock him. My big brother and Sally, who runs the place and is my good friend (who even Father doesn't sass), are always on my side. But this time, they have given me no help. They have just looked at each other, grinned and kept still like a couple of dumb clucks.

The time to dress is approaching, so up the back stairs from the kitchen to my room I go. From my back window I can see our big back yard with a board sidewalk running from our kitchen door to the stable. Our home is at the very edge of town and sits high on a terrace. It is a three-story frame building painted white with green trimmings, as are the stable, corrals and a picket fence that stands at the foot of the terrace on both sides and in front of the house. At the front and back of the house are large lawns with beautiful green grass sloping down to the picket fence. There is only one eyesore, the boardwalk to the stable. Several boards are broken, heads of many nails stick up, and Father is always going to have them removed but never does. I look out my window to the stable where

Bud's two cow ponies and Father's two fancy horses are quartered and to the corral where my two ponies are munching hay. I'm pretty proud of the whole affair, especially the three people downstairs. It is nine now and Sunday school starts at ten. Then church, where I am supposed to sing with the choir. Maybe something will happen before that.

Taking my time dressing, I am thinking of my new boots and saddle to come, along with my summer vacation. So if I get by today, life will be pretty good. Looking myself over in the mirror, big white collar on the outside of my coat collar, white lace cuffs over the ends of my sleeves, I am an awful sight.

Everything is ready, except Sally to brush my hair and put on the black ribbon tie, when I take a last look out the window. Here is something to gladden the heart of any small boy. On our lawn, eating our wonderful green grass, are five of the prettiest antelope I have ever seen. They evidently have just landed, because when I looked out the window before, they were not there.

Three of this bunch I have seen before, the two little guys are new. The three largest ones were here in the winter looking for food on a day when there was a big blizzard. Sally fed them some potato peelings and Bud put out some hay on top of the snow. Then they were very thin and didn't look good, but today they are fat and beautiful, with their big bunch of white hair for a tail and their slick coat. They are a sight to see. This is the only time I ever saw antelope this close to town in the summer. In the winter they are a common sight, especially around our house at the edge of town where they seem to know they're welcome. Today, these babies must have been just traveling and spotted our nice green grass. I start to call my family to see the sight, when I have a better idea. Gone is any thought of Sunday school, my blue suit, or future plans. I have immediate business. Down the back stairs I go, through the kitchen and the front room where Bud is playing solitaire and Father is reading. All this without attracting undue attention, and I am out the front door, down the steps and out the front gate. The coast is clear. Ducking down so I won't be seen, I run along the front and turn back to the stable, keeping well out of sight of my antelope until I reach the back of our corral. Here I slow up because it seems I have escaped safely from the house. My babies are still deep in grass.

Ignoring my ponies, I go through the stable to the front of the mangers where there is a runway between the manger and the door opening toward our house. Here hang three saddles, Father's, Bud's and mine. But what I am after is a dandy thirty-five-foot rope which Bud uses for front-footing. This is coiled up and hangs on the horn of his saddle. I remove it quickly. Looking out through a crack in the door, I spot my babies all happy with their heads in the grass, the largest of the five not ten feet from the door.

This is going to be perfect. If I can get my rope in position and open the door quietly but fast and get one shot. If I remember everything Bud has taught me. I will catch this guy, and will Father and Bud ever be proud of me! Clothes I have forgotten all about. Like I have been taught, I make a small loop for a quick throw, with the coil in my left hand, the loop in my right. I am about to open the door with my knee when I remember that, last month out to our ranch, I roped a wild horse going out a gate. I didn't only lose the rope, I got my hands rope-burned. And worst of all, it was one of Bud's best ropes and he spent a full day recovering it, which didn't make him too happy. This time I will be safe. I tie the very end of the rope around my waist, leaving myself plenty to cast. Putting one of Bud's gloves on my left hand, I leave my right hand free to cast my loop.

I am ready. All this has taken me practically no time. With one more look to see just where my prey is, I find everything to my liking. With a quick gentle push of my knee, the antelope and I are as one. My beautiful overhand loop has opened directly above and in front, so Mr. Antelope has no place to go. But go he does, straight up, turning in the air toward the wide open spaces.

This is possibly the first and only time a small boy has been attached to a jet-propelled antelope. This baby hits the end of the rope, jerking me straight up in the air and landing me on my belly, square on top of the broken part of Father's boardwalk from which nail heads stick out everywhere. Mr. Antelope has barely cleared our picket fence, what with having me on the other end of the rope, and is flattened out. By the time I have unscrambled myself from he boards, he is on his feet again and away we go. One jerk and I am flat on my belly in the nice green grass, sliding across the lawn and down the terrace, where my head hits the bottom of the picket fence with a bang. I am not feeling so good. A shadow passes over the top of me and the fence, and I know I am being rescued by my long-suffering but faithful brother, who grabs the rope and, hand over hand, separates the loop from a surprised and very happy antelope. I have come to enough that I am trying to climb the terrace on my knees when Bud gives me a hand and unties the rope from around my waist.

Reality has returned. I am standing up wondering how soon Father will show up. The beautiful white shirt is no more. The big white collar is torn half off. Green grass covers the front of my shirt and suit. One stocking is down, the other is torn and there is a large rip in the pants leg. My head hurts like the dickens and my left eye feels like it is shutting. Worst of all, it is beginning to dawn on me that I haven't gone to Sunday school. All of this has gone through my mind fast when Sally comes running out with "What has happened to my boy?" This is evidently too much for Bud and he starts to laugh and roll in the grass saying, "Sally, I told you he would make it. My God, Pard, you look terrible." Then Sally starts laughing, only she doesn't roll in the grass like Bud.

What I dreaded most is about to happen. Father is coming out the kitchen door. He takes one look at his bright young son. On his face is the funniest expression. His mouth opens and closes like a fish out of water. Finally he blurts out, "This is the first blue suit I have ever seen turn green so soon. What the hell happened?" Seeing the rope in Bud's hand, he inquires, "My God, what could he possibly rope to do this in such a short space of time?" So Bud tells him. His mouth starts the old routine — open and close. He wipes his hand across his face several times, like he has lost his voice. Then he heads for the back door, making funny noises like he was choking. As he goes into the house he says, "Bud, I'll make that deal of ours fifteen."

Boy, am I glad he's gone. I mention to Bud that Father didn't say anything about church. This starts Bud and Sally off in more laughter, which to me is not a darn bit funny. "Pard, why did you tie that rope to your waist?" After I explain about not wanting to lose his rope, Bud exclaims, "To hell with the rope. Don't ever do that again. I would rather lose all my ropes than lose my kid brother. And as for our father and church, I think you have convinced him that a minister you will never be. I don't think he will ever mention to-day's adventure, if you don't."

Sally pipes up, "Mention it? Did you see how hard he was try-ing not to laugh? I bet he will be down to that club where they all go, and everyone in town will know about that antelope." To me Sally says, "Darling, I am going to take you in hand and bathe your cuts and do something for that eye, because it's going to be a real shiner. And boy, you sure don't have to go anywhere today."

Bud says, "All right, Sally. You take care of our champion roper. I'm going to town. I can't let Father have all the fun. I'll make it fif-teen."

So I ask Bud for the meaning. It seems Father decided some time ago I wasn't going to live too long. He promised Bud three of his best horses if he would keep me going until I am eighteen. To-day he cut it down to fifteen. How do you like that?

My last week of school I am quite a hero with the black eye. Everyone seems to know about my friend, the antelope. The girls all giggle and look silly. The boys are all interested. Even our man teacher wants to know all about everything. My pals, the King boys, want to know what kind of a loop I used, and what did my father say, and would I teach them to throw the same kind of a loop. I agree to show them after school, but Willard has a little trouble with our lady teacher, so there can be no roping.

Teacher had Willard up in front of our class trying to read some-thing aloud. This was very bad, as Willard stammers. When he's ex-cited, it's awful. The words just don't want to come out, and when they do, they come all of a sudden. She had Willard try to repeat the same thing over and over, each time getting worse. "I just can't un-derstand you, Willard," she declared. By this time he is embarrassed and thinks she is having fun with him. He exclaims with an oath, "You, you, you thun of a vitch, see, see, see if you can unnerthtand that," and socks her right in the belly. She folds up like a punctured accordion. The girls all scream, "He's killed Teacher." By the time our man teacher appears, Willard has ducked out through the hall taking his Stetson with him, then home to his pony and off to their ranch before his mother has a chance to find out what happened. I don't see him again until after summer vacation.

3

School and Sis, Wild Horses and the Stinkenest Hog Wallow in the World

VACATION IS OVER. I have to go live with my sister Minnie, who is now married, and attend school. Father has to travel to Indian territory on business, and Sally is going home to her folks for the winter. I want to stay with Brother, but Father wants me to go to Sister Minnie. He is always worrying about me keeping my chest covered and my feet dry. You would think I was a little kid. I won't see my home or my ponies or Sally for nine months. But Father says we will all be together again soon. Nuts, I bet the kids where I am going, in Sabetha, Kansas, are a bunch of sissies. Bud says they don't have anything but milk cows. Who wants a milk cow? We always used canned cream, it's better.

And so in the autumn of 1903 it is my first time to take a train trip by myself. To leave Father, Brother and Sally is sad. They are so good to me. Even the thrill of eating in the diner by myself and wearing my special cowboy clothes won't make up for the loss I feel at leaving everyone and everything I love, but Father said it is best.

It helps some not having to carry a lot of clothes, just the cowboy clothes I'm wearing and Sunday clothes in a light suitcase. Father has sent my sister money to buy me a new outfit for school. Bud is going to take me to the train in Father's buggy. So I say goodbye to my ponies and Sally as Father takes my suitcase to the buggy. He

seems to be in a hurry and there are tears in his eyes when he tells
me goodbye, take care of yourself and Sister Minnie and be sure
and write. If I ever wanted to cry, this is the time. Having Brother
Bud to talk to real fast is all that saves me from being a baby. Brother
puts me on the train in a nice big chair, gives me my ticket, promising to take care of my new saddle and ponies. He assures me that
everything in my room will be kept just as I left it and that he will
look after Father. Just how is something beyond me, as Father is going to Indian territory. With the train beginning to move, we shake
hands. Bud gives me a friendly pat on the head and is gone. Oh
God, why do I have to go to my sister? I don't even remember her.
If it weren't for hurting Father and Bud, I would get off at the first
stop and rustle for myself.

My sister is at the station to meet me, where she makes a show
of herself mushing all over me, then to a horse and buggy owned by
a friend, where she introduces me as her baby brother. This is bad
enough, but when she says to her friend Marjorie, "Father, you
know, doesn't have any idea how to dress a boy. . . . Those horrible
clothes will be discarded for real boys' clothes," I want to sock
someone. But what can a fellow do with a dumb sister? My first day
and night with Sis are terrible. I inspect the yard, both front and
back. Not one horse in sight. My beautiful cowboy clothes and
fancy boots are in the closet. I won't be able to show them to any of
the kids. The damned knee pants with shoes are to be worn even to
school.

My room is a little place upstairs, which I don't mind so much,
only there is nothing to see from the window except houses. I am
lonesome and lost. All I can think of is how sad Father looked when
he told me goodbye and Brother Bud's last remark of how "Father
wants you to have a good education and then we will have a lot of
good times, so try and put up with Sis until next spring when you
will be home for vacation."

Here in a big bed where no one could see or hear me, I cried
myself to sleep, which wasn't being a man like Bud had always
taught me. I didn't even cry when the antelope almost killed me,
but this was different. I was only a small boy of eleven and so alone
and lonesome.

It was inevitable that Sis and I would have one real row, which came, of all things, about my hair. There was one spot that grew straight up and stayed that way. So Sally used to just brush around and everything was all right, but Sis said I had a cowlick. This was news to me, as a cowlick was where we put out salt for range cattle to lick. Where she found out about a cowlick, I don't know. So her idea was to wet my hair all over, then split it in the middle and brush down the sides. She wanted to make an impression on my new teachers, whom I was to meet on my first day of school.

I looked just like a fat baby's bottom. This was our first and only battle, but from then on she left my hair alone.

School wasn't bad the first day. Sis went with me. After that, I was on my own. I saw one boy looking me over the first day. I learned he was the school bully. The third day he knocked one of my front teeth out. It wasn't all one-sided, because when a teacher pulled us apart, I was on top polishing his nose with my fist and he didn't look so good. Sister's new clothes were in bad shape with blood, mostly mine. The professor looked us over, trying to decide who was the worst, and said, "Do you fellows want to shake hands or shall I take you both on?" We shook hands and went to my house to see my beautiful boots. How many kids I took upstairs to see those boots I don't know, but if my pony and saddle had been up there, Sis would have really gone nuts.

The winter has passed, spring is with us and school is about out. Sister Minnie is going to have a baby. She looks like she swallowed a watermelon and is as cranky as an old hen about to hatch. She will peck at anything, and her poor husband catches the dickens from all angles. I'm hoping Father or Bud will send for me soon. To get home is all I ask.

One night when I come home late from school, Sis meets me at the door with "Why are you so late? Bud has been here two hours waiting for you." My heart sank. But her next words did it. "Bud has gone to the stockyards and won't be back. He said if you came home in time, to go to the yards, where he has several cars of horses to feed and water which he's taking to Indian territory. If you get there in time, he'll take you with him."

This is all I need, all I have been living for. Grabbing a fast drink of water, I am out the door when I remember my manners and say my goodbyes almost on the run, leaving her bawling. I have no time for this foolishness. On a high trot, I start for the stockyards, which are over three miles from our house on the other side of town.

Taking the center of the road to avoid anyone on the sidewalk, I never slow up until in sight of the stockyards, where I can see a long freight train in the yard with a caboose on the end. Nearest me and close to the loading rack are several empty cars. All signs indicate that Bud has started to load and that I am in plenty of time.

Life is good. I'm back with my pal. All I have to do is find him, which is a cinch because he'll be somewhere around the loading chute. And there I do find him and inundate him with a few thousand questions such as "Where is Father, where is Sally, do you have my ponies and saddle and where are we going?" The guy doesn't have a chance to talk. He's just as glad as I am, so everything is swell.

"Father is fine, we're going to meet him day after tomorrow. It's time to load out, we'll talk on the caboose, here comes the switch engine to spot our first car. You work the fence like always, and I'll cut the first load into the chute."

Bud's words were like music to my ears, and loading was easy as pie. Bud had only some eight cars of horses, all wild except five saddle horses for his own use. My ponies and saddle he left home, explaining he would get me an outfit in the territory where we were going.

After loading, we went over to the caboose while the switch engine hooked our horses onto the front end of the train. From the upper windows of the caboose you could look along the entire length of the train. Bud had bought a couple of pies, a flock of sandwiches and some soda pop for me, because he figured I would make it. If I didn't, he could throw the pop away. Boy, was it good to be with him, on a big, long train going someplace new. Bud said it was plenty tough there. What difference? I was with my family.

We arrived at Minco Indian Territory early in the morning, about two o'clock. By the time the switch engine got around to spot our cars to unload, it was about three o'clock. Unloading would be easy, as the minute the door was open and one horse came out, the rest would follow fast. I'm in heaven and having a wonderful time. When we climb up to the unloading platform, Bud says, "Pard, climb up on that walk and see that all back gates are fastened good, because if this bunch of wild horses should get away, we will never get them. Just be careful, it's dark as hell." Doing something I have done many times before, I run down the walk to the runway. I have to climb down, cross the runway, climb up, then down on the other side of the fence and examine the outside gate. This would be fine, only it's dark and I'm in a hurry to get back to Bud before the horses start out of their cars. So where I should have climbed down, I jump off into space, expecting solid ground. Instead, I land in the middle of the stinkenest and deepest hog wallow in the whole world, I guess. That particular section of the stockyard was reserved for hogs, and me, I'm in the middle of it.

How long I yell, I don't know, but Bud and one of the brakemen pull me out in nothing flat. Having fallen forward when I finally quit going down, I am well muddied up almost to my shoulders. After fishing me out and finding I am not hurt, just my feelings, Bud says, "Damned if everything don't happen to you in the spring. Just like a rose only you stink like hell. Boy, you are overripe. Come on, I'll get you some sticks to scrape with while we unload these horses."

After unloading, we climb in an empty furniture car in back of our horses, where Bud puts his bed roll and traveling bag, saying, "We can't get you any clothes until morning, so you scrape while I take a nap. You have got to be clean enough that I can get you into a barber shop bath. I'll bury what you have on and buy some new. As you are now, someone might try to bury *you*. Where the hell are your good clothes I bought you, and where are your boots?" I explain Sis didn't like cowboy clothes and had never let me wear them, and I was in such a rush to catch the train I forgot all about them. He says, "We'll have her send them on by express. She should see the lovely ones you are wearing today. She would turn over and die. Damn the pigs, why couldn't you fall in a barrel of perfume or something that don't smell so bad? God, Father will really laugh when he hears about this. Stay with it, Pard. By daylight I will feel better and you won't smell so bad." Then he goes to sleep.

By eight o'clock I have removed the worst and have cleaned

my shoes the best that I could with some waste the brakie gave me. But the smell is still there, only not quite so bad, or I have gotten used to it. Bud wakes up. Cussing the railroad, he says, "It always happens. They never get anywhere in the daytime where you can unload without using a lantern. Let's go to town and see if we can rustle some food, a bath and clothes. You carry my hand bag, I'll carry the sleeping bag. My saddle I expressed before I left home."

Minco has one small main street, with a couple of general stores which are just opening. The barber shop will open in a few minutes. At least that was what the colored boy says, and pointing to me he asks what is the matter with that boy. "Is he sick?" This tickles my brother. "Yes, he's sick. Don't he smell sorta bad?"

"Boss, he sure do. He's dead."

The next remark of my brother's damned near kills me. Turning to the boy, he says, "Son, do you know where there is a blind pig?" Me, I've been fighting the dirty end of a pig all night, and now he wants a blind pig? But the boy quickly responds, "Sure, Boss, all you do is go to the back of that house, stick your five dollars through the slot and your package will be pushed out a little chute to the side. Come on, I'll show you."

"Come on, Pard, you smell too bad to leave alone. Someone might cover you over with dirt while I'm gone."

What comes out is a pint of whiskey. What a blind pig has to do with whiskey, I don't know. I am hungry, tired and awfully dirty. So on to the barber shop bath where Bud explains my trouble to the boss. Into the bath while Bud finds a place to lose my clothes. He buys me new ones and I begin to feel better and hope Father won't think I am too stupid. After the bath, I don the new clothes, which fit except the trousers are too long. We stick them down in my new boots, which aren't bad although not nearly as nice as the ones Bud had made for me. We really enjoy a good breakfast.

If I had any fear of Father being upset over the pig business, it was quickly forgotten when we met, for he seemed so glad to see me. I knew everything was good, we were all together.

Indian territory was a new country, with people from everywhere settling on the land, trying to make a living from the soil. They grew

cotton, corn and any crop that could be raised by rainfall and no irrigation. Father had a beautiful piece of land, also a large horse pasture he rented. He had it completely fenced with barbed wire to
hold the wild horses, which he and Bud sold to the settlers almost as
fast as they could ship them in from Colorado. Bud said he never
had it so good. He would sell out a shipment of horses, then go back
to Colorado for more, none of which he had to pay for until sold. All
he and Father were stuck for was the freight and shipping expense.
The JB brand was owned by one of Bud's best friends, who had
more horses than money. He trusted my brother to pay when the
horses were sold. As Father said, one hell of an arrangement for
everybody.

     True to his promise, Bud bought me a saddle and horse for my
very own. He didn't want to ship my ponies from Colorado to Indian
territory. My saddle was out to our home ranch for safekeeping until I returned, which Father said would be in the fall. No more Sister Minnie for me.

     With that one worry out of my mind, I had a swell time doing
the things I liked best, traveling with Bud and on my new horse,
which was bigger and faster than either of my ponies. With Bud's
help and advice, I was getting to be perfect with the rope and very
seldom missed when front-footing in the corral. A compliment from
Father or Bud meant more to me than money. I didn't even mind
learning to cook, as the three of us were batching. It's fun if you
don't have to, but grows very tiresome when necessary. Doing
dishes was the worst. Father solved the problem in a hurry. "Just
throw them in a deep pan, pour boiling water over and leave them
to dry." The only thing wrong with this was, if they didn't drain
good, they would rust, as everything was tin. But that was better
than wiping them with a rag. If too much rust, throw them away.

     The two largest towns near us were Anadarko and Okmulgee.
Minco, where we unloaded our horses, had the nearest yards for
shipping. It was just a small place, but one I'll never forget, especially the hog wallow. The folks who were trying to farm were a kind
people, working hard and hoping for the best. Some had a little
money, others were broke after building some kind of a place to live
in, which often was just a hole in the side of a bank with some kind

of a roof. It was called a dugout but was always clean, with the walls scraped down even and the floor being just the ground, but packed solid and firm.

Regardless of how poor the settlers were, we were always asked to stop and eat, even if only corn pone and sorghum. Many of these people Bud let have horses without any money, taking their note for a year until they could raise a crop. He would even help break them to harness if the farmer was too helpless, because all of these horses were wild and they often needed help. Father's prediction that the Indian territory would soon be a state was very true, for in a very few years, in 1907, Oklahoma came into being and more than justified those who had faith in its future.

Something is going on which I don't understand. Father has been talking to strange men. One day he says, "Son, we're ready to go home. I've sold the whole works and, Bud, we have quite a bit of paper floating around here which we'll put in a bank for collecting when due. You can come here in the spring with more horses or, if you think the market is shot, just come back on a visit, because some people won't be able to pay and we don't want the banker to press for payment."

Having been away from home for over a year, I am thrilled to death. Even if you are a boy, the King boys and my man teacher, Mr. Young, who I liked very much, and all the nice people in town will speak. Life is awfully good.

4

My First Big Battle

Home with Father, Bud, Sally and my ponies, I am in heaven. Even school doesn't give me any worry. I will be with the King boys, old Bean Soup, Dago and all my gang without Sis to mess with my clothes or hair, and everyone in town is my friend. I am about to bust with pride.

First day of school, 1904, is same old routine. New books, etc., except something has been added. We have a new boy in our grade. His father is a railroad man, and they are from Chicago. It seems this kid doesn't like anyone and is bound to be boss of the roost, a real tough guy. So, at recess in the afternoon, my gang gets together and who do you think is elected to battle the new boy? Me! Just me, such an honor. I'm not a bit happy with the prospects. In the first place he's bigger, and I am not mad at him or anyone else and have never had to fight but once, because everyone has been my friend. I have always done as Brother Bud said, help the little fellow, pick on no one, but let nobody push you around. And up to now, I have been doing well. Now I'm in an awful spot. No brother to advise. I'm on my own with just the kids to cheer me on. The do-or-die contest is to be back of the livery stable after school, and I don't feel like fighting. I'd rather go home to my ponies. Suddenly I remember the boy in Sabetha, Kansas, who jumped me on my third day of school, and I remember he didn't do so well and became one of my best friends. This waiting business is not for me. I like to do what-

ever there is to do, whether good or bad. I like action without waiting, so the rest of our afternoon was of no interest to me.

When three-thirty arrived, we headed for the bloody battle-
ground. Sure, the affair was pretty bloody — but with my blood.
This guy had been trained to box. No wonder he was so cocky. He
hit me, I hit the ground. I took a beautiful plastering, but I did succeed in blackening one of his eyes and separating him from his shirt.
And at least he never made me say "enough," although I'd had
enough before we started but was too stubborn to say so. The affair
ended because we were both completely finished. Evidently he
didn't have strength enough to hit me again and I wouldn't play
dead, so we parted with my gang in much glee. Why shouldn't they
be? None of them has a bloody nose or a swollen cheek, and their
clothes are all together, while mine are a mess of blood, dirt and
tears. I am in rags.

And now the worst is to come. This is my first day of school and
Father and Sally are home. Sally, I don't mind. But to face Father in
my condition is not good. While Father has seen me in pretty tough
shape, he has never seen his young son worked over by another boy.
This I know he won't like. But he can't feel half as bad as I do, so
home for more medicine. Boy, I only hope Bud is there. He always
knows the answers.

In the back way through the stable, then the kitchen where I
hope to see Sally or Bud, but no such luck. Father is in the kitchen
mixing up some of his favorite tonic. His first words are "Oh my
God, it can't be. Where is your brother, where's Sally?" As I have
just arrived, I know none of the answers, but answers Father must
have, so to the living room we go, where my parent makes himself
very comfortable while I tell him the facts of life.

Father is a swell listener. He waits until the end, then he surprises the pants off of me when he asks: "Hasn't Bud ever given you
any boxing lessons?" When he learns I haven't even had a boxing
glove on, he almost explodes. "No wonder, Son, you took a licking.
Did you do it like a man? And what about the other fellow?" After
my gruesome rundown, Father says, "Son, I have some news for
you. The next kid you fight will be sorry he jumped you, because
your brother is quite a boy with a boxing glove. Why the hell he

hasn't taught you before, I don't know. The idea of letting you grow up without any training is something I want to know about. Go upstairs and clean up while I find something to put on that skinned cheekbone. Sally will be home soon and everything will be all right. And Son, I think you did damn well. I'm right proud of you. I just don't want you beat up without a chance, and believe me, after Bud is through with you, things will be different."

I only hope Bud doesn't come home early. I don't want him blamed because I get skinned up. And right now Father is mad as a wet hen. If Bud is late, my honorable parent will have time to cool off. My poor brother and Sally always are blamed if I get in a mess. It makes no difference where they are. Sally comes home and takes over, fixing up my skinned cheekbone and skinned knee. As for the nose, it's swollen, which doesn't add to my beauty, and when I think of school tomorrow I don't feel so good. But I'm hungry. It hasn't spoiled my appetite, and here is my big brother with his usual cheerful greeting for everyone: "How's my family?"

Father starts with: "Take a good look at your young brother." But Bud beats him to the answer. "I know all about the fight. I just came from town, and Dago says it was a peach of a scrap and your young son sent the new boy, who is bigger and older, home crying. Pard, let me look at you and how do you feel? Tell me, where did he hit you most?" When I reply, "Everywhere except the bottom of my feet," Father explodes as though it was funny. To me, none of the business was funny, but at least all Father says is, "Son, just keep your sense of humor, and Bud, it might be well to give your kid brother some training in the art of self-defense." Bud promises he'll start next week when he returns from the ranch. The only reason he hasn't started before is I was always so busy learning the things I liked best, roping and riding, and me being only twelve — he hadn't thought it was quite time. "Next week, we will start, but the first lesson I'm going to give you, Pard, is for tomorrow at school. Look the new kid up and offer to shake hands and be friends. If he doesn't want to, go back to the livery stable again — soon. We shall see."

With this, there is a rap on our front door, which Bud answers. And of all people, it's Mike and his father. At Bud's invitation to step in, the man introduces himself as Mr. Mason, saying they walked all the way across town to our place to apologize for Mike and for Mike to apologize to me. He told Father he had requested a transfer from the railroad to our town just to get away from Chicago, because Mike had gotten in with a tough crowd and was always fighting and always in trouble. While Mike was only thirteen, Mr. Mason wanted to bring up his son and three daughters in a good community, and the very first day in school Mike had started a fight. He knew because he made Mike tell him the truth. Also, this was the first fight Mike hadn't won quick and easy, so his pride was hurt. He wanted to go back to Chicago.

Here my father takes over. He welcomes Mr. Mason, offers him a drink of his favorite tonic, which he accepts, and they get real friendly, which gives me a chance to look Mike over. I guess he looks just as bad as I do. He has a black eye and a swollen lip and must be awful tired, having walked all the way out to our home at the edge of town. I take Mike up to see my room and tell him about my ponies and our ranch. He is a nice kid and agrees to help me learn to box when Bud starts on me. And best of all, I don't have to look him up in school and offer to be his friend. This little matter has been taken care of by his father, who I like very much. He can't compare with my father, but he's very nice and I like Mike.

My first day of school in my twelfth year has ended well. Father won't let Mike and his father walk home. He has Bud hitch up his harness mare to the runabout and take them home. So, our family has some new friends. A fellow can sure be proud of a family like mine.

Nothing exciting happens to me for the next two years, except an incident involving two wild horses coming out of a corral gate. They ran over me, breaking a couple of ribs and skinning me up some. It was all my fault. I didn't see them until too late and they had no place to go, only over me. The doc tapes me up and that stops my roping for some time. One other thing which is worth forgetting: Our town is growing. The main street is now paved and the sidewalks in front of most stores are now cement. No more wooden sidewalks until you leave the main street. Also, the homes are having bathrooms. No more baths in the big galvanized tub, heating your water on the stove, or going to the barber shop for a bath. This, of course, the girls can't do, so the new improvement was much appreciated by many. Besides, people are doing away with the outhouse, or "chick sales" as they are called by some folks. These establishments are always a target at Halloween. Nothing bad, just a run and a push and they are over on their fronts. To re-enter, they have to be raised and put in place. On Halloween, the timid stay just as far away as possible for fear of being an occupant at the wrong time. Many things happen on this night in our town. Such as the time someone put a complete wagon on top of our city hall and opera house. This was too much work for my gang, which concentrated on a few of the "chick sales specials." One of our specials was owned by the biggest crank and miser in town. We didn't fail him. True to our tradition, one of our first calls was on this gentleman's outer resort.

At our usual speed, we had it down pat. Six of us would make a quick rush from the rear and over it would go, easy as pie. Not so this night. To what cost in time and expense he had gone, we never would know, but the frame had been picked up and moved just ahead of where it had always been and should be. By this time, I should be familiar with falling into places which I shouldn't. If the hog wallow was bad, this was worse, only I am an experienced hand. Heading for home, smelling like anything but a rose, I go into the stable through the back door so there will be no inquiries from the house. I disrobe, tossing my clothes in the corral. With a broom and a bucket of water from the horse trough, I give myself a bath. I then beat it for the back door, which for the first time in my memory is locked. What the hell to do? I'm stark naked and damned cold, so try the dining room window, which, thank God, is unlocked and responds to a tug like a good window should. I am all in, just stepping to the floor, when the light goes on and Father is with me. His only remark after hearing my story is, "For God's sake, can't you just once fall in something that smells good!" That finishes me for the night, which will be my last evening to participate in any Halloween festivity. Taking Father's advice, I heat a big pot of water and, with his help and some of Sally's tar soap, I have a good bath. When he inquires what happened to the other five and did I leave any of them in the hole, I tell him Bean Soup and Dago were sick at their stomachs, the two King boys are going to kill the old man and the last I saw of Pat, he was going down the alley in a hell of a hurry. This gives Father a good laugh. "Wait until tomorrow. Your troubles will really begin, so don't get sore," he says. "When someone holds his nose when you come close, just grin. They will only be kidding, Son." I never dreamed that old man could be so smart. He must have been planning this little stunt for the whole year.

My fifteenth and sixteenth years are a decided change and two of the most wonderful years of my life. Father wants to send me east to live with his sister, Josephine, known to all the family and friends as Aunt Jo, and go to school. I'm to spend nine months with Aunt Jo and three months of vacation at home in Sterling or on our ranch. I am not a bit enthused with the idea, but Father and fate always know best. These two years will remain in my memory all my days. My Aunt Jo was one of nature's noblest women.

My new home was up the hill from Marshfield Center, about halfway between Boston and Plymouth, in a beautiful white-shingle house at the front of a forty-five-acre tract of pine woods, overlooking the ocean and South River. Here everything was different from Colorado. I had no ponies but a beautiful Spaulding chainless bicycle to ride to school when the weather was good. When it was impossible to ride my bicycle, I took the school bus. My high school was Marshfield High. Here I met as nice a bunch of kids as I had ever known. They were friendly and kind and made me welcome from my very first day. I made the football and baseball teams, but my greatest sport was with a new shotgun Aunt Jo had for me. In the woods, which were full of partridge, quail and squirrels, I could hunt until tired. Then I had the South River to catch fish. And when the tide was out, there were always all the clams a fellow could dig. My time out of doors was spent doing the things I liked best, but the best of my life was indoors with my darling aunt. In our school we were through at one-thirty, as all studying was done at home. So my evenings were spent in preparing my lessons for another day.

At three o'clock Aunt Jo and I had dinner in front of the fire-place with just the housemaid to see that we had everything necessary. The food was always different. Some days it would be roast, with everything that goes with a roast. Other days partridge or quail, and always on Saturday and Sunday my favorite all of the time, Boston baked beans cooked in an earthen jar and brown bread, with raisins for me while Aunt Jo liked her brown bread plain. For dessert there was sea moss pudding; my aunt had hers with rich Jersey cream, and me she humored with Carnation canned milk, because I liked that best. After dinner I would study until I was through or until just before bedtime, when my darling would say, "Honey, take a pitcher and go down cellar and draw some wine while I warm up a raisin pie." Before bedtime, with home-made rhubarb or dandelion wine and either pie or cheese and crackers, we would talk about all our family, Father and Bud, my uncles and aunts and all the Libbys in general. I learned about Father and Uncle Robert going around the world on a tramp steamer when they were very young. I learned that all the family was originally from Bangor, Maine, and that Aunt Jo had always lived in Boston until she bought this beautiful place to spend her life away from the city. She told me when our family first came over, sometime around 1630, which seemed to me a long time ago, which it was. One thing I was sure of, they never, any of them, had an aunt such as I had. When a fellow eats raisin or mince pie and drinks some wine and goes to bed, he is supposed to die. This could only be a wild dream, for during my happy days with Aunt Jo, I never even had a stomach-ache and I slept like a child.

I only wish I were elegant enough to describe my darling aunt, who was all things to many people. She was gifted with the ability to help those who needed help with a grace and graciousness which made the recipient think he or she had helped themselves. And above all, she was possessed of a charm which was obvious in any company. While others might be turning handsprings to attract attention, Aunt Jo, without attempting to do so, would steal the show.

Through this great lady I learned the meaning of the word

"aristocrat," by just looking at my father's sister, Josephine Dame. God bless her. If it wasn't that I missed my father and brother and my horses, I would never have left for home in Colorado. But come spring, I couldn't get home to the ranch fast enough to hear Bud say, "Boy, am I glad you're home. I sure have a job for you." That was heaven, being with my big brother where I was needed.

5

Our Home Ranch
and a Man with a Gun

MANY MILES ACROSS THE SAND HILLS that parallel the Platte River is our home ranch. At the edge of these hills, where the hard soil formation starts, our ranch begins. Most everything is government land. On some of this land homesteaders are trying to make a living and provide homes for their families by farming, depending on rain which always comes at the wrong time. The soil is good for grazing land but not for farming, and the average stay of a homesteader is about two years. Then the poor devil is starved out, and the government has won again.

The buildings of our ranch, which occupies three hundred and twenty acres of deeded land, consist of a five-room house, a barn and corrals, large water tanks and two windmills. The pastures and grazing land are all leased from the government. Here, when not in school, I spent most of my young life. During my vacations I roamed at will, doing all the things I liked best and learning from my big brother all a fellow should know about horses and cattle. The horses I liked best. They were so beautiful and graceful. I could watch a corral of wild horses for hours, and when Brother Bud was breaking a wild one to ride, I was in seventh heaven, watching and learning every move my brother made, so that when I was big enough I could do the things Bud did in the same way.

Our ranch was perfect for handling wild horses. The house and barns were fenced off from everything with a four-wire fence. From this fence we had two small horse pastures for our gentle horses and those we were breaking. In the other directions, reaching far back into the rolling hills, was our large horse pasture of some two hundred and fifty thousand acres. Our wire corral, which surrounded our big board corrals, was a twelve-wire-high fence which would hold several hundred horses, with wide gates entering from all our pastures. Our two wooden corrals were round in shape with no corners and were made of broad, flat two-by-twelve boards with bolts sunk from the inside into large railroad ties, which were set close together.

The three heavy wooden gates working on swivels were easy to open and close, owing to the way they were balanced. Here the two windmills ran continuously, pumping water into our above-ground storage tanks. These supplied large sunken tanks, which were always full and available to all our pastures. There was plenty of rock salt on tap a short distance from them. Our horses and cattle never had it so good.

Our two windmills were located about a half a mile apart. From these our big pasture fence extended out for miles, except the one extending from the corral where our number one well was. This fence paralleled the other fence for about a mile, then turned abruptly for miles until it eventually tied in with the first to enclose all the leased land. With the two wire fences, half a mile apart and paralleling each other, we had a bottleneck to our main wire corral about one mile long, so that the wild ones hitting this narrow entrance would have no place to go except through the big open gate to the corral. Without this arrangement we never could have controlled the wild ones. It was in this pasture that the wild horses grew fat, having never seen salt, grass or water such as they enjoyed here.

Early in the spring, Brother Bud would buy horses from the Indians in Nevada or anyone who had been successful in trapping a few. Sometimes there were many groups to buy from, as the horses were owned by no one. These horses were the offspring of some who had escaped from the travelers in the early days of the covered wagon, at least that is one theory. But from whence they came makes no difference. They were the most alert and interesting horses in the world. The domestic or hand-raised horses were always slower to learn and never had the stamina of the original wild horse. Buying several hundred or all he could of these horses at five dollars apiece, Bud always got the colts free as well as many of the mares. They would arrive at our home stockyard in the Platte Valley poor, hungry and thirsty. With plenty of water and hay in the stockyard they would begin to pick up immediately. While they were thin and the hair was rough, they were still beautiful. Some were black with white markings, others were buckskin, palomino, sorrels, blacks with white face and legs, bays, browns, solid blacks, blues with curly hair, grays and always some big beautiful stallions.

Many of the wild ones had manes and tails full of cockleburs, matted solid. All of these we would front-foot and lay down, then clean their manes and tails, which would make them look good and certainly feel good. On each one we had to put a small brand on their left jaw, just enough to distinguish them in the event they should get away or escape from the pasture. After they were worked over at the stockyard to our satisfaction, there was the job of getting them to our ranch, which with several good cowboys on fast horses was usually accomplished without too much trouble. In our home corral, we would take our time letting them get used to their new environment, including the salt and water. Looking the bunch over carefully, we would pick at least thirty or fifty to be turned into the pasture with our gentle horses. These we would break at our leisure for cow ponies.

At fourteen, I was allowed to help with the breaking of the wild ones. At fifteen I broke my first horse without any help or advice, just Brother Bud high on the fence watching but not interfering. My first colt, Pal, was a young palomino that was quick as lightning and walked as though he was stepping on eggs. He was a little beauty, and we took to each other like real pals, so my brother gave him to me, and until the day I left Colorado no one else was ever on his back. When I left, I returned him to my brother, where I knew he would always be a pet. In this environment and under my brother's watchful eye, I was in heaven, alone in a corral with a real wild horse to tame. And there were some that were much more difficult than others. One of these was a little sorrel with a white face, a beautiful silver mane and tail, one glass eye and four white legs reaching up to his knees. This one we called Headlight, possibly on account of the blaze face and glass eye. He was not a large horse, but what he lacked in size, he made up in alertness and speed. I had been working him alone, and each time I rode the little monster, I had all I could do to stay on top until he quit bucking. The fifth time I rode Headlight, my brother was out to our ranch and I told him about this little sorrel and what a bucking horse he was. Big Brother wants to see how good he is, so saddling and stepping on, we leave the corral and start out for the big pasture when our little sorrel seems to fall apart. In three jumps, he has me all loose in the saddle. Then he quickly finishes the job, dumping me on my head with a pair of pants split down one leg. Damn, I am sure mad. I have been careful with him and he hasn't responded to good treatment, so I am going to work the baby over good. But Bud stops me, saying, "Son, this is a real bucking horse, so don't do anything to change him. If he wants to buck, we'll sell him to Buffalo Bill's show which will be in town next week, and at a fancy price. Next week, Pard, you bring Headlight and that big gray I shipped in from Nevada on my last trip, and I'll sell them both to the show. Just don't ride either of them again. Let Buffalo Bill's cowboys try their luck."

Two days before the show is to open, I am in town with my two bucking horses. Bud has made a deal with the show's advance agent for a flock of passes, and if their number one cowboy likes our horses, the sale is made at a fancy price. On the day of the big show, I turn our ponies over to the head man, who agrees to ride them that afternoon. This I am going to see. With the big tent, the band and all the noise, I don't know what the little sorrel would do. He might stampede and kill someone, but the big gray I knew would give any cowboy who climbed aboard a ride for his life.

This horse Bud bought because he was a bucking horse. He was not an original wild horse but a farm horse who resented anyone on his back. He was gentle to saddle and would stand perfectly still until the rider was seated, then the fireworks started. This I know because, unknown to my brother, I had tried him out. He damned near jerked my back in two. He could go higher and faster and hit the ground harder than any horse I had ever been on. Truly, he was a natural bucking horse. Nothing was needed to make him buck, such as surcingles or spurs. All a fellow had to do was try and stay put.

Mr. Cody, or Buffalo Bill, had done his act with the guns and it was time to ride our broncos. So the cowboys are out in the arena in all their glory, doing some trick roping, when they announce that one of their punchers is going to ride the big gray. This is what I have been waiting for. He stands still, doesn't seem to be worried about the tent and all the people. He acts just like the farm horse he is, until the guy is seated. Here all resemblance to a nice gentle farm horse is gone. His head goes down, he seems to go straight up in the air and makes a turn, and when he hits the ground the rider is loose in the saddle. One more twist and the puncher is on the ground. The crowd is wild. So what do the show people do? They tell the audience that they will ride the big gray at the night show, along with the bucking horse Headlight, and to be sure to see the show! After this, I find Bud, who has collected his money in cash.

Now Buffalo Bill has two of our horses, one of which dumped his rider at the afternoon show. Though they announced they would ride both at the night show, they don't try even one. Someone has gotten cold feet, and I don't blame them much. All the cowpunchers in our country are razzing Buffalo Bill's boys, so they evidently decided not to risk riding them here.

I only know that Headlight killed the fellow who tried to ride him on their third stop out of our town. He went wild and bucked into a couple of big tent poles. I was sorry we ever sold him. He could have been made into a good pony if we had kept him. All he needed was a real good working over. Bud says all for the best, but for once, I don't agree with my big brother.

On a real hot morning, about eleven o'clock, I come into the house to get myself an early lunch. I have been out in our corral breaking a colt to lead, when there are five short rings on our barb-wire telephone. Our phone is a telephone of sorts, having a party line of nine ranchers within a radius of one hundred miles. It runs on the barbed wire fence, where there is a fence. Where there isn't, it runs on a single wire attached to some small poles stuck in the ground. Each rancher is supposed to take care of his own line. As we are at the end of the line, we don't have too much of a problem. Sometimes it works, sometimes it doesn't. When it does, if a fellow wished, he could carry on a conversation with nine people. There was no privacy. This day, with the five short rings, it turned out to be Bill, an old friend of ours who lived alone about twenty miles from our ranch. He had a lot of cattle and supposedly a pile of money. But he was one hell of a drinker. He didn't just buy a bottle. When he was drinking, it was by the barrel — a big barrel, that is, with a tin cup attached. This only happened about once a year, but when it did, he was a person to stay away from, for at least thirty days. Today he sounded fine. His voice was good with his greeting: "Kid, would you come over and help me this afternoon? I have some young horses to brand . . . and will you do the front-footing and give me a hand?" It has always been customary for all ranchers to help one another. While I had other plans, he is a good friend of my brother's, so I promise to be over as soon as I can catch a bite to eat. Having a half broken horse in the corral, I decide to ride him. The trip will do him good as long as there is no roping with a horse. Anyway, my trip to town is spoiled, so the quicker the better and I am on my way.

To reach Bill's ranch house and corrals, one has to go through three wire gates all within half a mile of the house. With a half broken horse, this takes a little longer than usual. Reaching the first gate and giving a look, I don't see anyone near the stable or the house when I tie my horse to a wagon near the barn. There is still no life, and in the corrals there are no horses. I have about decided someone has been having some fun at my expense, which I am not enjoying in the least. Now I have a feeling that I am being watched and should get on my horse and travel for home. What the devil is going on I am going to find out, so I head for the house. Here is a sight for the Gods. Twenty miles I have to come to find Old Bill seated at the table with no food, but a big tumbler of straight whiskey out of a ten-gallon barrel perched on another table in a far corner. For sure, I'm in trouble now. He tries to have me get drunk with him. If the old guy was human, I might have had a few drinks, but his reputation I know well. When drinking he is always mean and loves to shoot people up and make them dance. He always carries a gun and is a dead shot. That is why he never killed anyone that we knew about. He just scared them to death.

There is nothing more unpleasant than a drunken old man, and one who loves to play with a gun is worse. I know it is just a question of time until this old buzzard makes a play for my feet, and out here a hundred miles from nowhere I don't feel like dancing. So, I talk to him about my brother, hoping this will bring some sense to the old boy's dome, because he has a handsome respect for Bud and may spare Bud's little brother. Staggering to his feet to get a refill from his barrel, the old boy starts to paw me and tell me what a great man I am, all of which I agree with as I lift his gat from the holster. While the old man is getting his refill and talking to himself, I head for my horse tied to the wagon. Here I leave his gun in the bottom of his wagon bed.

It is looking like a clear getaway with no trouble, when I see Old Bill coming out of the door, staggering, cursing and trying to run toward where I am mounting my horse to head for safety. The old boy gets halfway and falls down. By the time I am on my way for the first gate, I see Old Bill moving to the house as fast as his condition will permit. I am dismounting to open the second gate when the gentleman appears at the door with his rifle. The first shot hits about forty feet in front of the bronc. Without closing the wire gate, just giving it a toss, I am mounted and have one more to go when the next shot hits just back of me. The bronc has almost left this world. The old man is in his glory, having a wonderful time. He isn't shooting at us. Had he been, we would never have gotten past the first gate. He is just having himself a hell of a time. My horse is scared to death, and I am not feeling so good. I'm mad enough to murder the old boy. The only thing I am afraid of, in his drunken condition he might kill us accidentally by the gun slipping or any number of things.

At the third gate, I toss it open out of the way, then I have trouble getting on my horse. He's half broken and scared, is trembling like a leaf and wants to run, so I let him run while I do like we do in relay races, grab the mane of your horse and the horn of your saddle and with a running momentum toss yourself in the saddle without using the stirrup. This is fine with a broken and trained horse, but on a baby like I am riding, I expect him to start bucking immediately. This doesn't happen. My bronc is so damned scared that all he wants to do is run, and as for me, brother, he can't run too fast. Old Bill winds up his shooting exhibition by putting one shot down back of us as we disappear around a hill. The gentleman has had a good day.

Why he has never been killed on account of his private sport, I don't know. I remember one of his former stunts. He was going home to his ranch, having been on a large celebration in town, when he fell off his gentle old horse. About this time a car full of men and girls came along the clay road running through the sand hill. This clay road is narrow. If a car goes out too far on either side, said car is there for keeps. Of this the driver was aware, so with Old Bill standing in the middle of the road holding his horse by the reins, the driver had to stop. This was made to order. Out comes Old Bill's gat, and they all did a dance in the sand hill on a muddy clay road with the old boy as their only audience. Gals who had never seen a can-can learned their art under a tough teacher. When the old fellow was so tired he wanted to go home, he made a couple of the men help him on his horse, and the show was over. Nothing ever happened. The law waited until they were quite certain Bill was sober, then they arrested him, but no one appeared against him. Everything was forgotten. Quite a character in any man's country. And me, dumb sap, knowing all about this chap and his love of fun, I fall into his trap for target practice.

What to do? Nothing, just tell Brother Bud, who waits until there has been time to empty the barrel. Then he and our boy Bill have a talk. Bill was sorry, so what? There it ended. Who wants to kill an old man, especially a friend? So everything is just ducky, except I didn't enjoy the party, not even a drink. Our friend Bill I shall leave very much alone. Bud can have the old boy for his very own.

6

A Girl, a Jug of Whiskey
and Sheepherders

Oₙₑ Fᴙɪᴅᴀʏ ᴀꜰᴛᴇʀɴᴏᴏɴ, an old pal of mine shows up at our home ranch where I am breaking colts: Ray Rice, whose father is one of the best cowmen in the business and has a big ranch on the Platte River many miles from our home ranch. Ray is one of my closest friends, a peach of a rider and an all-around cowhand.

We don't agree about breaking horses, as Ray just wants to throw and saddle and ride, which scares a horse to death and in my book is a lousy way to treat a horse. This is about the only thing we don't agree on, so we leave the breaking of horses out of our conversation.

I know from past experience my friend has something on his mind, so I call it a day and we go in to prepare our dinner. While dinner is cooking we partake of a couple of liberal portions of Yellowstone, which Brother Bud gave me on my last visit to the village we call home, and my friend spills his mission, or plan, even before we eat.

It seems Ray met a gal at a dance in our town. Evidently she has what it takes to make a cowpuncher ride a hundred miles, for on Saturday night just thirty miles from our home ranch a bunch of sheepherders are giving a dance, and my pal Ray has promised his new girl he'll be there.

That sheep men have to live, there is no doubt, for they can always be found on the fringe of a good cattle range where the damned sheep spoil the range by grazing the grass too close. Then, there is the smell. No respectable horse or cow will ever eat or drink where a sheep has been. The cow business and sheep business simply don't mix, and I know we have no business going over to a sheep camp to dance. This friend of mine is nuts just because a silly dame has asked him over to a dance where there are nothing but sheep men who hate our guts even before they see us. Going into a hostile camp to see any gal is not for me, so I refuse and he shuts up on the subject until breakfast Saturday morning.

Away we go again. He is not only back on the subject, he wants to ride one of our best horses. If I will go with him, we will stay only a short time and then back to our ranch, thirty over and thirty back. And there is nothing over to the big sheep ranch I can't do without.

I offer to go to town and put the bite on Brother Bud for some dough and take a train to Sidney, Nebraska, where the boys have open shop and a fellow can get a suitcase full of booze if necessary. This doesn't interest my pal, so by three in the afternoon, I agree to loan him one of our best horses and go along for the trip, providing he and his girl make love fast and we get the hell out because I don't like the smell of sheep and neither do my horses.

I give Ray Keno, one of our best horses, and take War Whoop for my mount, and we start out on two of the best trained and toughest horses on our ranch. With plenty of time we hit a leisurely gait to Ray's vision of a sheepherder's delight. On two top horses the thirty miles of open range go fast. Then we reach a fence with sheep wire on the bottom and we know whatever is going to happen will not be long in coming. The night is dark as the proverbial black cat. Which way to a gate? We guess and guess right, for in about a mile we not only find a gate but see a dim light in the distance. This, Ray says, is home sweet home to the sheep men and is where we will find peace and contentment and his new doll. Taking it easy toward the light where we won't strike a wire fence, we are pretty safe, for our horses can both see better than we can at night and a fence is something they know all about. Getting closer to our light we can see, off to the left, some haystacks and sheep corrals. So, riding to a spot not too far from the house, we drop the reins of our horses. I know they will be there no matter what happens. Come hell and high water, they will be waiting. Ray is all dolled up like Puss Irwin's butler. He even has on a tie. Me, I'm in my cowboy working clothes. I throw my big pair of angora chapps over the saddle and we sally forth to rescue Ray's dame — if she needs rescuing.

Here we find she needs rescuing less than any gal we know, at least that is the way it turns out. Keeping my eye cocked to know my way back to our horses without running into anything, I hear much shouting and laughing, when the door opens, giving us a view of a house full of females. But what attracts my attention most is the seven men heading for the sheep corrals.

As though we owned the joint, or were a special celebrity of these parts, Ray knocks on the door and we are in the midst of a bunch of gals. Ray's virgin of doubt was there and looked pretty good. So did the gal she introduced me to, who is her best pal. They had a couple of fiddles and a beat-up piano for music, so the dance was on. We were introduced to two or three men, who showed no signs of fainting from the honor of our acquaintance.

Then the line of men returned from the sheep corrals. These fellows showed more of the same enthusiasm when we were introduced. This didn't worry me much, as we hadn't made a thirty-mile ride to see any men and certainly Ray was going strong, quite oblivious to any cool feeling with the male members. And the little dame is trying to show me a good time, and she don't smell nothing like sheep. She smells real good and interesting. Ray gets me off in one corner with the news that the boys who were breaking toward the sheep corrals have their drinking whiskey hidden there, and his gal has told him just how to find the jug. As long as we're not invited to have a drink, it's customary to help oneself, so let's go. I ask if his girl is going with us. Apparently not, for she had been there before. She would come later when everybody was real tight. Slipping out a side door, the way to the sheep corral and refreshments is a new path, but I watched the way the first contingent had traveled, so I lead to the low fenced corral where Ray takes over. The gal told him right. The jug is there and over three-fourths full. You would think they would offer a fellow a drink, but they hadn't, so here goes, and I take two big swallows before I hand the jug to Ray. He is downing his first gulp when all hell breaks loose. Over the fence like a bunch of sheep come the sheep's masters. Before I can turn around, I am knocked flat. It is so cockeyed dark a fellow can hardly see, but I could feel. I'm on my feet but quick, and not at all happy, so I do a little punching on my own when some big clown says, "I'll teach you to make love to my wife," and boom I hit the dirt again.

I have discovered by now it's high time to get to our horses. I plant one in the big boy's belly, duck out under another fellow and, running low and making time to the fence, I see a shadow going over the top. Pal Ray has had enough. He is not going to say good-bye to his gal and, as he spots me, he remarks, "Those fellows are real mean. Where are the horses?" The poor sap doesn't even know where our horses are. This I do. As it is so dark, there is no rush. I think they are still fighting each other back in the corral. I hope they are, but good. Our horses are where we left them, and so are my hat and the chapps with a big forty-four in the right-hand pocket. Glad I brought it along for the ride. We are through the gate to the open range and I am close enough to see Ray is carrying something when he says, "Let's have a swig." He has escaped with the jug, three-fourths full of booze. The guy is smart. He put the jug up in front of him for a shield. Every time a sheepherder swung he hit the jug. I bet there are several broken hands among our recent hosts. My left hand feels like I had hit the jug. It's all swollen and hurts like no-body's business, and my left eye I know is a pip. It's always my poor left eye that gets popped.

"And Ray, did you hear the big calf crying about his wife? Evidently this dame your recent girlfriend introduced me to was married. No wonder she wanted to hit a haystack, married to that guy!"

What a wonderful time we have had when we reach home. We have traveled sixty miles to get beaten up and acquire a jug of booze. When will I ever learn? I have the rest of the night and Sunday to put a poultice on my eye and soak my hands for Monday. Bud is bringing some horse buyers out to buy some of our wild horses. Corralling this bunch of wild babies is real work, and if my hand is no good Bud will have to do all the roping, which isn't going to make him very happy. When he sees my eye, I know I'm going to catch hell for going near a sheepherder's whiskey. It has finally dawned on

Ray that his girl told the gang where we were. She wasn't so hot for my friend or had found it safer to cry wolf. Anyway, he is through with girls. Nuts to him and his love affairs.

So I now have a bad eye and an awfully sore hand and may have a damned sore brother on Monday morning when he takes one look at me. This is about par for the course. He should be used to me by now. Come Monday I'll know. Lady Luck, stay with me.

7

Wild Horse Roundup
for Polo Ponies

Monday morning I am up early, so I can have my breakfast and get the saddle horses in the corral before Bud and his party arrive. I'm determined to make the best possible impression on my big brother, because I know I was dead wrong in looking for trouble at a sheep camp.

Ray left me early Sunday, taking a half pint of the sheepherders' whiskey with him, leaving quite a few drinks in the jug for Bud and his gang if they need an appetizer. My eye is better, although much discolored, and I see rather well. The left hand is still sore and means no roping, so Bud is stuck if there is any work with a rope.

The guys must have left home in the middle of the night, for it's only nine o'clock and a buckboard with four men is crossing through the pasture toward our house. I open the gate, letting them in our big wire corral, where at the barn they unload. Bud has brought two good riders to give us help in corralling the wild horses, and his buyer, Mr. Miller. Before they are all on the ground, everyone yells, "What happened to you?" This I knew was coming, so I spill the works and don't give myself the best of it, because it wouldn't go over with Bud. He has taught me always to give it to him straight, so now he has the worst, and I feel better.

Everyone gets a hell of a kick out of Ray and his jug for protection, and when I make known the fact that there is some left, everyone heads for the house before going to work. Here my big brother looks me over and decides I came out rather well, except the hand which he says we'll have X-rayed tomorrow.

Bud and the two punchers, Blondy Arnold and Dave Collier, have their saddles, so will ride three of our top horses. Bud will ride Silver, his very special. I will ride War Whoop and the other two fellows will ride Keno and Rowd. All were originally wild horses but now are four of the fastest and best of all, and they can run all day.

As we saddle up, we leave the buyer, Mr. Miller, at the windmill, where he can't be seen but will have a good view of what takes place. The four of us ride out into the large pasture about a mile, where the one fence turns right for miles. This is the end of our bottleneck.

Since I am light weight, I always have the key spot to turn the horses toward the entrance to our big wire corral. The trick is starting the bunch from the far side of our large pasture toward this spot and keeping them coming until they're pushed into the corral. Today should be easy. We have about nine hundred wild ones, but about two hundred are yearlings and two-year-olds which were shipped in as babies, so are not as wild as the others, which is a big help in controlling the others. All are nice and fat and full of run, but thanks to the windmills and salt and a few half gentle ones, we don't anticipate too much trouble.

Bud sends Dave to the far side of our pasture, leaving the three of us to hold them in the bottleneck so they can't get back out to the large part of the pasture. As we're waiting for Dave to start them running, Bud tells me about Mr. Miller. He was sent to Bud by a St. Louis commission man who knows all about our wild horses and how wonderful they are if properly broken and trained. But Mr. Miller only wants thirty, which don't make sense to me. All this work to sell thirty for forty-five dollars a head seems silly, when always other buyers buy two or three hundred or all we have at a price. This thirty business surprises me indeed — until I learn he is out for polo ponies, and all said ponies have to be a certain height, of a certain weight, and trained to follow a ball like a cow pony follows a cow.

Bud says he's sure we have the kind he wants, and may get as much as one hundred and fifty apiece if they're properly broken. He don't have to say any more. I know what's coming. I'm stuck, and here they come following the fence to our number two windmill. Here in the flat, with fences on three sides, they will mill around and finally settle down, while we close in and gently ease the entire bunch into our number one wire corral.

At this point Bud says to leave them while we go in and have some food and they get over their scare. I take the two punchers who I've known for years with me to help with the food, which won't take long, for everything is out of cans, except biscuits, beans and sow belly. The guys are more interested in the jug than in helping me, which is fine, as I do better alone.

Bud and his buyer come in and Bud has a couple bottles of his favorite, which he brought out this morning. So he and Mr. Miller ignore my jug, which is more than all right with me.

This Mr. Miller is a nice guy. A little on the short, pudgy side, but awfully jolly, and he wants to know all about my deal with the sheepherders again. He can't seem to get it out of his mind when my big brother, who usually doesn't put me on the spot, has to come up with "You know this isn't my kid brother's first contact with the sheep boys. He damned near got killed the first time. It was almost identical to what happened in this affair. I sent him to represent me at a roundup some eighty miles the other side of the Platte, up in the Buttes. So a gang of punchers went over to a sheep camp and were messing with the gals when one of the sheep men started shooting. My young brother headed for his horse. While he was bent over, climbing through a wire fence, the guy put two holes through the inside pocket of his coat. I thought that would cure the taste for sheep, but I guess not. What about it, Pard?" When I assure him I am cured for life, he only says, "I hope."

The guys eat like horses. They clean me out of everything, which Bud says is good, for I am to go with them to town to have my hand X-rayed. While I was preparing our meal, Bud and his buyer were looking the horses over, sitting on the high board fence, and Mr. Miller was as excited as a kid. He had never seen such a magnificent band of horses all together at one time. There were all

kinds of colors, but best of all were the style and movement. They
were in a class of their own. He keeps asking Bud to put a price on
War Whoop, Silver and Pal. This Bud would not do, explaining that
Pal belonged to me and was the first horse I had ever broken by myself, while Silver was his own pet and War Whoop was the number
one horse in my string of ten cow ponies.

For some reason, this seemed to please Mr. Miller. Anyone
who thought enough of their pet horses to refuse money, the horses
and man must both be all right. Bud did tell him he could have a
little gray horse I broke the year before — we called him Possum —
as a start toward his thirty polo ponies if they could agree on a price.
So out to the horses we go, where we are going to let Mr. Miller pick
forty of the horses he thinks will be best.

With Dave and Blondy working the larger wooden gates to the
board corrals, Bud and I cut out the ones Mr. Miller chooses. This is
a slow job, but finally we have forty of the most beautiful little
horses separated from the others. All except this forty we release to
the big pasture. I have never seen any man so pleased and happy as
our buyer, Mr. Miller, is with these ponies. They are all about the
same size, and he has picked mostly blacks, bays, sorrels, grays and
only one palomino. With the forty where Bud and Mr. Miller can
look until they deal or else, Dave, Blondy and I leave them to their
trading. It isn't long until Bud calls me and walks me off to a place
where we can talk. "Pard, how long do you think it will take you to
break thirty-five of these babies the way we break horses like, say,
Possum and Pal? The reason I ask is, if we can do the job by September, I can get one hell of a price, but they must be perfectly broken. If we can make this sale, we will have something good going
every year and while I don't know anything about polo, these ponies
will be different and better than anything the East has ever seen.
He wants to take delivery on the tenth of September, and I will fur-
nish you with some young puncher and his wife to do the cooking
and help you and will give you twice your wages each month, plus
ten dollars for each horse we deliver. This way, you will have quite
a bank roll for this winter."

This is too much, and I tell my big brother he doesn't have to
give me that kind of money. I would almost work for nothing, just

for the pleasure of training such a nice bunch of colts. All I want him to do is not give me any cheap cowboy with a wife to get in our way but a top boy like Dave and pay him top wages, someone who can help, not be in my way.

Bud is sure a peach. He understands and agrees to let me hire Dave and one other good hand and pay them tops and, best of all, he will help until the thirty-five have been broken to lead and I have ridden all of them once. With this, I'm in clover. We can't miss, and I almost drop dead when I learn that Mr. Miller is going to give three hundred per head for thirty and he might take the thirty-five. Bud is going to give him a demonstration of what a trained wild horse looks like with Possum, the little gray. Bud says, "Just think, with this sale we will have more than twice the cost of all our horses and have them all free and clear, and Mr. Miller is to sign a contract at the bank and put up some money tomorrow to cinch the deal, and will Father be pleased?" Yes, and what about Father, when he sees me with this eye and fist. "Look, Son, if Father sees you walking, he will be satisfied. As long as they don't carry you home feet first, he will be satisfied. Besides, I will be there to run interference for you. Only, tell him the worst, don't hold back. He knows you are far from being a choir boy."

It doesn't take Bud long to show how well Possum works, which is really my job. As I have a bad hand, he does it better than I could with a good hand. He takes the little gray out to the open by placing his hand over his mane, and then, bareback, without any hackamore or bridle but by holding on to his mane with his left hand, jumps on his back and by the pressure of his knees and holding his mane makes the little gray pivot, run and turn in a way Mr. Miller said he had never seen any polo pony do, and he has a finishing school for polo ponies.

As it is now the tenth of July and my birthday is the fifteenth, Bud was going to have me home for that day anyway, even if I didn't have a bad hand. Sally is going to make a special cake and I will be eighteen, which is more years than Father expected me to be around. Up to now, I have fooled all the family except Bud. He always expects the best.

I am to take our own team and buckboard with Dave and follow Bud, who has rented the outfit he is driving from the livery stable. When I come back to start work I will need to bring a load of groceries and two boys with me, because we won't be going to town for a couple of months. We don't reach home until midnight, and Father is asleep, which is perfect, so in the morning I am in no hurry. I let Father and Bud eat some of Sally's hotcakes before I appear. They are always up early, which gives my big brother time to tell Father all the news and, I hope, have the way all cleared for my entrance. My appearance is just right. Father is in a beautiful mood. He takes a look at my hand and wants Sally to look me over, as she is a honey at mending eyes and hands, but they all agree I need an X-ray. This is wonderful. I'm not even told to stay away from sheep camps. I guess everyone thinks by now I have had enough to last me a lifetime. They are so right!

I have a letter from Aunt Jo that has been waiting for two weeks, enclosing a fifty-dollar check. This I proudly exhibit with the remark, "She knows you fellows are starving me to death." This isn't very smart, for Sally hasn't fed me my hotcakes yet, and "Boy," she says, "you can eat oats with the horses this morning." Nevertheless, with a lot of soft soap on my part, she feeds me breakfast for a king.

Driving Father's famous mare, we all leave for town in high glee, me for the doctor, Father and Bud for the bank to meet Mr. Miller. The contract is completed and Bud has some of Mr. Miller's money as a guarantee, and our gentleman buyer wants to buy my little palomino for five hundred dollars, which is no dice. As long as this pony lives he stays with us, where he has a good home. We don't sell our pet horses. Besides, Pal is special.

Summer is almost over. With my two helpers, Dave Collier and Hal Day, we have worked every day, even Sundays, with good results, far better than we expected. Every one of the ponies is full of pep but thoroughly broke. We have even gotten them familiar with a mallet, as Mr. Miller sent Bud two polo mallets with polo balls, so in a flat part of our pasture we have given them practice in following the ball.

Mr. Miller arrived three days early and has stayed at the ranch with us overnight and is happy as a fellow could be with his ponies.

They are now his. All we have to do is deliver them to the stock-yards, where they will be loaded on special horse cars attached to a passenger train. No freight car for them. He tried to hire me to make the trip east with the ponies, but I don't want to go. Besides, Bud wants me to join the roundup wagon in a few days, so Mr. Miller hires my two helpers, Dave and Hal, with a round-trip ticket and good wages.

No wonder he wanted to buy Pal so bad. He finally, the night he stayed at our ranch, after a couple of stiff Yellowstone highballs, confessed he could get at least twenty-five hundred for him from some of the millionaire polo players. It is evidently a rich man's game, and I'm glad. That's good for my family. Bud has paid me more money than I know what to do with, except to spend it. So I buy Sally a couple of pretty dresses, Father a couple of horse blankets for his harness mare and gaited saddle horse, which pleases him more than anything I could have possibly bought him personally. It was Bud's suggestion. My big brother I buy a beautiful automatic forty-four with a light shoulder holster and two of the best special hemp ropes in existence. So, for myself, I go to Sidney, Nebraska, which is a short distance from our home, where the town is wide open. I buy a dozen and a half of the best old Yellowstone, six for Father, six for Bud. The others I take to the ranch and prepare to join the roundup.

8

Phoenix, Wild Horses,
Wild Steers and a Broken Leg

THIS WINTER, 1910, I AM EIGHTEEN. But now it seems the weather has caught up with me. The thing that brought on the crisis, I got wet this fall and developed a hell of a cough, so Father is sure I must have consumption. Between Father and the doctor I am shuffled off to Phoenix before Christmas. Phoenix is wonderful, the prettiest place I have ever seen. The city is full of people who have what Father thinks I have, only I don't. By the time I stepped off of the train, my cough had completely disappeared. A two-page letter to my honorable parent informs him that I want to come home.

There are all kinds of cowmen around the wagon yards, and I have already been offered a job breaking horses, but I decide to wait until I get word from Father. The cowmen only come to town twice a year, hauling out enough supplies to last six months each trip. If I hear from home before Mr. Wilbur goes back to the mountains, I am his boy, because the wages don't scare him one bit.

Never having worked in the mountains, this will be a new experience, providing there are no objections from home, and the news from home is good. "Take a job for three months until the weather breaks at home," Father writes. "If you must work, find something easy — not breaking horses." Father will have me milking cows yet!

If Mr. Wilbur is still in town, I am going to work for him. It will be for six months, but no one will mind so long as I am not breaking horses, which is just what I am going to do. We are off to the Mazatzal Mountains, which Mr. Wilbur says is across the desert. After the desert comes the Verde River. His home camp is close to the river and at the edge of the Mazatzal Mountains. His upper camp is some twenty miles up in the mountains, where travel is impossible except on horseback, which makes it necessary to pack everything needed. For this purpose he has ten Spanish mules and a couple of horses for a pack train.

The big wagon, pulled by four mules, is loaded to the guards with every known kind of supplies. The first part of our trip from Phoenix is through the desert. It is hot and dry and we drive at night to avoid as much heat as possible. To my surprise, when I join the wagon Mr. Wilbur's wife is with us, parked up in the seat where I was expecting to enjoy the eighty-five-mile trip, so I find a spot to ride among the supplies.

The trip we're making is for men. A woman is in the way, but the lady hadn't seen a town for six months and won't be back for another six months. She must be nuts or something. It's a cinch I wouldn't have taken the job had I known there was a Mrs. Wilbur.

When we arrive about noon the next day, the number one camp proves to be a beauty. There is a small three-room house and a corral close to the Verde River, surrounded by the foothills at the edge of the Mazatzal Mountains where the grass is just beginning to turn green. Here I meet Chico, a Mexican cowboy who has worked for Mr. Wilbur for many years. He is considerably older than I, knows all the tricks of mountain cowpunching and teaches me the art of packing a pack train, something I knew nothing about.

It dawns early on me how smart Chico is. He won't break horses, and that probably accounted for the old man's not squealing at my top wages. The horses to be broken to ride are at the upper camp, some twenty miles away, mostly up. I reason that if it took a pack train to get there, it will be rough and dangerous to ride a bad horse. After Chico telling me just how tough it is, I realize that, as usual, I have moved too fast, and it's eighty-five miles back to Phoenix. Damn it, Father is always right. How right, I learn later.

The land where I grew up and learned about horses and cattle was level except for a few sand hills and the odd prairie dog hole, which were a rider's worst hazard. Any resemblance between the prairies of Colorado and the Mazatzal Mountains? There isn't one. In these mountains you are always looking straight up or down. There just isn't any level spot, and here is where I am supposed to break five colts to ride. Then Chico and I are to work the back country and gather cattle that have strayed high into the mountains. As long as I am going to be killed, we might just as well get it over with.

Chico and I crawl out bright and early to corral the five horses which are to be my saddle horses and, with Chico as my assistant, we waste no time. One by one I front-foot and lay them down where I tie up a hind foot so they can't kick, then clean out their manes and tails. I break them to lead by using a war bridle until they follow me like a dog. When they are good, they get a petting. I get them familiar to the saddle, on and off, while I have a foot tied up, get on and off a few times with the foot tied until they get used to me and find I am not going to hurt them. Then, while standing, I untie the foot and, before the horse is on to me, step back in the saddle. He is then free to buck or run, or whatever he wishes.

All these preliminaries are done in the corral. What will happen when the gate is open and you are on the outside, one never knows, but with a good man like Chico on a gentle horse riding herd for you, if he don't go crazy and jump over a cliff, everything is fine. Which isn't likely, for most horses will buck with their eyes open and won't do anything that will injure themselves.

By night, all five have been worked over and old man Wilbur is more than pleased, and so am I. The worst is over, at least as far as I know. Brother, I have a lot to learn about mountain work. On the level or in a corral, I can rope with the best, but here in the mountains, I have to learn a different method. This Chico will teach me.

One week after arriving at our mountain retreat, I have my five horses partially broken and ready for further training. So with three of these and seven real cow ponies, Chico and I go over a couple of steep ranges of mountains to Deadman's Creek, where we join ten other ranchers from other outfits. We have ten saddle horses and three little mules for pack animals, carrying our food and bed rolls as we are to be out two months. Here begins one of the most interesting experiences of my young life.

Starting early and with Chico taking the lead with our pack mules, we wind our way back and forth over trails that are not visible to me but must look like boulevards to Chico. Deadman's Creek, I find, is just a wide spot in a very wide canyon with a fast stream of water running by a large, high rail corral. Unpacking and hobbling our horses so they can't travel far, we proceed to make camp. While ten other men will join us, each outfit works separately in teams of two. You have separate food, individual cooking. Everything is done in teams, except when there are a number of cattle to move.

As we are a day ahead of the others, we have plenty of time. While enjoying our evening meal, Chico brings me up to date on our mission. "High and back in the chaparral and manzanita are hundreds of big steers, seven and eight years old. They escaped back there when they were branded, quite young, and have never been out, can't be driven out and are real wild cattle. Every spring representatives from different brands gather here for the purpose of catching as many of these steers as possible. This is the reason for the high rail corral, for steers can jump any ordinary corral. Here they are held with some gentle cattle until they are tame enough to move to pasture. The only way they can be brought out is to lead them, which is why we have those twelve eight-foot ropes you unloaded from the pack mule, and it is also why we work in pairs.

"Tomorrow we will go early on a trail coming in back of some big thickets and try to catch some grazing cattle in the open, where I will try and rope one. If I catch him, you hind-foot him and we both stretch him out while I tie one of the short ropes around his horns and saw off the sharp ends so he can't gore our horses. Then we tie him to a tree, where he will stay all night, and the next day we lead him down the trail to our corral. We take turnabouts in catching, which is why I brought another sixty-foot ratio. You will find it better roping in the brush because you throw a small loop hard and fast. You have only one chance."

This seemed almost unbelievable, that two cowpunchers would climb for hours to get a throw at one steer and, if they caught him, would have to lead the animal out. One of you ahead on a long rope, the other behind, so Mr. Steer could only go where you wanted him to go. If you missed your throw, the day was a total loss. This, Chico explained, had happened to him, but he thought we would make a good pair. While I had no experience with a light rawhide rope like he used, I would do all right heeling and stretching after he caught the steer and, with a little experience, the rest would come easy.

Chico said if we could average one steer each day, Mr. Wilbur would be very pleased. In my opinion, the old man was damned easy to please. I thought we could surely do better than that, which we did.

Early in the morning before it is light, we have our breakfast and are saddled and ready. I take a big blue roan that Chico says is a honey on the end of a rope. I hope to hell, in these mountains, I am half as good as my horse looks. Today will tell. We have climbed back and forth up the side of the mountain to get above where the big steers are hiding. For the last hour we have been walking and leading our horses across slag slides, around big boulders, so they won't be so tired when we go into action. All of this to catch a damned steer!

I have never walked so far in my life, even where it's level, especially leading a horse, and with a good pair of high-heeled boots. My chapps are hanging on the saddle horn. At least the horse is carrying them. He is certainly in better condition than me. Chico has the lead, for he knows where we are going, or at least thinks he does. He is like a mountain goat and just as sure footed, while I slide and puff. I am getting thoroughly unsold on this kind of cow business, when he finally stops for a breather.

Chico assures me the long climb is over, so we mount our horses and head for the deep thickets where we have a chance to catch some of the big babies out in the open. His plan is to go ahead of me and do the catching by the head, then I can catch the heels and will stretch our steer out so Chico can work on his horns with safety. This action is something I am anxious to see, for in my country when we cut the horns, we cut them close to the head. Chico says they just saw off enough horn so they can't gore your horse if they should get that close. The little saw he carries in a small leather case attached to his saddle doesn't look like much to me. It seems so tiny.

From where we are, I have time to see the view. On every side of us there are mountains covered with timber. In places there are open spots with no trees, and in some of these open spots are horses and a few cattle. The mountains appear to run in every direction, but their bottoms are in Deadman's Creek. This is my first time to see a country like this. It is so vast and magnificent, no wonder cattle escaped into these mountains for safety.

Starting toward a thicket slightly off to our left and below us, we have our ropes unbuckled and laying over the horns of our saddle, so with a quick slight swing you have a small loop that you can throw hard and fast. I have my own rope, as Chico's long rawhide just didn't seem right for me. Not wanting to be a complete loss for the first day, I stuck to what I was used to. Going through our first thicket, we hear a hell of a commotion, and out headed for the opening is one of the big steers with the largest pair of horns I have ever seen. He's traveling like a race horse. I am completely taken by surprise, but not Chico. He is after him, and with the fastest and best throw and under the least favorable conditions, he catches Mr. Steer just as he hits the chaparral. As for me, I'm struck dumb, but not for long. Coming down the trail and past me is an even bigger steer. Without any effort, my loop is opened and thrown. It settles just over the baby's horns. With the speed he was going and down-hill, I simply turn the big roan uphill, lean forward to help take the shock. The big steer hits the end of my rope and hits the ground with a thump. Before he can start to recover, leaving the big roan to keep him stretched out, I am on him, and with the tie rope all cow-boys carry attached to a loop in their chapps I have him tied where he won't be going anyplace until I'm ready.

The big roan giving me slack in my rope, I remove it and go looking for my friend Chico, who is wondering what has happened to me, because I wasn't supposed to do any roping. For if we both caught a steer and they both got into the thicket, we would have no way of helping one another. The only thing that saved me was having a short rope and a close catch on my steer. He was turned upside down about ten feet from the chaparral. Chico's steer was back in a clump of trees tangled around, so Chico couldn't get a chance to bust him. Without someone to stretch said steer out, neither one of them were going anyplace. That is why two men are needed.

It wasn't long until the sharp part of his horns were sawed off and he was tied to a tree with one of the head ropes Chico carried on the back of his saddle. Here he could fight the tree until tomorrow, when we would lead him down the trail.

The fact that my partner was pleased to find me with a steer tied up down-trail made me feel good all over. He was so sincere that to work with this Mexican boy was something to be proud of, because he was the fastest and best roper in the mountains. Without him, on the flat or in a corral I had a chance, but when we hit the mountains and thickets I was lost, unless a lucky stab like my first steer coming out of the thicket into the open.

I never worked so hard in my life. We were always through breakfast and on our way before daylight and wouldn't return to camp until long past dark. Then we would cook up something to eat. I was always hungry and feeling better than ever and wished Father and Brother Bud could see me. They would quit worrying about my health.

We have wound up our chore this spring and are to return to camp where Mr. and Mrs. Wilbur are and look forward to having some home-cooked food for a change. The ten men who joined us are a congenial bunch. Two of them have not seen a town for five years. They had a run-in with John Law, who knew they were hiding out in the mountains but never made a search for them, probably figuring it was a lost cause.

All of the men are experts with their ropes, but Chico and I have caught the most steers, averaging two a day by plugging away relentlessly. Everyone in the crowd carries a gat, with the exception of me. I feel undressed. A sheriff would surely get fat coming in here to get his man. It's a good place to hide out after robbing a bank, only there is no place to spend your money. Not even for a soda pop.

The old man is pleased as a kid with a new red wagon when Chico gives him a report on our work. Evidently, the steers we caught will bring him some extra dough. He wants me to break five more colts and has agreed that Chico and I can return to his home camp on the Verde River, where the ground is not so rough, and we won't have to hurry like we did on the first five. With the Verde to fish in, a house to live in and only five colts to break, we are in clover.

The first morning we started to work, everything went perfect. I rode two, then we stopped work for a midday meal and decided to only ride one in the afternoon, then catch some fish. The afternoon horse was a little buckskin and tough. I worked him over as usual, and when we came out the gate into the open territory, he started to buck toward a dead mesquite with a lone branch sticking out. Before Chico could get between us and the tree, this bronco had hit the tree and somehow the dead limb was pushed through between my right leg and my stirrup. One jump and I felt my leg go and fell off on the other side with a badly broken leg.

Cutting the boot off, Chico straightened the leg, which we wrapped with cotton batting out of one of the bed quilts. With part of a shingle on each side, Chico wrapped it tight with strips from a towel. It is a good thing we were not at the upper camp, or I could have twenty miles on back of a horse with my leg hanging down. As it is, we turn all the horses loose in the pasture and at sundown start for Phoenix, eighty-five miles away, me in the back of the buckboard on the bed roll and Chico driving the mule team. The trip will take all night with only one bright spot. About halfway to Phoenix, we hit the desert and meet an outfit coming out with a bunch of bulls, traveling at night to avoid the heat. This was the Cavaness boys, one of whom had worked with us on Deadman's Creek. Upon hearing what happened to me, he gives me a quart of good bourbon. By the time we reach Phoenix at daylight, I feel no pain and have no bourbon.

We are a sight when we reach St. Joseph's Hospital, as neither of us has shaved for a week. I have one boot off and hobble to the hospital door and without any delay or commotion I am in a bed. A doctor shows up and removes the homemade splint and packs my leg in ice bags to reduce the swelling. Chico says he is going to feed the mules, take a little rest, then head back to the Verde River where he will catch a horse for the upper camp, see the Wilburs, collect my three months salary and return, pronto.

What a hell of a disturbance I have caused. Before my new doctor leaves the hospital, I ask him if he would write Father, making it easy so he wouldn't feel too badly. Boy, the doctor is a peach. He not only tells me to relax, that he will handle Father, but he'll have a barber work me over, as he put it. But he wouldn't be pinned down as to how long I would be laid up. "Just take it easy and enjoy the rest" was his sound advice.

One week to the day since I landed in the hospital, the doctor came in with a letter from Father. It contained a check for two hundred dollars, which Doc says he will cash. Father tells Doc to send the bill to him and to get me home soon as possible. And the doctor tells me that Father isn't stuck for the bill, since Henry Wilbur, who is a good friend of his, is going to pay my expenses, as I was hurt while working for him. Chico is back with a check for three months wages and a nice letter from the Wilburs, which raises my spirits because I felt bad causing everyone so much trouble.

The best news of all, however, was that Chico had done such a fine job setting my leg straight that it would be placed in a cast and I would be up and about on crutches. My letter from Father was a peach. No bellyache about my getting hurt. "Just cheer up, Son. We are all glad your cough is gone. Your brother suggests you get a job in the 'Bed Pan' department." He must be crazy or something.

I don't only have the best father in the world, but the best looking one. He is built just like the guy who used to be on all the police gazettes, Bob Fitzsimmons,* only Father is better looking!

I have now been home four months. The old leg is as good as new, although I favor it a bit. Have been out to the ranch with Bud helping him break a few colts and am going on the fall roundup for two months. I have been drawing top wages, even if I haven't been doing too much. I am surely lucky in the brother and father department.

---

*The storied English boxer, who won the world heavyweight title from Gentleman Jim Corbett in Nevada in 1897.

9

Christmas Eve,
with Hundreds of Dead Cattle

It is Christmas Eve morning, 1911, and from the only door in my two-room sod house, through the blizzard that is raging, I can just barely see the sod stable, some five hundred yards away, where my three very special cow ponies are warm and snug. Around me, death is everywhere. Huddled close to each other and close to the house are hundreds of cattle. All are doomed. Hundreds have already died, or have been killed by me from a tap on the head with the blunt part of an axe. The ones I killed were mercy killings, as their feet and ankles were frozen and they were unable to stand. There is no food or shelter for them. There has been no food since the tenth of October when this storm started, and the temperature has been continually below freezing.

Stock that died in the freeze were thin. The white part of their bodies had turned yellow and they were covered with lice. Their eyes were pitiful and sunken and held the most helpless and sorrowful expression. Their death was a blessing.

Going from the house to the stable, I can walk most of the way on dead cattle. Some are covered with snow, others are visible where the wind has blown the snow away. Some I have pulled away from my door and the only two windows in the house, where they had huddled trying to live. The weak were trampled where they froze and stuck. So, with my cow ponies, I drag them away. This performance I shall repeat when the storm subsides enough for me to see to do my work without freezing. Every day I have to dispose of some dying in their tracks and beyond hope. This will go on until all have died or there is a sudden change in the weather, which is unlikely, and even if that should happen tomorrow, not very many would be saved. It is too far from food and shelter, and the snow is drifted too high between us and civilization. But my guess is that it will be April before any great change occurs.

Smart boys who know everything will say this is an act of God. This I can't swallow. While I am only nineteen and not too well versed in God and his ways, I am sure no God would have anything to do with thousands of cattle suffering and starving to death as they are doing this winter.

Perhaps the cowmen have erred. It has always been their custom to depend on the range cattle to come through the winter on grass they can rustle. Even if a big storm comes, it doesn't last too long. The wind usually leaves some spots of grass uncovered, and the sun obligingly melts other spots. So the cowmen don't do too badly. There is always a certain percentage of loss, but with the coming of spring, there is new life. New grass is like a fresh tonic. The will to live revives. The winter has cost the cowman a few cattle. With practically no outlay of cash, with the new calfs in the spring, together with a year's additional weight on the older cattle, the cowman is much more than ahead. But this is a winter to end all winters, the like of which has never happened in my lifetime. Early in October the rains started, then turned to sleet. Freezing weather followed to form ice over all the grass, freezing it solid. Then more snow, with no sun to ease the blow. Just snow and wind. Even the bare spots where there was some grass were frozen over with ice. The cattle have had no food for three months. There is no hay — no nothing.

Early in the storm, some cattle drifted into the deep canyons for protection from the winds and were soon covered with snow. They died in their tracks. Others drifted up against some building or fence, where they hump up in a huddle and wait for the end.

I have been here at Battle Ground Springs for two months and twenty days. How do I know? I have circled the days on a large calendar which came with the cases of canned food and groceries that are my winter supply. If only I could share some of my comfort with the poor devils outside my walls! In my house, which has three-foot-thick sod walls, plaster on the inside, and only two windows, I have shelter from the storm.

The windows I have boarded on the outside, leaving only a four-inch space for light so some steer won't fall through. My domicile is a two-room affair, the larger room acting as a storeroom and bedroom. Here are all my canned goods, such as Carnation cream, canned corn, tomatoes, peas, different kinds of fruit, also dried fruits. This room is always cold, as the door between is always closed except at night when I am in bed. The kitchen is small. It has an excellent coal stove that burns nut coal, keeping the room real comfortable as the fire is never permitted to go out.

At the back of the stove is sourdough working in a stone crock. Out of this crock comes the best hotcakes and biscuits known to man. In another pot is beans and sowbelly, with the usual pot of coffee close at hand. I have no problem of survival with all this food. As for my three cow ponies, they are living it up. Their quarters have thick walls like the house, and large spacious stalls with sliding windows in front of their mangers through which I poke alfalfa-baled hay that was hauled out before the storm along with the coal and food for my winter supplies and cracked corn and barley for their one meal a day. Their water comes from a spring from under a bluff, running down and back of the stable. But today they will have their morning drink out of a bucket, as last evening I carried up three buckets of water to the stable so their morning drink won't chill their insides.

When the weather is half decent and one can see, I give each pony a workout, dragging dead cattle out of the springs where they have tumbled from a steep bank. On the very edge of this bluff is one end of my house, leaving only three sides for the poor devils to huddle against. The stable they can't reach, as it is protected by a high board corral against which many cattle have perished.

Today isn't fit for man or beast. It is Christmas Eve. Even my ponies will have a treat. No storm for them. A drink of water, not too cold, plenty of hay and the usual brushing with a good stiff brush to keep their manes and tails beautiful and their coats slick and glossy. It is the first time in their lives anything like this has happened to them, and they like it! In the past they have been treated like ordinary cow ponies, and now, the first time we have been together, their status is royalty.

With me, it is something to do and gives me pleasure. They are my only friends, the only ones I have to talk with, and to say they don't understand would be foolish. I like to brush their coats and make a fuss over them. They are badly spoiled, and the next cowpuncher that comes into their life will get a surprise, because the two younger ones, the buckskin and the gray, are very touchy and take some understanding, while the light bay is older, with more experience, and is the best cow pony I have ever seen. He works easy and sure, never takes two steps where one will do and is always poised to move, which he does without apparent effort. In other words, he's one hell of a rope horse and can make even a poor cowpoke look good.

I was told when I picked the trio up at the river ranch to watch the two young horses or I might find myself in trouble such as had happened to others. To this advice I paid very little attention, for I have learned by much experience, young as I am, that horses are smarter than humans. They know the minute you come near if they can trust you. Also, if there is any fear, they know immediately and act accordingly.

During my short span of life, I have broken many horses to ride. Many of these were wild horses that had never seen a human until trapped, many were domestically raised and others known as bad actors who were classed as outlaws, but regardless of what they were or where they came from, I have never seen a horse I didn't like. All are different, in many ways, but all are quick to recognize fear and equally quick to know their master. If tough treatment is necessary, the man who shows no fear and is kind but firm will soon gain their control and respect.

A bad horse is the result of a bad cowpuncher who wants a horse to buck so he may show off, or a bad-tempered, inexperienced person doing something for which they are not qualified. There are no bad horses — just bad people.

My three pets have never made a move to hurt me. Although the buckskin is my favorite, I try not to show my favoritism. He does like to buck around, stiff legged, when I take him out to work, but it is only play and to warm up. For when I fasten the rope over the horns of a dead steer to move it, he is all business. He stands still with the rope taut while I cut the frozen body loose. Then, when I climb aboard in all my heavy clothes, he could make it plenty tough if he did not like and understand me and that we were working, not playing. This buckskin has the most beautiful markings of any cow pony I have ever seen. There is a black stripe running down his back, with four legs black to the knees, a luscious mane and tail, and he is unusually wide between the eyes, as are the other two ponies. While all three are exceptional, this guy has a habit of whinnying to greet me mornings before I reach the door. The other two show their happiness by jumping around in their stalls, but the buckskin seems to be the only one capable of making some sort of vocal greeting. He seems to be saying, "Where the hell have you been all night? I'm hungry."

It is no wonder that I love these three. I haven't seen a human since moving in on October tenth and it is not likely I shall for the next two or three months. We are completely isolated, which is not the fault of anyone. It is something that no one expected, and were it not for the suffering and tragedy and the utter helpless condition in which I find myself by not being able to help the cattle, I wouldn't mind. The fact that my brother hasn't shown up is understandable. Between the ranch and the river where Bud is, the snow drifts are piled mountain high, particularly through the sand hills, which would be the shortest route. We are just too many miles from civilization or any passable road. Of one thing I am certain, could Bud get here, he would, just to see how his little brother is doing.

I know Father and Brother are worrying some, but both know I have coal, plenty of food. I could get sick and I can hear Bud say, "Don't worry, the kid is tough as they come." I don't know, but I think I have had the mumps on one side, because one side of my face swelled up so I couldn't open my mouth except to drink coffee and cream of wheat, thinned out, with lots of cream. On this, with a couple jiggers of bourbon, I have managed to keep going as there isn't even a blooming bit of iodine, aspirin or any medical supplies. So, one does without.

The bourbon Brother sent out with the wagon of groceries is a Godsend, with the weather as it is. It is the best barrel whiskey, put up in two gallon jugs, and careful as I have been, one jug is empty, so I shall nurse the remaining jug, even if it is Christmas Eve. I know there are other days coming which may be worse.

The damn storm is worse, all I can do is hole up by the cook stove and play solitaire, which I have done until the cards are worn out. I reread some of the stories in the old magazines for the fourth and fifth time. I have three *Saturday Evening Posts*, several detective novels and one magazine, with a story about Tahiti. This one I have read the most. The picture of the gal in a grass skirt looks best to a lonely cowpuncher with no place to go.

So help me God, this will be my last job as a cowpuncher. In the future, I shall be near people, and it may just as well be Tahiti where it is warm. I have seen all the snow and enough dead cattle to last me a lifetime. Surely, there must be some place in a warm climate where they have horses to break, even for less money. Nuts to the cattle. They are strictly dumb. Horses are the smartest animals living — including humans. By now I should know. What is to be will be. Come hell and high water, otherwise I wouldn't be here by myself on Christmas Eve. Last winter was a pip, the first I didn't go to school. I lived in town for free with Father and Brother, had plenty of hay and grain for my cow pony and made more dough working when I wished than I could by breaking horses, and the weather was good. So, this first winter in a camp, I catch the worst in history. I should never have gotten into that stud game. Now I know.

Coming in off the fall roundup, I was looking forward to another winter like the one I spent with my honorable parent and brother the year before. I had been with the roundup wagon, where some thirty cowboys representing different brands had been going through the usual routine of gathering the big steers for shipment and returning the strays to their own range. We were continually on the move, and moving ahead was the cook and bed wagon. From this cook wagon comes the kind of food that cowboys like. Cooked in dutch ovens on a long bed of coals would be steaks, corn, beans, tomatoes, and in one would be a fruit cobbler, peach or pear, whichever Cookie had available. This, with canned cream, was a dish not to be found in the best hotels. There was the usual pot of coffee, except when Cookie was moving. We were never all together at the same time, but when one did arrive, you simply grabbed a tin plate, a tin coffee cup and dug in.

Cookie, always in a hurry, had two helpers to rustle fuel for the dutch ovens and to harness the horses. His moves came just as breakfast was over, usually as it was getting light, and were executed at a high gallop across the prairies regardless of roads. It was nothing to have breakfast at daylight, the midday meal twenty miles farther on and supper at a spot thirty miles distant.

We were continually changing horses owing to the number of miles we traveled. The horses had to subsist on the range alone and we had nine to twelve horses each, depending upon how long we expected to be out with the wagon. On this trip I had twelve which I used for everyday work. One I kept for my night horse because he was wonderfully trained and gentle and would stand saddled at the foot of my bed roll, so that when I was called by my puncher going off duty I could grab a quick cup of coffee and lose no time getting to the herd. Guard duty was usually two hours but could be longer, depending upon how many men were working and how large was the herd we were holding. After guard duty, you either returned to your bed or, if the last shift, you stayed up and caught a fresh mount out of the remuda, grabbed breakfast and were ready for the day's work.

Turning my twelve horses loose in what is to be their winter headquarters, I catch my pet cow pony for the winter, parking him in the family barn. I give myself the usual yearly cleanup, haircut, shave and bath, and decked out in a new suit feel no pain. Tomorrow I will collect several months salary, which since my seventeenth birthday has been top wages of sixty a month found. The found means food and a place to sleep. Place to sleep was usually on the ground, unless at the home ranch where there was a real bed. Not just your bed roll.

To earn this kind of money, you had to be a top roper, not a trick roper but able to front-foot when necessary. An all-around cowhand must, above all, be able to break a string of horses for cow ponies in the right way. That was the real mark of a cowboy. In all the cattle outfits I know, there are only three older men who were paid as much as I receive monthly. So, considering my age, my brother who trained me hasn't done a bad job. He is known as one of the finest cowboys in the business and the most perfect hand with wild horses in any man's country. Of this I am very proud. Without his help, I would be just one of many.

Collecting my wages the next day, I am of a mind to go to Denver for a few days to let off steam, a fact I don't mention to Father. Brother Bud thinks it will put me in condition for my winter rest. I think he was kidding, but I am not quite sure, so while waiting for tomorrow's train I visit an old friend in a pool hall, where I am cordially invited to sit in on a stud poker game. With nothing to do except kill time until train time, and holding plenty of moolah, why not? By seven I am convinced that I won't go to Denver tomorrow because said bank roll has shrunk to less than five bucks. This fact causes me no great agony as I have a swell place to eat and sleep. Jobs are easy to come by. All I need is a little spending money for entertainment if I am not going to Denver, and this I know how to remedy fast.

There is always one guy who understands and comes through, without a lot of questions and advice. Brother Bud! Knowing that at this time of the evening he will be upstairs at a club for men, I head for this spot, where I tell the clerk I would like to see my brother on business for a few minutes. One word from him suffices. I see Bud playing pool with a gang at one of the corner tables, and when he spots me he hands his cue to one of the boys, motions to a chair and asks, "What can I do for you, Pard?"

Without any shame or hesitancy, I ask Bud to loan me twenty bucks.

Bud's hand reaches for his bank roll. "Sure I will and glad you came up. I want to talk to you and a decision has to be made by tomorrow morning. What did you do with your dough, put it in a bank?"

When I break the news that I lost the works in a stud poker game in one hand, he looks me over, saying, "How much did you lose?"

"Well, Bud," I reply, "you paid me. You should know."

"My God, you mean you lost all summer's wages on one hand? Pard, you really went first class. Tell me, who did you play with? . . . There is nothing I can do about your loss because the fellows who got your money don't cheat. They are good poker players, best in town. You were simply outplayed, which is natural because you can't sit still and wait. Your curiosity is too much, you take a chance. Hell, son, the only time you are not in a hurry is when you are roping or breaking horses. As a poker player you are the world's best bronc buster and now you are broke."

Here was a fact I couldn't deny. Bud wanted to know if I wanted a winter job with top wages, even five a month more than I had been paid. If I did, he said I'd be working for Mr. Williams and himself, and that it was Williams' suggestion I be hired. "You will have to batch and live alone at Williams' summer quarters at Battle Ground Springs and will have three of his cow ponies for your winter horses. They are up the river at his ranch, where they have done nothing all summer and will be full of pep. You will need grain and hay, coal and food to last six months, and supplies must be hauled out before the weather changes, as we will have four thousand three-year-old steers and five hundred two-year-olds here soon. They are coming up from the South and should be in top condition, and in that big pasture which hasn't been grazed all summer they should go through the winter fine. As it is late in the year, we won't even dip, but move them on before winter hits."

I mulled the thought over as Bud continued. "It should be an easy winter for you, just keeping up the fences. With three good winter horses, you can even visit some of the homesteaders that live back on the flats. They are all hungry and will be glad to see a cow-puncher, especially the mothers with daughters."

"Nuts to them," I replied. "Why don't we use our own horses for the winter, rather than Mr. Williams'?"

"Well, Pard," said Bud, "I offered to, but two of his three are badly in need of work and the old man knows your ability in this department. They are wonderful cow ponies, only the two younger horses are very touchy and will buck at the drop of a hat. Besides, the kind of men Williams is hiring are afraid and the horses know it."

I thanked Bud and took the job. I asked him not to mention the poker game to Father, as he might think I was careless with my dough. Bud cracked right back, "Son, you lost Father a long time ago. I think it was the Sunday you roped the antelope. He has never been the same since and anything you might do will come as no surprise to our parent. He has done given up long ago. I won't tell him because I don't want him to know how rotten a poker player he raised. Tell him about your new job. This Father would like." Bud's parting words were: "Have your outfit ready to move tomorrow. The sooner those steers are in pasture and you are on the job, the better I will feel."

So, here I am on Christmas Eve, going through a nightmare on a job that appeared at first to be manna from the Gods. Bellyaching will do no good. I am just stuck until spring. I don't even have the old Edison with the big horn. Why I didn't bring it over from the home ranch, I don't know, unless it was the rush act to get settled here.

Boy, oh boy, the licking Bud is taking in his pocket book! I can't help but worry, he's such a swell guy. If he isn't broke in the spring, he must have more dough than I figured. At least I don't have to stick him for any wages. It isn't his fault the damn weather blew up in our faces. But his partner is different. I will need some of the old man's money because I am through being a cowpuncher for anyone, and I will need some traveling money to get the hell out of this country.

So, Mr. Williams, if helping cattle die has any value, you will owe me some wages. Everything comes to an end, either good or bad. Spring is here, even the sun. A little over three hundred cattle of forty-five hundred survived, and now they have hay and will probably live to die again. They are the thinnest, most sickly few cattle to survive a winter. How they lasted is beyond me.

The hills and flats are dotted with dead cattle. Their bodies are mangy and they are not worth the skinning. True to my promise, I am through with the cow business. Where I shall end up, I don't know.

I have told Bud and Father I'm going south. Of course, they think I am just fed up and will return soon, but I know better. I have had my belly full of anything that looks like a cow or is remotely connected with ranch life. I shall be twenty in July, and surely to God there is something other than cows and horses in this world. I am giving my saddle and ropes to Bud. He insists on paying me my wages, but I don't feel right, because I know that to keep going he will have to borrow an awful lot of money. But as he says, my small amount of wages won't help him much, which it won't. So with over four hundred dollars in my pocket, Denver will be my first stop.

10

Denver, Where I'm Rolled of My Loot by a Pimp

IT IS ALWAYS HARDEST TO SAY GOODBYE, especially to Father and Brother Bud. Father appears so sad and lonesome, yet is apparently pleased when I assure him I am through with breaking horses and never intend to spend another winter in the snow. If I had only known what the future held in store for me, I would have gone home and crawled under the bed and stayed there, but one doesn't know, which is well. It makes each day yours to live as it happens. If it's a good day, all well and good. You go ahead. If a bad one, you survive. Tomorrow is another day, and fate may be kind. There is always hope. If one could live by a motto I once read, "As we journey through life let us live by the way," everything would be just perfect.

For my travels I have said all my goodbyes and done a complete switch in wardrobe, taking only my nice boots and spurs in my suitcase. In the event I should see some easy money in a rodeo, I could then borrow the other necessary equipment. My ropes, hackamores, saddle and ponies are in my brother's keeping forever.

Catching the morning train for Denver, I intend to spend one day, then on to the place which appealed to me so much and which the advertisement said was paradise.

Going to the cowmen's hotel, the Albany, where visiting cattle people make their home while in Denver, I am sure there will be someone I know, even if only the night clerk. My hunch is right, for the clerk informs me that there are six characters upstairs from home, including my two old pals the King brothers and four other fellows about the same age as my brother Bud.

While it is almost noon, the clerk tells me they never come in until the wee morning hours and have been living at the hotel for thirty days and are tight all of the time. Getting their room number, I go up to see what my gang is up to and how come they are leading the life of Riley without me. Here is where I should have gone back to the depot and taken a train for anywhere, so long as I was going away from this gang.

Their hotel room is unlocked, so I walk right in and think I have waltzed into a bad distillery. Three of the boys are in the first room, and looking through the bathroom into the adjoining room are the other three characters, my old pals. When I open the windows to give the joint an airing, the two King boys come to life and pounce on me like a long lost relative.

With this hell-of-aballoo everyone asks, "Have you any money?" and upon my answering with the affirmative "I'm loaded," one of the lads grabs a telephone, calls the bar and orders a quart of bourbon, some ice and glasses, and I hear the story of why they are parked here in swell rooms but have run out of money and credit. They were all hired to join a Wild West show in Denver and start here with the first week's performance that would put the promoters on Easy Street, then travel east. The promoters hadn't paid the hotel bill or paid the gang any dough, nor had the stockyards been paid a feed bill for some thirty bucking horses. Something had gone wrong with their finances.

I have known this bunch all of my life. The King boys are old school pals, the others are older but wonderful fellows who have worked with me and my brother, so I do what Bud would do — give each a twenty-dollar bill, pay for the hooch and have breakfast at my expense.

When I ask how the hell they can get high every night without dough, Paul Lambert says, "Son, we'll show you. Down Seventeenth Street is a bar run by one of our best friends. He is an old cowpuncher from our range who quit the cow business and has been carrying us on credit. The hotel stopped our bar business long ago, but the promoters are stuck for our room and wages. Look, Son, Walt Perkins says, 'Join us, we can get you a job easy. You will only have to ride two bucking horses a day, ride in the parade and you can get some extra money for trick roping.' Hell, they promised us we would travel everywhere."

I don't have the heart to ask them when, but join them to see their friend down the street. By this time, my bank roll has shrunk to a little over two hundred and sixty dollars, which is causing me no worry, for if I get out of town with a couple of hundred, everything will be good. Even if their promoter should show today, I am not going with any Wild West show, but decide to spend the rest of the day with the gang just for old times sake.

The money I have staked them will buy a lot of cheer and is something they would do for me, if they could. So, in high spirits, we go to their favorite rendezvous, where we meet more kindly souls, all our kind of people. By nighttime everyone is happy. I haven't a care in the world, when one of the boys mentions going down to a new joint which had just been opened and was run by a gal, with wonderful gals, where money was no object. This joint had a player piano, a dance floor, an excellent bar.

My six friends have some money left. I haven't been hurt much, so we pile into a taxi, the seven of us, and head for the promised land. The house looks nice from the outside and on the inside it is very plush. Anything for free I don't see. I buy a couple of rounds of drinks. My gang is in the dance hall, either drinking or dancing, and I am standing at the end of the bar having just finished a drink, thinking of beating it out the back door and catching a taxi for the hotel and calling it a day. Without warning a long glass with a highball complete slides down in front of me from the opposite end of the bar where the bartender is standing with another fellow. With a signal from him, it is on the house.

I remember taking several swallows slowly, then the lights go out. My next recollection of anything is at daylight. I am in a big wide bed with all my clothes on with the exception of one shoe. My hat lies crushed in bed with me. I have a head that reaches from here to there and a taste in my mouth with the flavor of a dead cat.

When I sit up, my head just about bursts. Taking it easy, I feel for my money. This, I know, is an unnecessary effort, for I have a definite feeling I am clean.

Upon my staggering to the door, it opens into the kitchen where a big fat colored woman is cleaning up. She greets me as if it were an everyday occurrence. "How is you, boss? Can I give you a cup of coffee?" She evidently knows I've been rolled, but as to where my gang has gone or what happened, she is a total loss.

The only unlocked door is the one leading into the alley. The dirty bastards haven't even left me taxi fare, and it is a long walk to the hotel. I don't feel too good and want to get the hell out of the kitchen to fresh air, with a promise to myself that I will be back but not as a paying patient. I go through the alley into a street, where I catch a taxi.

Depending on the kindness of the hotel clerk to pay my cab fare upon arriving at the hotel, I put the bite on him for ten dollars, which he hands out like it grew on a tree. Nice guy. He tells me my friends were in early looking for me. They apparently think I ditched them to hole up with some gal. When they learn what happened, they will want to clean the joint out, which may be what we will do, but first I am going to see a real wise fellow at the stockyards.

Billy and Louie Degan are commission men, have known me since a boy and are great friends of my father and brother Bud. These gentlemen know their way about and will advise me right. I didn't want to get my head busted and didn't intend to be rolled and let some damn pimp enjoy my dough. Here I've been away from home almost twenty-four hours and am stone broke and owe the hotel ten dollars, plus. I just can't be too bright.

As the bar is closed, and having seven dollars left after paying the taxi fare, I am going to try the rear door and see if there is anything this bartender can do for my head without cutting it off. I have several reasons for seeing my friend Billy Degan. First, to find out what I can do about my two hundred, which I'm sure a pimp has. Next, to see if he has a free ticket to some place far away and also loan me fifty bucks.

Billy is out in the stockyards when I arrive at his office, but his brother says he will be back. When he does return, he has with him one of my best friends, Russell Brown, who is two years my junior and has just run away from an Eastern military academy where his father thought he had him parked for safekeeping. The guy landed home, called my house and, finding out I was in Denver, stayed just long enough to telephone his mother and catch the next train to join me. This is a pleasant surprise, as I am very fond of Brownie, who has always looked upon me as a big brother, and his father and mother are always pleased when we are together. When I explain to Brownie that I am going south and am not going to do any more cowpunching, he's pleased as punch.

I tell Billy what I want, only I now want two tickets. He says this is no problem. He has two return tickets to Flagstaff, two for Deming, New Mexico, and several others which he will look over and we can have our choice.

When I tell Brownie what happened at the new joint run by a gal by the name of Mabel, and that I am clean out of something to use for money except what I have from the hotel, he says, "Why, boy, I have some money. Let's go get the gang at the hotel and clean the joint out. It will be fun. Those guys at the hotel, with two drinks under their belts they can really scrap. Let's go."

Billy says, "Wait a minute, Brownie, not so damn fast. That won't get the money back. They will cry 'copper' and you will all make the can, then I'll have to bail everyone out because the joint has a license. How they ever managed one in the first place, I don't know, but I don't want you fellows to get into trouble."

I know Billy is right and there is no good reason for getting everyone in trouble just because I am simple enough to get taken by a lowdown bum of a parasite, who lives off the proceeds of a dame wiggling her bottom. Sure, I would like to murder the bum, but it's my fault, so to hell with it. I know Bill will loan me fifty bucks, and I'm not going home and I am not going to wire Bud.

All this reminds me of the previous fall's poker game when I lost all my summer wages in one hand. I wouldn't mind so much if I had lost my two hundred in another poker game or out of my pocket, or been rolled by a dame. But this I am ashamed of, so let's keep it quiet.

Billy asks when I want to leave town. I assure him the quicker the better. He says to be here tomorrow morning and he will have the tickets for Flagstaff okayed by the railroad and give me a letter to the Babbitt people. He says they are the largest outfit in that part of Arizona and will give us a job. Calling his bookkeeper, he has a check for one hundred dollars made payable to me, which I endorse and his bookkeeper cashes, so once again I am in funds but feeling plenty stupid.

Billy is a hard guy to thank, he is so gracious and decent, with his remark, "We have all had a bad winter, but your family have been our friends for years. Don't worry about the hundred bucks. It's only money. See me early tomorrow and stay away from Mabel's."

Brownie and I head for the hotel to kill time until morning. It's good to have the kid with me. He is good company, full of enthusiasm and afraid of nothing. His father is one of the wealthiest men in our town and a swell fellow, even if he and his young son don't see eye to eye.

About eight o'clock, Billy makes his appearance at the hotel bar with our tickets. They are shipper's first-class return in the chair car. We will have our meals in the diner. Our train leaves at seven, so Billy has saved us a trip to his office. With a letter of introduction, money and tickets in our pockets, our future in the distance, we are on the move.

11

More Wild Horses
and a Big Gray Outlaw

W<small>E ARRIVE IN FLAGSTAFF ON A BEAUTIFUL SUNNY MORNING.</small> Why we should have chosen Flagstaff, I will never know, except it was the end of the line for us or as far as our free tickets would take us. After all, we had to light somewhere and make more dough before taking off again. It is just as well that it be here in Flagstaff.

Taking a gander at the town and surrounding country from the depot, we find ourselves in a very picturesque setting where the railroad runs almost through the town center. The main business block is just across the street from where we are standing. Saloon signs are heavily displayed, and we are close to refreshments.

The surrounding district is high, with mountains looming in the near distance. A large observatory perches on a hill overlooking the town. The most conspicuous place in sight is Black's Saloon, and as we cross the street to have breakfast, we run into a real friend of ours from home, Guy Galbrieth, a very old friend of our families and a fellow we have both known all our lives. Guy is a cattle buyer and is in Flagstaff to accept shipment on some steers he bought last fall and had enough sense not to ship home late in the season but wintered in Arizona on the Little Colorado. Otherwise, had he shipped them home, he would have lost the herd.

Guy is so glad to see us that the whole world looks better just by meeting this old friend. We are introduced to Mr. Black. Set up in business on the main stem in town, just across from the depot, coming or going he has the first and last crack at the thirsty. His is the welcoming tavern for the coming and the weeping room for the departing. A nice arrangement.

After several portions of Mr. Black's best and a very little breakfast, we give our friend the lowdown on Denver and our future plans. At least I tell him I am all through with cattle and breaking horses. I want a nice quiet job with lots of money, no work and, above all, no broncs.

Guy knows everyone in and around Arizona, so we feel pretty sure of a good job. He wants us to go home with him when he ships out his train of steers for Denver. Finding we are not interested in going home, he gives us the picture as it is, in and around Flagstaff. There are three possibilities: be a lumberjack, a cowpuncher or a sheepherder. Take your choice. At the word sheepherder, we damned near killed the guy. No respectable cowhand will even eat sheep, and as for a lumberjack, what the hell could we do in a lumber camp? Then we think of our letter to Babbitt from Billy Degan. This he reads and says, "Brownie, I'll take you and the letter over to their office. They will give you some kind of a job, but I have a good job for Fred — it's tough but big money, and I will recommend you both."

I say, "Listen, Guy, not so fast. I have a suspicion you didn't hear me when I said no more bucking horses for me. I gave all my equipment away to Bud except my boots and spurs. And of one thing I am sure, there is a horse or horses back of this fancy job, so tell me the worst."

"Well, Son, you are no lumber man. You are too damned lazy to herd sheep. Anyway, I wouldn't recommend you to do either. But you can ride, so listen. Yesterday I was talking to Tom Aikens, the brand inspector who has a cattle ranch out near Lake Mary, and he wants a good cowpuncher to join the Thursten Wagon, down Apache Maid way. You would fit the job perfectly, with better money than you have ever made, and you will be out three months before you see Flagstaff again. Look at the dough you will save."

"Listen, Guy, tell me the worst. Why hasn't this inspector hired a local boy if the job is so swell? Who does one have to kill, or what the hell is eating you? You have talked all around the bush. Now, how many damned horses does a fellow have to break? I have no saddle, and I am not going to take the job."

Brownie is a big help. He comes up with: "You can have my entire outfit. And this fellow might take us both and we can borrow a saddle."

While we are arguing what I am not going to do, a big moose of a fellow with a hearty handshake and infectious grin joins us at the bar with the greeting "Guy, have you found me a top hand?"

You would think I was a bottle of nothing when Guy says, "Tom, I sure have, brought him all the way from Colorado. In fact, two of them. Can you use both boys? They would be a good team."

This bird I like, but not his job. He starts on me as though I am hired, saying he will get Brownie a job wrangling for some outfit if I will go to work for him. All I have to do is stay at his camp near Lake Mary and break ten horses to ride good enough to take on the roundup to last three months, then travel to Apache Maid, which is the name of a big mountain many miles from Mormon Lake. And this would be through heavy timber country, even more so than in the Mazatzal Mountains out from Phoenix where I broke my leg.

No wonder he hadn't anyone to take the job, to batch and break this string of wild horses all by oneself with no one within miles. A fellow would be crazy to work alone in a rough country full of rocks and trees. He would be nuts. So, I take the job. Right away, Mr. Aikens is full of glee. He offers us both an advance of dough, which for once we don't need, with his promise to take care of Brownie. I borrow all the kid's riding equipment and agree to start for the Aikens camp the next day with Brownie's saddle and a buckboard of groceries driven by a Mexican kid. I start on the toughest and most dangerous experience of my life as a cowpuncher. It is unbelievable to me, but it all happened.

With a team of mules and leading a saddle horse, the Mexican boy and I leave Flagstaff early in the morning. The first few miles out are easy, but then we run out of road. Any resemblance to a road is only a trail over boulders and hills for the next thirteen miles to the Aikens camp at the edge of Lake Mary. During our trip to camp, the Mexican boy brought me up to date on the kind of trouble I was in for and why no one had taken the job before. He was not trying to scare me, only giving me the facts. The rest was up to me. It seemed there were ten unbroken horses and only one well broken cow pony at Aikens Ranch. And among the ten unbroken horses was a big iron gray outlaw that had severely injured two cowpunchers who had tried to ride him. The other nine had never been touched. A fine prospect to end a brilliant future — mine. Dropping down a mountain only fit for a goat to travel, we and the buckboard and groceries arrive at the one-room frame shack that is the Aikens headquarters. There is a cook stove, a bed in the corner, a table and a cupboard for groceries, and one is surrounded with all the comforts of the Aikens home camp. The shack is on the edge of a creek, and across from this are the two rail corrals, one a real large high corral, the other much smaller in the corner of the large corral.

Telling the Mexican boy to take his saddle horse and run the horses in the corral while I cook something to eat, I get busy and cook some bacon, open a can of pork and beans, make some biscuits and put on a pot of coffee. With a can of cherries for dessert, we have a good meal, and my Mexican companion, with food under his belt, is on his way. He was only hired to bring me out, not to see me slaughtered, so he is gone.

It is just past twelve and I am alone with a corral of unbroken horses except one. This is against all the laws of humanity, but worst of all, I don't only have horses to break, but they have to be shod before I go to the roundup, as the rocks are murder on their feet. Even without carrying a man, their feet get very tender. This is a country where a cow pony must have shoes. Now the Mexican boy tells me this on the way out — the boss didn't have the guts, was just going to let me learn the hard way. And shoe a horse I never have, not even a gentle one, as in our country we only use shoes in winter on our winter horses, and that very seldom is done and, if so, it is always done by an expert blacksmith. To hell with the shoes. I have to break them before shoes are needed. There is no reason to worry at this time. Shoes can wait.

Taking thirty minutes rest before wandering over to see my future steeds, I wonder how anyone can get in this kind of a mess, without even trying. The day is beautiful and I have no business here, but here I am, alone with the kind of work ahead of me that no one person is supposed to do alone.

It is not a question of help, it is just some human being around in the event of an accident. Promising myself one thing, that as I am alone, I shall take every advantage, I wander over to the corral to see my ponies. Sitting on the top rail of the corral, I size the bunch up. They are wild but don't look too bad. The big gray has rollers in his nose. When he throws his pretty head in the air, he lets out with a noise which scares even him. He is a beautiful iron gray, with a long mane and tail, a wide forehead and deep chest, but regardless of everything a good eye. This baby I like immediately and decide he is a big bluff. All he needs is a friend, so I call him Gray Eagle and head for my rope and saddle. Running all the others except the big gray into the smaller corral, I am left with Gray Eagle, who senses something different from his past experience with man, because he turns and faces me, not with fear but wonderment, as though he would like to make friends. All my disgust of a short while ago has gone. I am in my glory, alone, with a beautiful animal with whom I am soon to be good friends.

Just the two of us and I hate what I have to do, but the big boy is powerful and I have to take the advantage, for I must thin out his mane and tail and break him to lead so I can pet that beautiful head. It has to be done, so here goes! I push him into a corner with my rope ready. When he breaks past me, I toss the rope over his front feet and, when he's off the ground with them, give a stiff pull. The beauty hits the ground, hard. Quickly pulling his right hind foot up to the front feet, I have him down where he won't go anyplace. I put a war bridle over his pretty head to teach him to lead, and tie up his left back foot with a cotton rope to his neck so that when he is up, he can't kick. His foot will just touch the ground. I release his front feet and right back foot, and he is on his feet with sweat breaking out all over. The big bad guy is now mine. I am in no hurry. His left hind leg is so he can't kick me, but when he stands still, it just touches the ground. The war bridle over his head is a large loop in his mouth with the rope over and around his head, so when I tighten the rope it pulls up on his mouth and is damned uncomfortable. If I pull on this slightly, he will soon find that when he comes to me, the rope slackens and the hurt in his mouth is less. Soon he will be following me like a dog.

Petting the big boy and pulling his mane and tail, I pay no attention to his objections to having his tail cleaned out, and he quickly gets the idea that I am his friend and don't want to hurt him. The big boy quits all foolishness. All he wanted was to be friends in the first place. In less than thirty minutes I have removed the rope from his neck to his foot and he is following me all over the corral and is enjoying being petted and talked to, just like a human. I have a real good friend that has to be saddled and taught the art of being a good cow pony, but this will all be easy, so while I am in the mood, I again tie up the left hind foot so it will just touch the ground, putting on a hackamore in place of a war bridle. I pet and play with him, getting the big boy used to the smell of my saddle blanket and saddle, put it on and take it off till he is completely used to the feel and knows it won't hurt. I quickly tighten up the cinch and he is saddled. Continuing to pet and talk to my friend, I put my weight in the stirrup, then gently slip into the saddle. This I do a dozen times until he is used to me climbing on and off, then quickly untie my rope to his foot so he is free to buck or do anything that he wishes. With a light pat on the neck, my beautiful gray trots around the big corral without even one buck. He seems glad about the whole thing. Climbing on and off a few times, I give my new friend a rest for the day. He is a beauty. A fellow could almost work for nothing just to have a horse like Gray Eagle.

Having made better time than I expected working with the big horse, I took on one more for the day, a big bay. He was almost red. His hair was so slick he just glistened. This horse had none of the wild characteristics of the gray and was just as quick to respond to kind treatment, and I had nothing but time. I gave the big bay a lot of petting and the name Red Bird.

I had now on my first afternoon acquired for myself two beautiful new horses. They needed much work, with much to learn, all of which would come soon to them. The other eight would be easy. I would be on time at the Apache Maid roundup. Only the shoeing was going to be tough for me. Having never shod a horse in my life, I would have something to learn.

After a good night's rest and with the satisfaction of work well done with Gray Eagle and Red Bird, I take the gentle cow pony which I held in the corral for the night and run the bunch of ten future cow ponies in the big corral. Putting all the horses in the small corral except the big gray, I toss my rope over his head. He doesn't even tighten the rope but lets out with a big whistle and snort, throws his beautiful head in the air and trots up to me with no fear, just a little nervousness, which quickly disappears with a few words and a little petting.

He shows no fear of the hackamore I slip on his head. I then try saddling him without tying up his back foot, and much to my surprise this beautiful horse that has been classed as an outlaw gives me no trouble, stands for the saddle and my mounting without even trying to buck. In the big corral, I give him quite a workout, which he seems to enjoy. He moves with a strength and grace of power unusual in most horses in such a short time. Now for the real test! I step off and open the big gate to the outer world, where, if he throws me off or goes wild and stampedes or falls, I have no way to catch my horse or saddle. This is always the danger of one man working alone. All this I knew when I took the job. I should have taken a job as a ribbon clerk in some department store, where there are no horses, just dames and that's good. There's nothing wrong with dames.

Gray Eagle and I seem to be just right for each other. He gives me no trouble, and anything he learns once he never forgets. He is the very finest out of hundreds that I have broken. With him and the big bay, I will have a couple of fine cow ponies before the roundup is over. At the end of my eighth day at Mr. Aikens' camp, I have ridden all of my ten horses. Only two gave me real trouble, a little sorrel and a curly-haired blue. This pair were about the same size and didn't respond to kind treatment like the others. They were determined to be bucking horses, whether I liked it or not. After three days of playing with these two babies, using no rough tactics when they bucked, hoping they would see the light and respond to kind treatment, I reversed the procedure and worked them both over, but good. The results were amazing. They were the kind who only understood rough treatment; once conquered, these make good ponies but never in a class with the others. They were strictly a one-man's horse and would always give a stranger trouble.

On the tenth day, Mr. Aikens showed up from Flagstaff with some shoes and shoeing equipment for the eleven horses I would take to the roundup. The guy was so pleased with my work, he even agreed to help shoe the bunch. Damned nice of the old boy. After all, they were his horses and I didn't even know that the nails holding the shoes had to go in a certain way. It is an old story to him, but when we come to the big gray, who lets a couple of snorts go when Mr. Aikens comes in the corral, this scares the hell out of my honorable boss so I am elected.

Patience and kindness with Gray Eagle and Red Bird, with advice from the boss on how to fit the shoes, pays off. They are both shod without too much trouble, and I am proud of my first lesson in the art of shoeing a horse. After I talk Mr. Aikens into staying over one more day, we shoe the remaining eight fast. I had to take a great deal of time with my first two pets, the big gray and the bay, as I didn't want to scare or hurt either of them. As for the others, I laid each one down and tied him solid so no one could be hurt, then shod them real quick, which was better and safer, but shoeing horses is not for a cowboy — it belongs to a blacksmith. These were my first and only. Never again!

12

Fourth of July Celebration, Susie, Cyclone and a Wild Beautiful Brown Stallion

B EFORE MR. AIKENS LEAVES FOR FLAGSTAFF, he gives me the direction for Apache Maid Mountain. I am to travel on a trail to Mormon Lake through the heavy timbered country about twenty-five miles, where I find a camp with a small horse pasture and a cabin with supplies for cooking. Here I am to stay the night, then continue my trip to the big mountain. On the day I leave for the roundup, I tie my bed roll on the curly blue pony and, riding the old reliable cow pony of my outfit, I head for Apache Maid via Mormon Lake. I was told that if I traveled in one direction I couldn't miss Mormon Lake, as it was twenty miles long, and when I reached its shores to turn right and I would run into a camp at the end of the lake. I am on my way with a string of green horses, half broken, to join a real cow outfit where punchers with green horses are seldom welcomed.

The past two weeks have been my worst experience as a cow-puncher, much worse than in the Mazatzals. There I had a companion. Here at Mr. Aikens' camp, I was completely alone where anything could happen, only it didn't.

I have been awfully lucky with no trouble. Following directions, I arrive at the Thursten headquarters where many punchers from many other cow outfits are rendezvousing for the start of the spring roundup. This fellow Thursten is a real cowman, greatly respected by all the cattle folks in Arizona. He is a big man with an understanding of cowpunchers' problems. To say he is amazed that I have landed to start on roundup with a string of half broken cow ponies, all of said ponies having been broken by me in the past fourteen days, without help, is putting it mildly. In no uncertain terms he expresses his opinion of my boss, but gives me the assurance he and his men will help me anytime I am in trouble. Here I am, meeting with some of Arizona's best cowmen. They are all older than I and all experienced in this territory, where cowpunching is different than in Colorado or in the Mazatzal Mountains, which are the only three places in my short life where I have worked as a cowhand.

The cattle range of Flagstaff and surrounding country is similar to the Mazatzals in that there is a lot of timber, only of a different kind. The Flagstaff country doesn't have such terrible steep mountains, and here the cattle aren't so wild. In the summers the grass is fattening, so the cattlemen are able to ship beef to market in the fall without the usual feed yard.

Among the representatives of different outfits is Lee Miller, whose headquarters are on the Little Colorado, where he was boss for the Babbitt people of Flagstaff. Lee was one of the best riders, ropers or all-around cowmen in any man's country and became my good friend in the days to come. Working under Mr. Thursten as boss with my string of half broken colts, I had a most enjoyable and different two months than any I had ever experienced in the cattle business.

One of the first things I learned as a cowhand in this territory was that altitude has a great effect on many things, especially cattle. Here they were quick to stampede. That was why, when working herd, they always tried to find a real rocky piece of ground where the cattle would have sore feet and couldn't run. This was also a reason for having shoes on all horses, as they could work in the malipi and the cattle couldn't. Another thing, one should always be alert for skunks, which would go mad with the altitude and would bite anything. Also, in the fall when beef were real fat, there was a tendency to stampede, and when holding a herd at night the cry of a coyote or timber wolf or the rustle of a slicker on a rainy night would stampede a herd instantly.

Working our way from Apache Maid Mountain back past Mormon Lake toward the Little Colorado, we ended up near the shores of Lake Mary, which was July the first, when Mr. Aikens joined us for our last day of work before the roundup ended. I had made many friends and was offered a job by Mr. Thursten any time, any place, all of which he told Mr. Aikens, who only grinned. I learned from my boss that Flagstaff had a three-day rodeo and general celebration starting on the fourth of July, with riding contests, relay races and all-around general sports. So, turning my string of horses loose in the good pasture, the boss and I go to Flagstaff to see my pal Brownie and celebrate.

While I have been out on the roundup, my new saddle I had ordered before leaving Flagstaff has arrived and Brownie has been using it, so we exchange saddles, although they are both just the same. Brownie's is broken in and a new saddle needs use. I have three months of pay in my pocket and am all dressed up with no place to go. With three days celebration coming up, Brownie tries to talk me into entering the bucking contest. Inquiring as to the prize money and the rules, we find the prize money is not very big and that each person riding furnishes his own horse. I have no bucking horse, but Aikens has three pretty fast ponies that I just turned loose at his ranch which I think might win the relay race worth a couple of hundred bucks.

When I tell Mr. Aikens about the three ponies, he says, "Go get them. You can have all you make, and if you want to enter the bucking contest, my uncle Tom Fryer has a real bucking horse you can have, only I suggest you ride him first, just to get the feel. I'm sure with this horse you can win first dough."

Leaving late, I am back with my three relay ponies and the little sorrel bucking horse. In the morning, going out to the track, Brownie and I work the three relay ponies, just getting them used to the fast change of saddle and mounting. I am quite satisfied. At the suggestion that I try out the bucking horse to see if I can ride him, I laugh this off as ridiculous, it isn't the way we do it in my country. You drew for your horse, which you had never seen, and either rode him or you didn't. It didn't seem like cricket to me to ride a horse before the contest, even if they assured me everyone did.

Looking the little sorrel over, I tell Brownie if I can't ride him, I don't deserve any money, which is exactly what I got — no money.

The relay is for two o'clock, so Brownie and I are on the job. It calls for saddling your first horse when the signal is given, all starting at once around the track, changing horses, then around to another change of horse and home. With Brownie holding, I do the saddling and riding; we are away first each time and it looks like we will win, but my last pony wasn't quite fast enough, so we finish second out of nine contestants, which is good going for three horses that three months previous were green broncos.

Now comes the riding. I am fifth to ride, which is a good spot, and Brownie and I think we have a cinch. There is no chute, you saddle out in the open, so with Brownie pulling the sorrel's head down and twisting his ears, I quickly saddle, give the cinch a good pull and step on. Brownie steps back. Without paying any attention to this baby's head or what he is going to do, I have hat in hand, throw the right spur toward his shoulder and start to look back at the crowd for a grandstand ride, when this little monster falls apart. He doesn't go ahead but lets out a bawl and starts bucking backwards and sideways. I lose both stirrups on the second jump, and by the fourth I have to grab the horn to even stay on. This I manage to do. I could well imagine what my big brother would have said had he seen my noble exhibition. It was every bit my fault. I was careless and too cocksure. I rode like a farmer. It served me right. Well, at least we won a hundred and twenty-five dollars in the relay, which was expense money for our celebration. Better than spending our own dough.

I was all for drifting south but accepted a job with Mr. Aikens to stay with him until the beef roundup in the fall, when I could go down to the Little Colorado and join my friend Lee Miller. Of one thing I was sure, I wouldn't winter in Flagstaff. I had enough snow and dead cattle the previous winter to last me a lifetime. Besides, I wanted to travel in the direction of warmth and sunshine.

Back at the Aikens camp, I unpack the groceries and canned food to put things in order before visiting the other cow camps. I find no Carnation cream. Although my boss has been charged for a case, there is no cream. Someone has pulled a boner. Here, eighteen miles from town, over a damn tough road, I am without my Carnation for my canned fruit, for my rice, my coffee, my gravy. The joy has gone out of my eating department — immediately.

It is a fact known to all cowmen that there may be ten thousand cows in the back yard but who wants to milk a cow? The canned product is the stuff every cowman has in his home, at the ranch, with the roundup wagon. Hell, children grow on it. I was raised on Carnation cream, and here some damn clerk has left me high and dry.

The closest ranch is three miles, owned by my boss's uncle. I know he isn't at the ranch, but this makes no difference. The place will be open, as no one ever locks a door in this country. This is tradition with cattlemen. A fellow eats and sleeps, cleans up afterwards and goes on his merry way. It is a nice custom and never abused by real cowmen. So, over I go, hoping to grab a half dozen of Mr. Carnation's best, which will, if I am real careful, last me until I join the roundup wagon. Anyway, I will be visiting the other camps some of the time. Mr. Fryer's camp is deserted, but as usual everything is open, so I raid the joint. There is everything to eat, beans, canned fruit of every kind, but only one poor, lonesome small can of Carnation cream, which I haven't the heart to take. Someone may need it worse than me. By now, convinced that a clerk is a clerk and mostly a jerk, I am headed back where I started from, when I pass a nice looking red cow with a nice pair of horns and a young bull calf she seems mighty proud of. Here, I have one of my greatest ideas — why don't the young bull and I become partners in the milk department? There is only one little problem. He knows how to proceed better than I do. So, without further thought, I drive young Mr. Bull and his mother toward my camp and the big corral. Now I have me a walking container full of milk, only I know the lady is going to object. So what? Ladies have objected before. Why, I don't know, but I name the lady Susie and her little monster Cyclone. Had I thought for a hundred years, I would never come up with a more appropriate name for the little bull. He was all of that and more. Putting the little monster in the small corral, I leave his mother in the large corral with the gate open, so Susie can go out and graze or have a drink. But young Cyclone has a rail fence between himself and his mother for the night. He doesn't have any manners, he wants to eat all the time, but he is going to share his breakfast with me. I don't know how, but for once I am going to learn about cow's milk.

There is one bad feature about fresh milk after you get it — what to do with it? With a can, you just stick a plug in the hole and the milk keeps. No wonder cattlemen don't bother with taking it away from the cow and then trying to find a way to keep it fresh without ice. Me, I have a thought. Taking two stone jars, which were once full of apple butter, I am going (if I can get some milk) to put the small jar with the milk in the large jar, tighten both lids, dig a hole in the sand in the springs near our shack and let the cool water run over them. If this doesn't work, Susie will only have one to support. Tomorrow after breakfast, I shall talk the matter over with the lady and see how she feels. I have my doubts.

On my way to the milking department to be, I am about to call the whole thing off as being too much trouble. Then I remember how flat breakfast tasted. I decide, just once and no more. Young Cyclone is bawling and raising hell. The pig is real hungry, so for once in his young life he is going to have seconds. His mother is up against the little corral fence as close as possible, when I throw my rope over her horns and pull the lady's head up next to a post so she can't stick one of those nice horns through my middle. This takes care of the front end, but the dairy end is free and kicking and it's here I have to operate. So, wasting no more time, I rope and tie her right back leg to another post. This leaves the faucet department open to attack, which I do. With a tin cup in my hand I grab number one faucet and squeeze and pull. Nothing happens. Susie is a real lady, she resents the addition to her family and has turned the faucets off.

With my head against her side to keep her from falling on me, I try them all. I have one more chance. I turn Cyclone loose on the lady. This guy knows all the answers. Giving his mother a butt in the milk department with his head, the gentleman grabs a faucet and goes to work. Soon there is a stream of fluid running down the little monster's neck and I go to work with my little tin cup on the other side.

Evidently Susie can't turn the faucets off one by one, for very quickly I have extracted three tin cups full of nice milk, which was all I wanted. The rest is for my partner, and does he understand what he is doing? While I am untying the lady, he is punching her with his head until he has drained the container dry. Then with milk all over his white face like a little pig, he looks at me as much as to say, "Son, you just don't know your stuff."

But I know something he doesn't. Today he and mother are free in the pasture, but tonight it's back to the small corral for him. I have decided to give it a try for a few days if the milk keeps in my jar under the springs.

With three tin cups of milk every morning, I have plenty and everything tastes better. My hole in the springs works perfect and Susie doesn't put up so much fight, although I think she would still like to stick a horn through me just for having disgraced a perfectly good range cow. For it's back to the range for her when I head for the roundup, and it's me back to the canned article, no work, no trouble, just poke a hole in a can. Nothing could be easier or sweeter.

With Susie and her offspring, I have a nice arrangement. When I am away for a night or two, my young friend Cyclone does the milking, and when I return and want milk, I just pen the little fellow up for the night and, come morning, we both battle for our share. I have grown very fond of the little guy. When he is not busy in the dairy department, I pet him and he has no fear, even if his mother is worried and disgusted with the entire affair.

I am having an easy time, visiting other cow camps, and join in a wild horse roundup where I catch a big, wild, dark brown stallion, about seven years old. This fellow is all horse but wild as hell. So this beautiful horse I take to my home camp where I have plenty of time, and, just for my own satisfaction, I break him to ride.

The big stallion starts out full of fight, but with patience and kindness and by never allowing him to win a battle, I soon have a big powerful horse with greater stamina than any of the colts I broke for the roundup.

When my boss comes to visit me and to tell me to go down to the Little Colorado and join the fall roundup for beef, he is amazed

at the big brown stallion. But what to do with him? I can't take him
on the roundup with the other horses, since he's an original wild
horse and a stallion. So Mr. Aikens decides to turn him loose on the
big range from whence he came, where he could join his own kind
and be free again. I hate to part with the big boy. While he is far
from being a gentle horse, with me he was always very friendly,
would push me around with his head when he wanted it scratched
or petted. So I turn him loose with a farewell pat, never expecting to
see him again.

Taking six of the top cow ponies, I join Lee Miller and his gang
on the Little Colorado. The work is, as usual, long hours from early
to late, with two hours night herd. The cattle are beautiful and fat,
more so than any range cattle I ever saw on a fall roundup. Truly, the
Flagstaff cowmen have the world by the tail. In the winter they drift
off the mountains, out of snow and cold, down to a warmer climate
and good food.

We have completed our fall work. The beef have all been
shipped. All I have to do is turn my string of cow ponies loose in the
big pasture where there is plenty of good grass and water. Here they
will remain until spring, when some puncher is hired for the spring
roundup.

Coming down over the mountain into the small valley with the
frame shack and rail corrals of Aikens' ranch, I see several horses
grazing near the stream which runs past and between the shack and
corrals. These horses spot us at about the same time, throw up their
heads and start for the hills, all except a big brown horse who dis-
putes our way with his head held high and nostrils blazing. He is a
beautiful sight. Here is my old friend that I had turned loose to freedom a couple of months before. He circles around us, not knowing
if he would be welcome or not. So, pushing my ponies through the
corral into the pasture, I leave the big gate from the range open to
see if he will come in. With all the horses out of the way except my
saddle horse in the small corral, I walk out to the open range. The
big boy hasn't forgotten. While I was away he has gathered up his
old family of mares, who are now waiting on a hill a short distance
away, and has brought his family back from their own range, where
there are no fences or humans.

He is magnificent! A stallion returned to a place he had never seen but once in his life, and that time by force, returning to visit the only human he had ever known, where he had been treated like the gentleman he is, with petting and kindness.

Standing outside the big corral gate on the open range, he is tossing his head, making up his mind that I am the right person. I start talking to him, then hold out my hand and say, "Let's go, son." I turn and walk toward the corral gate. Without a minute's hesitancy, he follows me like I thought he would, through the gate and inside. Here I stop and he is up against me to have his head rubbed, just the same as in the old days.

I have just passed my twentieth birthday and have broken many wild horses — not the domesticated wild horse, it is always the real wild horses that make the better cow ponies. They are tougher and can stand more hardship, are more loyal and friendly than our domestic breed. Always, in choosing the best horses to break out of a large herd, we tried not to pick one over four years of age, as the older horses were real tough to break. But here was this beautiful brown stallion who had roamed the mountains with his family of mares and was at least seven years old, never touched by a human hand until, veering to escape in a wild horse drive, he passed close to my rope and it settled over his pretty head and the battle was on. As he traveled down the mountain with a terrific speed, I had just time enough to head Gray Eagle uphill to take the shock, and even then he almost upset us. It was a foolish thing to do, but I wanted this fellow who was so beautiful and graceful in flight, and I acted before I thought. With an ordinary rope horse other than Gray Eagle, we could both have been severely hurt, but my big gray was no ordinary horse, so before any help could arrive we had the big stallion tied fast. I was the only one with a wild horse, as the rest of the herd went through and over the new corral, which was built as a trap. For once the king had made a mistake by deserting his herd to go over the side of a mountain.

Now, here on a range where he doesn't belong, this magnificent animal with his family of mares has returned. How long they have been here, I don't know. I only know it is dangerous for them. They belong far back in the mountains, where only on special occasions are they ever bothered by man, and where the odds are a hundred to one they will never be caught.

In a big corral, where I have left the gate open, I am being nuzzled by this king of all wild horses. Whether he is trying to thank me for turning him loose, or thank me for not making a slave of him by treating him like most wild stallions are treated, I will never know. It is getting late. Soon the sun will be down and I have eighteen miles over a rough trail to Flagstaff, but I can't push this fellow around. He seems so glad to see me, so I clean his mane and tail and trim one of his front hoofs which is broken.

Taking him out the big gate to open range, I pet his beautiful head, and with a few pats I tell him to get the hell back where he belongs. My friend trots off to join his family, which is waiting near the top of the big hill. I watch him and his group disappear and, as sad as I had ever been in my life, I start for Flagstaff in no hurry.

I have plenty to think about. A big beautiful stallion, with a greater understanding and affection than most human beings I have ever known. Him, I shall always remember. I only hope he wasn't fooled by his one touch of civilization.

I have my mind made up when I get to Flagstaff to draw my pay and go south. I don't want to be caught in any storm or freezing weather, and tell Mr. Aikens of my decision to move and about the big brown stallion returning. He says, "Son, your friend Guy Galbrieth told me right when he said you had a way with horses. If you would stay with me, or come back in the spring, we could catch a lot of wild horses using your big brown for a decoy, for I'm sure you could find him again." This doesn't appeal to me, but I do agree to live at his house and break two thoroughbreds he has bought. They are a couple of young, nervous colts he wants broken real gentle to keep in town and train for racing. I agree to do this, but at the first sign of snow, I am gone.

My pal Brownie isn't going with me. He is going home for Christmas, so a young cowboy, Berry Carter, is going to join me, and on November the seventh we depart for the south to a spot in Imperial Valley, Calexico, on the border of Mexico. We are at least near a foreign country. To us it is foreign.

Imperial Valley was new. Many farms were in the making, with new land being leveled, new irrigation ditches being built and various crops being planted. It was a garden-spot-to-be under development. There were no paved roads through the valley, just in some of the towns and then only the main streets. Here, in one of the worst dust storms Imperial Valley had ever known, we arrive in the town of Calexico.

13

God's Country — Imperial Valley

THE DUST IS BLOWING SO THICK AND FAST that visibility is almost nil, but on the one main street of the town we see a sign, SCRUGGS POOL HALL. This establishment will offer protection from the wind.

Mr. Scruggs' pool emporium is a rendezvous for many. He has the usual barber shop along with soft drinks and cigarettes and cigars, and chairs lining the sides of the room where pool and billiard tables are running full blast.

The boss is a nice guy, very friendly, with a good word for everyone, and on a day like this a friendly word is appreciated. From Scruggs we learn that Mexicali, the adjoining town, which is separated from Calexico by an imaginary line, is wide open with hard drinks and gambling going full out, while in Calexico it is a sin to take a hard drink. So the town of Mexicali is doing real good. There is no passport or anything needed to visit Mexicali. All one needs is the strength to walk two blocks across the imaginary line, and the world is different.

Carter and I are enjoying watching a billiard game, waiting for a break in the wind, at which time we intend to visit the bright lights of Mexicali, when we are approached by an individual about my weight and height and a very few years older, inquiring if either of us wants a job. He introduces himself as Clint Wylie, with the statement he has a ranch about four miles out of Calexico and is looking for someone to break four colts to ride and at the same time help on the ranch.

He has a wonderful personality, an infectious smile and a cheerful greeting which remind me of my brother Bud. I am completely won over. He should have been a greeter in the White House, only people would have believed him. There is nothing phoney about this boy. Why he chose us, we don't know — we are in no hurry to go back to work, as we both have money burning our pockets — but it finally ends with me taking the job with his assurance that my pal will have no trouble getting all the work he wants.

With a promise to meet a week from Saturday at Mr. Scruggs' pool hall, I leave for the Wylie ranch. Wylie is driving a Pope Hartford, one of the few cars in the entire valley. As of 1912, horse transportation is still the main way to travel in Imperial Valley. I find on our way to his ranch that the Wylie family is from Montana, and they have several ranches and have moved their horses and sheep here. Sheep I don't want any part of, but I am quickly assured the sheep are taken care of by someone hired for that purpose.

Life with the Wylie family was always interesting. The foreman, or boss, of the Wylie ranch was Sam Jones. He and his wife Bonnie, together with Clint and his wife May, were the life of the surrounding vicinity. Clint Wylie took on the Cadillac agency, the first car agency in Imperial Valley, only there were not many buyers. Everyone was using their money to develop their land, especially those who were just getting started. Sure, we were the only two-car ranch in the valley, and from Saturday noon to Monday morning there was always someplace to go.

With these lovely people I stayed through Christmas and until July, when I was offered a job with more money bossing a crew of Mexican labor for the California Development Company under the supervision of Mr. Peck. This job, without any effort on my part, was the life of Riley. We started work at eight, were through at five. All I had to do was hire my own crew, keep their time, while we worked six days a week on a big canal well away from civilization.

My problem was to keep my crew happy and a full crew on the job. With a very limited knowledge of Spanish, this was not always easy. But it was a lazy man's paradise, and I enjoyed every minute working under the supervision of Mr. Peck. I liked the Mexican people. They were never in a hurry in this land of mañana. Life was free and easy, and the town of Mexicali was no exception.

On weekends people came from all parts of the valley to enjoy the freedom of Mexicali, where they could drink or gamble until from their money they did depart, then it would be back to work for a fresh supply. Mexicali would always be there waiting. If your luck was good, there were always friends. If it was bad, there were still friends, as in this warmth and sunshine there was a pioneer spirit where friendship seemed to thrive.

My pal Berry went to work punching cows for an outfit below the line in Mexico. So every other Saturday night we would meet at Mr. Scruggs' pool hall. From here, after the usual barber treatment, we would see the town of Mexicali where we made many good friends, both on the American and Mexican side of the line.

One of the finest pioneer families of Imperial Valley was the Lyons boys. They were hard working, hard drinking, and the most regular good fellows in the entire valley. These fellows became my good friends, particularly Frank, the younger of the clan. With Frank, Chuck Stanton, the Litzenberg boys, Berry and me, we made quite a group with a spirit of all for one and one for all. We were young and the world was our oyster. Here I had a home forever if I wished to stay with my pal Chuck and his parents, Mother and Dad Stanton, two of nature's noblest people.

Why I ever left this wonderful valley to travel I know not, but the urge was on me to move, so my pal Berry and I had a session and agreed to both quit our jobs on a given day, meet in Calexico on a Saturday night, say goodbye to our friends and take the stage to San Diego. From San Diego we would decide our future.

We have both thought about going to South America if there was a boat going our direction. I give my good friend and boss Mr. Peck notice I am quitting to travel somewhere. Comes the eventful Saturday, I am in Mr. Scruggs' pool palace when I am told my pal Berry has sent word for me that he can't join me until Sunday night. This blows my plans. I am all set to get out of town and be in San Diego Sunday morning. So what to do for twenty-four hours? Nothing but to go across to Mexicali and gamble a little. Hell, I have enough dough. I can afford to lose a little and I might even win.

There are days and nights where a fellow can't lay up a cent, and this was one of the nights. I lose a little, I lose a little more, then I lose the works. When I cross the line for the American side to go to bed, I am stone broke with the exception of a few loose silver half dollars. I have visions of calling Mr. Peck in the morning, telling him I'm still his boy, and tomorrow is another day. If that pal of mine hadn't taken one extra day, we would be on our way. Evidently things weren't supposed to work like that, for here I am broke.

Damn my ignorance. I sure need a guardian. I always shoot the works. Stopping in to my friend Big Foot, a Chinese boy who owns his own restaurant and is the smartest Chinese I know, to have a sandwich before hitting the hay, I find the place almost empty, so I have an opportunity to have a good visit. Big Foot is the only fat Chinaman I have ever seen. He evidently eats his own food. To kill time while waiting for my sandwich, I tell him what a chump I am. He says, "Mister Fred, you go back tomorrow, get all your money, all same bank, you put in now, you go take, I loan you some money, you savvy? I go get you hundred, you lose him, tomorrow I give you some more, you see?" Disappearing into the kitchen, he is back with a hundred dollars, so tomorrow maybe Lady Luck is better and will smile. If not, there is another tomorrow, so to sleep.

Taking my time in the morning, I have the day before me to re-gain my lost dough. It's like Big Foot says, my money in a bank. All I have to do is go get it. That's his opinion, not mine. But with a guy like my Chinese boy pulling for me, how can I lose with his money for a stake? I wander over across the line full of breakfast and feel-ing no pain over my loss of last evening.

Running into several of my pals, who are whooping it up, I de-cline all refreshments, as I am strictly for business, no monkey busi-ness. Ditching my pals, I slip down to the Owl, the most famous gambling house in Mexicali, where I had left my bank roll last night. Catching a half idle crap table, I have a feeling of confidence and away we go.

In less time than it took me to lose my stake last night, I have my lost fortune back with three hundred plus, and for once in my life I pass the dice, take my returned wealth and beat it to my friend Big Foot's restaurant where I try to split my three hundred winnings with the guy. He takes his one hundred and says, "You savvy, I told you all same bank." Leaving all my money with him for safekeeping except some spending money, I go back and join my pals, who haven't even missed me. The world is good, our trip is on, thanks to my Chinese friend. When my pal Carter arrives we are on our way, for God knows where, but it is spring and time to move. Our only reason for staying so long in Imperial Valley is the marvelous climate and the nicest people on earth. They are hard to leave, even if a fellow is young and full of ideas. Someday I shall return to this beautiful valley that has been so kind to us and settle down for life.

When I tell my pal I lost all my dough waiting for him, the old boy promptly says, "Don't worry, I have enough for us both." There is no use trying to kid a boy like that, so I tell him I have recovered my loss, we can travel faster and farther, so are on our way to San Diego, the first leg of our journey somewhere.

Having visited the wharf to see what boats were running and where, for no reason at all we decide to take the *Yale* to Seattle, stopping at Los Angeles and San Francisco. This will be the first trip on water for either of us. I think we are going in the wrong direction, but my friend Berry says Canada is a land of opportunities, and Seattle is close to Canada, so it's up the coast for us via a new mode of transportation.

Our last evening in San Diego, we go to Chinatown for dinner, where for the first time in our life we mark a Chinese lottery ticket known as a nine-spot ticket, for which we pay thirty-five cents each. The drawing is for nine o'clock and our boat leaves at midnight. We have worlds of time and can go to bed on board anywhere past ten. After killing as much time as necessary until the drawing, Berry jokingly says at nine-fifteen, "Let's go pick up our loot." The boy is a prophet. We have an unbelievable shock when the Chinese boy says my ticket has won one hundred and ten dollars. The boy is as happy as we are. We are paid in ten-dollar gold pieces. For his happiness we slip him a gold piece, and he shows us why we are being paid. I had accidently marked seven spots of the nine in the right place, which gives us each fifty bucks after giving our boy ten. It looks like a good beginning for our trip — at least a fellow can dream better with money in his pocket than he can when broke and hungry. Truly, if one is lucky, brains don't count.

Our trip was slow and easy, with nothing to do, just eat and sleep and enjoy the coastline, which was in view all the way to Seattle. With the two stops at Los Angeles and San Francisco to break the monotony, our trip was a real pleasure and came to an end much too soon.

Our stay in Seattle was limited, just a couple of days to see the town, then by train to Wenatchee, the apple country on the Columbia River. Here we did something I have always wanted to do. We took a trip on a side-wheeler up the Columbia to the town of Oroville, Washington. This boat trip was a joy. The boat stopped many times to unload passengers and freight. The scenery was beautiful along the banks, and everyone seemed to bubble with the joy of living. Oroville is a mining district with cattle, farming and always the Columbia River to draw from. It is a thriving community. Here we meet a Mr. Read, a cattleman whose ranch is on top of a mountain far back from Oroville in an isolated spot where he has trouble finding anyone to work for him. The gentleman batches, lives alone and has four colts he wants broken to ride.

I still have my saddle from Flagstaff, my boots and spurs, although I haven't used them for some time and didn't expect to use them again. For some reason I couldn't part with them. Berry sold his outfit before leaving Mexico. He was through with cattle, but for some reason it just don't last, and again we are talking to a fellow about breaking four colts to ride, which in itself is nothing. We don't need the dough. The job would be easy and, after all, I would have a good time. I always was happiest when handling an unbroken horse.

Mr. Read is desperate. He has to return to his ranch and feels he must take someone with him. This fellow is a decent sort, so we agree if he takes us both we will break his colts. If he is satisfied, he pays us whatever he thinks it is worth, providing he will loan us a pack animal and some equipment for a prospecting trip after he is satisfied. This he is more than happy to do. It was something he hadn't expected, though. It made him wonder a bit if we knew anything about horses or were a couple of four-flushers looking for a place to light.

The ranch on the mountain was forty miles by buckboard, where if we could have taken off across the mountain in a direct line it would be about ten, but once we were on the summit and Read's property, there was a beautiful little valley where he had a small farm and raised feed for his horses in the event of a real bad winter. His four colts were not wild. They had been raised on a ranch, were gentle to start with and were like four tame old cows, so we finished it up real fast. We were both glad we hadn't asked for any money. Mr. Read was such a decent person we enjoyed staying with him.

Berry and I were used to batching, so we did most of the cooking and helped build some fences and repair his house. Here we stayed a month where two weeks did the job. Making our headquarters at the ranch, we did some prospecting but then decided to cross over into Canada. When at last the day came for us to leave, we considered we had enjoyed a month's vacation, something neither of us had ever had in our life, so it was "Mr. Read, you don't owe us, we're even." This wasn't the way the gentleman wanted it, and he insisted on giving us fifty dollars after all the grub we had eaten and the pleasure we had roaming the country with his horses.

Returning to Oroville, we caught a stage to the town of Penticton at the end of Lake Okanagan, a beautiful, clear lake with boat transportation to Vernon, British Columbia, a small but picturesque town where many retired English people lived in an atmosphere of luxury. Here I sold my saddle and boots to a nice English chap who wanted them more than I, as he paid me more than their original cost. While they were not new, they were well broken in, and with a saddle and boots that is something to consider. Now I was really out of the riding business, and while I didn't know it, I had ridden my last bucking horse. To make the gentleman happy, I threw in my rope. So my new English friend was a cowboy without a cow, and with a rope he didn't know how to use, but he was happy.

From Vernon we traveled to Revelstoke, where we connected with the Canadian Pacific running from Vancouver, British Columbia, to Calgary, Alberta. Why we should go to Calgary rather than to Vancouver or Victoria was possibly the fault of our friend Mr. Read in Washington, who told us the wonders of Canada and the support the Canadian government would give a person who filed on the land, either for mining, ranching or any reason, just so the person was reliable and sincere. This appealed to us, for in our own country where you can file on one hundred and sixty acres, our government bets your land you can't live five years without starving to death . . . and the government always wins. Here in Canada, you have more land and financial help.

With high hopes we grab the main line for Calgary, our land of opportunity. Our trip en route to Calgary via the Canadian Pacific was the most enjoyable train ride with the most wonderful scenery we had ever dreamed of seeing. Every mile was something different. To a couple of country boys raised on the flats, this was life at its best. Mountains in every direction for hundreds of miles, with their different formations and changes of color, were to us something wonderful and different.

Any resemblance between Calgary and our mountains there isn't. Calgary is like our cattle country of Colorado, rolling hills with plenty of flat land, where the people are younger and more aggressive than the folks we left in Vernon, where things are much the same from day to day. Here in Calgary everyone is busy, everyone is optimistic about whatever they may be doing. It looks as though we have hit the right place on the edge of a boom. A few days here and my pal and I are as full of optimism, or whatever it is that makes the Calgary boys and girls run, as they are.

It is certainly high time. This is the last of May 1914 and in July I will be a really old man of twenty-two. Carter has already passed twenty-three and he is about through. So if we don't get rich soon, it's over the hill for us both, and they keep building the poor house further and further away.

14

Calgary, Investment in Oil
and a Soldier of the King

We each have twelve hundred bucks that we left Calexico with, so after much investigating and much talk, we have decided that when the country freezes real tight we will go to Edmonton, Alberta, and shoot the works for some big dough.

We have found out that now is the wrong time of the year, but when it is below zero and all the country is frozen solid, a fellow can go overland with a pack and snowshoes from Edmonton to the Peace River and the Mackenzie River country, which are rich in minerals. All that is necessary is to get there in the dead of winter, stay over summer and come out with the next freeze.

I, who hate snow and cold and have sworn to never be caught again in a blizzard, have succumbed to the lure of gold or money in any form. It is too early in the season to go to Edmonton. October will be soon enough. So we look around for a way to make a few extra bucks while waiting for the freeze. We are both pitched to a high level, with the world our oyster. Truly, we are congratulating each other that we landed in Calgary — we could have gone the other way. Carter says twenty-three is too young to be a millionaire, but when I remind him it will take two years to go where we are going and return, the guy is just as happy. He is a good sport, never worries, and is always ready for anything. A swell companion at all times, good or bad.

Here fate takes a hand and gives us a boost. Going across the street to our favorite restaurant of five days, we see a crowd a block down the street in front of an office building, which we decide to investigate after we have disposed of some waffles and eggs. It might be something we should know about.

After ordering said breakfast, we ask the waitress if she has any idea what the crowd is doing down the street. This gal knows everything. It seems Calgary is in the throes of an oil boom, and we have been so busy with our own ideas this was our first news of it, which proves a fellow should always look around. Without any urging our gal explains that if we hurry, it's possible we can buy some shares in the Pilgrim Progress Oil Company, that her mother has hocked all their furniture to buy stock and all their friends are trying to raise money to invest.

How lucky can a couple of fellows be? Here my pal and I have never invested in anything except a few crap tables, and without any work on our part, if we hurry, we may be rich. Asked what she thought a fellow could make with a couple of hundred, she said the man told her, with her hundred invested, she would never have to work again. So what are we waiting for? We can finish breakfast after the first oil well.

Reaching the scene of activity, we find the broker's office is full of people. There is a policeman on duty outside a big window, where the broker is throwing the dough he and his assistants take in. They don't have time to stack it, just count, give a receipt and toss the loot in the window. This is opportunity at its best. There are as many women as men. The question is how to get some before it's all gone. Again luck is with us, for a nice looking guy says, "Boys, do you want to buy some stock? If you do, I'll take you in the side entrance we reserve for our special customers. As you boys look like smart people, I'll take care of you."

He did. The gal was right one hundred percent, and we had it made, so Berry and I parted with five hundred apiece, for which we got a receipt with a promise of our stock tomorrow in Pilgrim Progress Oil Company. With a name like that, how could we miss?

Feeling like a couple of fresh made millionaires, we go into a tailor shop and order a blue serge suit apiece, then decide to hold the rest of our dough for our winter trip in the event our oil well doesn't come in on time. After a strenuous day of investment, tailoring and what have you, I challenge my pal to a pool game just to relax, when a gentleman introduces himself as Mr. Frazier. He is looking for help on his farm. With a pool hall full of men, he has to pick on us. When I ask him why, he says they are all a bunch of bums and won't work. He has tried them all before. The poor guy is desperate, there's hay ready to cut and soon the grain, and in a town full of men he can't hire a man.

Neither one of us has worked on a real farm, but this fellow seems a decent sort and will pay us more than we ever earned, considerably more than I made living alone batching, taking a chance with my life every day breaking horses. Certainly Canada is the place for us. They just won't let you starve. Besides, he wants us both for at least two months, so we promise we will take the job if he will wait until ten tomorrow, that we have some business to transact, then we will be free for two or three months.

I am liking Canada more every minute — never an idle moment, always something doing. We would get our stock, put it in a box in the bank. When we came back to town, our new suits would be ready and we would have more money. As long as we were going to be gone for two months, we counted our wealth and decided to put it all in the man's oil well. If he had any stock left, which we doubted.

Keeping just a hundred apiece for use if needed, we found our stock ready when we arrived at our broker's office, but there was no more Pilgrim Progress. It had been oversubscribed, so the man said. But he would let us in on a secret. There was another company just starting to sell their stock, the Black Diamond Oil Company, which he felt was just as good if not better. The man was right. It was just as good. The only thing was, we couldn't have the stock for a few days, so we took a receipt for our dough, which we were assured was just as good as stock. Again the man was right.

We were a little late meeting Mr. Frazier, who had just about given us up. Without any delay, we started for his property, some thirty miles out of Calgary. We learned as we traveled along that Mr. Frazier was an older son, that there were six brothers and six sisters, together with mother and father quite a large family. Why he needed men with a family like his was a puzzle to us until we reached the farm. This family was loaded with land and crops. They were old timers and a nicer family never lived. They all worked like hell. The girls helped in the field or wherever necessary. The youngest was eighteen, so without hiring outside help they had a large operation going. They all lived in the big house, and mealtime was like a hotel. At ten in the morning something was always brought out to the field and again at four in the afternoon.

These folks were the hardest working people I had ever known, but the kindest and gentlest to each other as well as everyone who worked for them. It was no wonder they were happy and prosperous. We were with these nice people on August the fourth when the First World War broke out. They had taken us to their hearts like part of the family. Through Berry they found my birthday was in July, so they baked a big cake with twenty-two candles and turned home-made ice cream. It was a wonderful gesture and made one feel good just to be around such people.

We had no news of our oil venture — in fact, very little news of anything except war, though I couldn't see how that would affect Canada, it was so far away. Our job would be over on the fifteenth of August. We were anxious to see what had happened in Calgary during our absence and to find out how rich we were.

Our work took a little longer than anticipated, so we don't arrive in town until the twentieth. Calgary has gone nuts. Since five empires declared it the war has been on just a few days, but there are uniforms everywhere, as well as many recruiting offices. War has arrived with a vengeance. Canada is rushing to get a first contingent together. Still one hears from many sources that the war can't last, that Germany isn't strong enough. It's sure to be over by Christmas.*

War or no war, we have things to do. First, our tailor with our new suits, then to see about our oil investment. And the time is not too far distant to prepare for our trip to the Peace River in

---

*In fact, it wasn't, and when it finally did end four years later, nine million men would be dead.

December. Our tailor is a most depressed Canadian. He is talking of going out of business. He hasn't sold a suit since the day war was declared. Who wants tailor-made clothes with a war on? He thinks he may join the army. Besides, he lost some money in an oil deal, some company other than ours. Of our company he knows nothing, so we hasten to our broker or the man who sold us our stock and find the place closed. Why, we can't find out. Berry suddenly thinks of the waitress who gave us our first information about Pilgrim Progress Oil, so we rush over to the restaurant where we first met the young lady. We find her working and very unhappy.

The little lady tells us the sad news. It seems the brokers and the men who sold the stock had closed their offices sometime in July and had beat it to the United States, together with the oil men. According to her information, they were American promoters who got rich from the sale of stock, then departed for the good old U.S.A., leaving their Canadian stockholders sadder but wiser.

Whether they had drilled a well, she didn't know. She only knew that she and her mother, together with all their friends, were broke and wouldn't be able to make the payments on their furniture, as they had borrowed money to buy stock. She told us business was bad. People still bought food, but where they used to tip a quarter or half dollar, they now left a dime or nothing. The poor kid was in real trouble, so for a dollar-and-a-quarter check, my pal gives the gal a dollar tip.

When I ask him why the hell he didn't marry the gal, the big bum just grins. Quite a boy, this pal of mine. While our little girlfriend didn't know it, the American promoters hadn't just left Canadian stockholders behind, they had two American stockholders with one thousand apiece of our money in somebody's pocket. At least we weren't broke. We were both too young to retire.

There were many places to go, so to hell with the boys. They were sure accommodating, even gave us a receipt, stock and everything, even took us in a side entrance. Next time I'll wait. That way I'll have my money a little longer. When I tell Berry it might be a good idea if we don't mention we are Americans unless someone guesses it, he agrees one hundred percent. Someone might hang us to a lamp post. Americans in Calgary are not too damned popular at the present moment. To ask anyone if they wanted to buy our stock would not be good. So just in case someone might be buying or trading, we get our stock and receipt out of the bank box. While it may not be worth much, the paper is beautiful and the seal is sure a honey. If worse comes to worst, we can take it with us this winter to use in our cabin as wallpaper, nice and expensive.

My pal has a brilliant thought. "You know," he says, "when you went broke in Calexico, you got all your money back with a profit on a crap table. Why can't you do the same thing here?" This guy is nuts. First, there are no crap tables here that I know about, and second, I could go bust and there is no big-foot Chinese boy to stake us if we wind up broke here. Another consideration is that, with this stock in our pocket, we could land in jail for life. Someone might swear we were part of the gang the American promoters left behind. I'm all for getting out of town. We have enough money thanks to our two and a half months with the Fraziers. I'm for Edmonton, where we can prepare for our trip.

It's amazing what and why people do things on the impulse of the moment. Someday when I get older I am going to stop and think, but now I still act and then think, and sometimes repent at leisure. Today is no exception. It is the second of September, 1914. We know of a waffle shop where the food has been excellent. So at about six o'clock, we bounce up to the counter for our evening meal, as tomorrow we have decided to leave for Edmonton.

The place is full of young men, some in uniform, others talking about joining the army. Seated next to me is a fellow in uniform with a load of stripes on his sleeves, none of which means anything to me, but what he says does. This character is a recruiting sergeant who is all full of his subject. At first his conversation doesn't ring a bell, until the old boy says travel at the government's expense and see the foreign countries. I was sunk the minute I asked if the government returned you to your recruiting point. I was quickly assured that they didn't only return you, but gave you a bonus and big pay while in service. He further explained that the unit he was recruiting for paid big money from the day you joined, with uniforms and everything free. If we would come up to the basement of the building where their headquarters were, his captain would explain all the advantages of being a soldier.

Glancing up toward the top of the wall facing us, we noticed some joker had pasted a sign: BROKEN DONUTS AND BURNT WAFFLES EXCHANGED FOR PILGRIM PROGRESS OIL STOCK. Whether this had any effect or not, I don't know, but we promised to come up after finishing our dinner. This wasn't good enough, for the old boy knew his recruiting, so he waited and grabbed the check.

Away we go. We don't have to join, just look. When we reached the basement, there was more activity than on the streets. If we thought there were uniforms upstairs, we were crazy. They were all down in the basement. Some fellows were drilling, some were learning about rifles, everyone was busy. The minute said captain took us in tow, I knew we were done for. Just think, three dollars and thirty cents a day, every day including Saturday and Sunday, with everything furnished, a chance to travel, starting immediately, tomorrow, no training required.

The gallant captain was recruiting for a motor unit to go to France at once. He had to have thirty-three men to leave on the two o'clock train tomorrow. Without asking, he says I know you boys both drive a truck, and as first driver you draw top pay at three-thirty per day and you have a second and third driver with loader for each truck, so all you do is boss and once in a while drive the trucks.

Here I explain to the captain our plans for the winter of going to Peace River. This is right up the old boy's alley. He counters with, "I think that is marvelous. You are the kind of men we need, someone with ideas. While the war is on, there will be nothing doing in the North. Join, and by the time you return you will both have a big bank roll. You will have seen a lot of the world, and Peace River will still be there."

What can we lose? So he turns us over to a sergeant where we sign up and are sworn in to His Majesty's service, with orders to return at eight in the morning. Upon our inquiring what happens if we don't show at eight, said sergeant leaves us with no doubt when he says we will send for you. In joining and being sworn in, the fact that we were Americans didn't trouble anyone. So long as we were twenty-one, there were no questions. They were evidently scraping the bottom of the barrel to take us, for two more ignorant individuals about army life they couldn't find had they advertised in all periodicals.

We stay awake most of the night laughing and talking about our new investment, as Berry puts it. I know nothing about a truck, and my pal knows less. Just wait until they put a truck in front of you and say take off. His quick answer is, "Dig in the spurs and pull the horn." With this we have a good laugh until the roomers all over the joint start pounding their walls. Berry wants to lick the whole crowd, but I have had experience with this business of licking a crowd. I am now a hero of the King's army and shall reserve my fighting for the war, and if the man is right, the war will end about the day we land in France. Just a pleasant trip with refreshments and pay. They started this war just in time for us. Always something happens. Never a dull moment.

We report promptly at eight as per orders for fear they might send for us. Now they have us. There is no rush. We are too early, so the sergeant gives us a chit on a restaurant across the street. In the army one night and breakfast on the house, it's unbelievable. And we don't have to report back till eleven, which gives us plenty of time to pack our things, get some travelers checks with our dough. We are a couple of kept men leaving for Toronto at two o'clock. Where or how far to Toronto, we don't know, but the sergeant says it is our first stop on the way to France. Of one thing I am sure, it is closer to the U.S.A. and our American promoters than here in Calgary. Which doesn't mean anything, only these boys may be working Toronto, and we could buy some more stock, I think.

At one o'clock, thirty-three men in civilian clothes and carrying their worldly goods lined up on the street in front of the recruiting basement for our march to the railroad station. Here we were supposedly going to France via Toronto, with no one having a uniform or a physical examination. All of this would be taken care of in Toronto. Up to now there had been no one interested in trucks. The captain said we drove trucks, so we left it at that. A captain couldn't be wrong. We were a hot looking bunch marching through town, Berry and I each with a suitcase and an overcoat, the rest of our bunch dressed similarly. I'm sure if the mayor had seen this crowd of recruits going to defend Calgary, he would have surrendered without a struggle. The walk was more than we expected, but we bore up like a couple of real heroes without too much griping and were more than pleased to find we would have a private car for our little group all the way to Toronto.

15

Loss of Citizenship, Sergeants Moose and Little Moose and the Motor Transport

W E WERE ALWAYS SERVED FIRST IN THE DINER, just our group, then the civilians. After all, weren't we soldiers or something special? One would think so with the special attention we received.

Having three days to become acquainted with our fellow passengers, we found a nice crowd of fellows, only three having previous military experience and only three admitting to knowing anything about trucks. One, Andy Ross, later known as Fish, was an expert mechanic. Bob Roberts was supposedly a good driver, as was Goldie. These three were as far as we could ascertain the only ones who had ever driven a car. After canvassing our group to see if anyone knew as little about what we were supposed to know as we did, we didn't feel badly. Everyone seemed to be in the same boat. Certainly Calgary had been easy. We would worry about Toronto when we got there. If they kicked us out of the motor transport, we would join the cavalry, anything, if we didn't have to walk.

Our group had been placed under the charge of a boy with some previous experience and training by the name of Thompson, who we felt sure would land a non-commissioned officer's post once we landed, wherever we were going. But for the time being, he was in command.

When we arrived in Toronto, we were met by a reception committee of one, the biggest, tallest, most hard-boiled sergeant major of the regular army imaginable. Taking over from Thompson, he lined us up with the group command "Fall in." In what he didn't say, but we assumed he wanted to play follow the leader, so with overcoat and suitcase in hand, we take off after the big moose.

The walk in Calgary was just a breeze. Here it is getting dark and cold, and still we walk. Neither Berry nor I have ever walked such a distance in our life. My damned shoes are full of feet and I am tired of playing soldier, when we go through a big arch into what appears to be a fairgrounds of sorts. Here the moose lets out with the only kind word he knows how to utter: "Halt." This comes just in time, for two of the King's best are finished. God save the King. I am just sitting down on my suitcase, hoping this is the end, when he bellows, "Attention." Then another move into a building where there are bunks one over the other. We are told to leave our suit-cases and coats on our bunk.

Then another march for blankets. This we do on a trot, or on the double, our new sergeant calls it. By this time I guess the moose is pooped, for we have a new sergeant in the picture. Not so big, not so loud, but fast on foot. We are issued blankets in a hurry and back to our bunks where, in the language of our new sergeant, we fall out for fifteen minutes, to wash before we eat. This has been our first contact with two real soldiers. They haven't scared me to death, but made me damned tired. I knew it was too good to last. You don't get something for nothing for too long a time.

Here we go again, to the mess hall which is two blocks away. You think they would walk this distance. Not our boy. He's away on the double again. If they have enough of these fellows, they can wear out all the army with this double business. Me, I'm going to be a horse soldier, to hell with this double stuff. Boy, will I sleep late to-morrow. So I think.

The food was wonderful. With no one to push us, no one to yell on the double, we walk back to the building to our bunks, where we have to make up our bed army style. This is new to us, but with the advice of a corporal who says he is assigned to our outfit, we are ready for bed, only you don't go to bed until they tell you. This we find is the exclusive privilege of the army. They tell you when to go to bed and when to get up. The "up" business they never forget.

They might keep you up all night, but never in bed all day. Everything is done for you. If you think, you're crazy. It isn't necessary. We find that our quarters are in the poultry building in Toronto's famous Exposition Park, which has been taken over as a training center for the Canadian Army. All the beautiful large buildings have been converted into living quarters or whatever is necessary to train an army. Here very soon will be twenty thousand men learning to be soldiers under the supervision of many old regular non-coms from the English Army. Certainly Canada is going full out for the mother country.

Despite the rumor of the war ending soon, it was evident no one in the higher command gave this rumor any attention. When we returned from our first army dinner, there was a new crowd of civilian soldiers in our part of the building. This new group, who had been recruited as motor drivers in Ottawa, were to be part of our unit. These boys were going through the blanket routine. It made us feel like old timers. We had learned two things: fall out and on the double.

Berry and I grabbed the bunk nearest the big stove and directly on the aisle toward the washroom. We matched for the lower bunk, which I won, so when they blew a bugle for bedtime, the poor old man of twenty-three climbed into the upper bunk with difficulty. The bed was hard, but to two old cowpunchers used to sleeping on the ground it was all the same feather to us. Also, our on-the-double business might have had some effect, for we were both asleep immediately.

The next thing I know, Berry is yelling, "For God's sake, don't that guy ever stop blowing that bugle?" He was of the opinion that this was the call he went to bed by. The only difference, this was the call to get up, five-thirty in the morning, dark as a black cat, with a loud-mouth sergeant bawling, "Fifteen minutes to dress and fall out in front of the side entrance." This boy is determined, with lungs to prove it. His gentle howl can be heard all over the big building.

We feel our way out to where our lovely sergeant is waiting. The old boy wastes no time messing around. Old Leather Lungs yells, "Fall in, count off in fours and follow me, left right, left right, pick 'em up, forward," and he hits a double, never a single, always a double. One thing for sure, *he* isn't lost. He heads straight for the race track, and on the double we make half the track before slowing down to a walk. Then he's off again for the rest of the course, just a little conditioner before breakfast.

Back to our building we are told to wash up for breakfast, after which we will have time to shave and prepare for the day's activities. They must have a relay of these sergeants, for we never have the same one twice. Always a fresh boy, full of whatever a sergeant is supposed to be full of. We are shaved and cleaned up and allowed to walk to breakfast by ourselves. They are beginning to trust us. For at least no one has given us any orders for about an hour. It's too good to last.

Sitting on our bunks, we're trying to analyze our plight when we are told to fall out in front of our building where there is plenty of room. What's coming is anybody's guess. Everything is always a secret until they get you lined up. Here we see the moose with a sergeant and a corporal. Berry and I are sure as hell making progress, for we have both found out how to tell the sergeants and corporals apart. The one with the loudest bellow is top. The others have poorer lungs. For once the moose keeps still. We are given a lecture by one of the lesser lights about how to line up, how to form fours, how to march, and above all, to eyes-right or eyes-left whenever we pass an officer. Up to now there have been no officers, so we are a cinch. The non-coms have the army under control.

Now the moose takes over. He is really a magnificent sight. He is straight as an arrow, with a tight fitting blue uniform all littered up with ribbons and stripes with a round, tall black beaver cap. The guy looks like a million and sounds like the whole army. His mission in life is to call roll, just to see that no one is lost or is still asleep. Fat chance. His mission complete and, all accounted for, we are turned over to an ordinary sergeant, who marches us to the quartermasters for uniforms.

Contrary to all reports about handing a new soldier a flock of clothes with instructions to fit himself, our outfit was different. It was almost eleven o'clock before Berry and I returned to our bunk loaded with everything a soldier should have from the skin out and beyond. Never had either of us had so much to wear. They even furnished us with shaving soap, razor, hair brush, and the best looking topcoat, called a pea jacket. It looked as good as an officer's British warmer, only a little shorter. If some joker had yelled "on the double" with this load, we would have both fallen dead, but being left to ourselves, we staggered back to our bunk with our loot and a problem. Our problem was what to do with our civilian clothes. We knew no one to leave them with. We each had three suits, including one beautiful new tailor-made blue suit. What to do we were trying to decide, when I left our bunk for a few minutes.

This pal of mine has an awful temper and will fight a buzz saw anytime. He may not always win, but the kid will always try, and this was one of his best days. When I return, I am just in time to jar him loose from the throat of a motley looking individual who starts apologizing immediately he could breathe. He blurts out, "If I knew the goods ver new, I vould hed offered you five."

Heading for the side door with my pal after him, the departed victim was one of several civilians I had noticed hanging around the bunks when we arrived with all our uniforms. While they were not allowed there, they had taken a chance and were buying the old clothes from the boys changing into uniforms. What had upset my pal was, he had been offered three dollars for his new blue suit. The guy raised the ante to five, making him even more hostile. It was lucky I returned when I did, but luckier there was a side door for the gentleman's exit, or my boy might have been shot or hanged or whatever they do to a soldier for killing a civilian.

Thinking everything is all over except disposing of our surplus clothes, we see a young punk who looks like a pug coming around the bunk with "Where's the so-and-so that choked my father?" Berry is on his feet with "Here I am, you blankety-blank so-and-so," when there is a bellow like an old bull with the mumps which freezes everyone including our visitor. Here we have moose number two. He's not so big, but just as tough, loud and hard, only this one is in khaki. The woods must be full of these fellows, and this one I am real glad to see, for I'm sure if our sergeant don't stop the brawl, it is a cinch that I will be mixed up in this affair of honor, some way, somehow.

Young moose, in a voice the world could hear, inquires if we belong at this bunk, and we assure him we do. He lets out with "What the hell are you doing here?" Our civilian friend is real tough. He has come in to beat my pal's head off and starts to rave about how good he is, when the young moose pulls a whistle and blows once. Before you can catch your breath, two real big boys are at his side. They have bands on their arms marked M.P., with big forty-fives hanging on each side. They look like the business. With one word out, they start for Mr. Pug, only he has seen them first and is on his way. It seems at the appearance of our M.P.s the place was fast clearing of all the civilian vultures, and we are still owners of a bunch of clothes we don't need. Our new sergeant stops for a few minutes to see what the fuss was all about. His name is O'Brien and he's to be our permanent sergeant, has just been assigned to our unit. This fellow we like much. He has all the appearance of what I thought a good non-commissioned officer should be like. We both find out later he is all this and more.

We have been here two weeks. We have given all our clothes to a Canadian organization to do with as they will. The few dollars we could receive for a sale would only be an insult and they might help someone. Today is our first payday. Everyone is lined up and receives his pay in cash as his name is called. We are all paid one-sixty per day, which is the low wages in our motor unit. While the man in Calgary rated us first drivers, neither one of us knows anything about trucks, so we are lucky to be paid anything. The foot soldiers only get one-ten per day. That is their top unless a non-com.

Our motor unit is made up of small groups from different cities in Canada. Among the Ottawa boys are several Americans, one a young fellow named Coapman who becomes one of my best friends.

Of our officers we haven't seen much. We have in command of our left half a Lieutenant Ellard, Sergeant O'Brien and a couple of corporals. Our unit as a whole is divided into a right and left half, each under different officers and non-coms. We have a couple of captains and a major who haven't put in their appearance on the parade ground, although Captain Parmalee and Captain McKinnon have been in our barracks on payday. Two of our Calgary contingent have done real well. Bob Roberts has been made sergeant of the right half, while Thompson has been made a staff sergeant.

Berry and I are lucky to still be privates. It is almost unbelievable that a green group of men with so many left feet could be trained into a snappy group of soldiers in as short a time as we now have. Our unit is the envy of the entire camp. We have the best dressed soldiers and fast are becoming the best drilled unit on the parade grounds. We have just stood inspection by our major. This fellow is the keenest officer I have seen at any time. We were lined up, he came down the line looking everyone over carefully. Some of us he stopped, inquired our name. When he came to me he knew I was an American, had enlisted in Calgary and could ride a horse. Once this fellow knew you, I would bet he never would forget. Either good or bad, he would see a fellow through. He was Major Red Harris, a regular soldier who I immediately took a liking to. With him I wanted to go overseas.

Today the only bad luck since joining the Canadian Army has fallen. We have been notified that all Americans serving with the Canadian troops should quit or lose their American citizenship. With this news, the Canadian Army agreed to release every American who wished to be released. Here my pal Berry quits to go home to Oklahoma. I think he is worried about his parents. He is one swell guy. It is tough to see him go. We have had some wonderful adventures together. So Berry and most of our Americans leave. My friend Coap and I stay.

I am only afraid we won't make the other side. Not that I am looking for a war. I just want a trip, and then back to Calgary for me. The soldiering must be good for me, the training and walking or doubling. I am hard as nails and feel better than at any time in my life. If I just knew a little about a truck, this would be an easy life, with top money for nothing. Soon we will be rated. How, I don't know, but whatever it is, I know from nothing.

They have finally found out that the Calgary contingent had no physical examination, so this we have just completed, and me of all people didn't do so good. About five years previous I was hurt by a bucking horse throwing me on the saddle horn and wound up with a small hernia. For this I wore a truss two years and was completely healed, so threw the truss away. But the examining doctor says cough, and there you are, he finds I have been ruptured. Otherwise

I am all to the good. The doctor is a peach. He says, sure, you go to the General Hospital for an operation which amounts to nothing. The Canadian Army will pay all expenses, you will lose no time and will be out and be able to go overseas with your own unit. Otherwise you will be discharged. Time is wasting, and I know it. My outfit may go any day soon, so with the doctor's promise to rush me through, I agree and he arranges with my CO and a well man walks into the General Hospital of Toronto, Canada, for an operation so he can go overseas.

16

An Operation, an Examination, Mutiny and War

THE ONLY TIME I HAD EVER BEEN IN A HOSPITAL BEFORE was when I broke my leg out from Phoenix, Arizona, where a horse bucked into a mesquite tree. That was a wonderful, small hospital, but this Toronto hospital is something to write home about, all full of pretty girls, and them I need bad.

Evidently the staff has been alerted that I am in a hurry, so I am given a fast shave and told they will operate in the morning. I am in a large ward where there are many sick people. I am possibly the healthiest person in the hospital, here for an operation I don't need but may need some day if someone kicks me in the stomach.

The hospital believes in starting early. I am wheeled in their operating room at seven o'clock and moved onto a table, and before I can catch a fast breath they throw blankets over me from both sides. Then, some chains. When I was placed on the table, I spotted a gal who I supposed was the head nurse standing at the head of said table. She was a good-looking old bag, I guess about twenty-eight. While they were clamping the chains on to keep me from jumping off the table, I was trying to tell this dame something. She responded by dropping a mask over my face and I began to choke to death. Did she give a damn? No, she kept doing what she was doing while I passed into a beautiful field of flowers, hating this dame like the monster she was.

When I came to I was surrounded by a screen of curtains and was sicker than I had ever been in my life. Every once in a while a student nurse or some dame would peek through the screen, snicker, then go away. It took me all day to recover from the ether they had used for an anesthetic and take some interest in my surroundings. It seemed by some circumstance I was one hell of a curiosity to everyone.

Beginning to feel better, I asked my neighbor in the adjoining bed what all the laughter and curiosity were all about. It seems, a person recovering from an ether anesthetic talks a lot and usually expresses what is on their mind when they pass out. In my case, it was this old bag of twenty-eight. I went under hating her like nobody's business, so when I started to talk she was my subject and my language was evidently not fit to eat. They should have brought me back to this world in a soundproof room. I didn't relive my past, it was all my opinion of this gal who gave me the works and didn't even say goodbye.

What was so interesting or pleasing to all the student nurses and most everyone concerned was the fact that my particular hate for this gal expressed their own feeling, only I did it with a vengeance. I was damned ashamed of myself and terribly embarrassed and very much wanted to apologize, but I never saw the young lady again.

By morning I had completely recovered and asked the doctor when I could go back to my unit, which he said was one week from date of operation. During this week, it seemed like our entire motor unit was in to see me. They came three and four at a time, both afternoon and night. Fellows I barely knew. The word went out that I had been operated on so I could go over with the gang, and they damned near made a hero out of nothing. Best of all, my major, whom I had never expected to hear from, came with Sergeant O'Brien. Now I was sure I wouldn't miss the boat. I was sure to go with my unit. With what kind of rating I didn't care, but here in the hospital I worked out a way to go as a first driver if they didn't get me too soon with the examination.

Back at my bunk everyone was glad to see me. You would think I had performed a service for somebody other than myself. I was excused from drill for a week and allowed a weekend pass. But I had something on my mind, because the rating examination was coming up soon and I knew from nothing about driving a truck. Getting my friend Fish Ross in a corner, I tell him my troubles, which he more or less realized, as the Fish was one of our Calgary crowd. This boy is the most efficient all-around mechanic in our entire motor unit. All I want him to do is teach me all he knows in a few days. I want him for a godfather or something. The Fish is a prince, and assures me I have nothing to worry about. Even if I should fail and fall on my face in Toronto, this can all be remedied when we reach overseas.

So on the weekend we go into the city, where my friend rents a truck and tries to convert a cowpuncher into a first-class truck driver. If one knows about trucks, there is nothing to learn, but in me the Fish has a real dumbbell. Yet through Saturday and Sunday I have developed my driving enough to pass any driving examination as long as the boys don't get too technical. As to why a truck goes and stops, I don't know, but Fish says never mind, I'm in.

My idea has paid off, thanks to a real pal. The day for the great test arrives. We are to be examined in the mechanics' building, where those who are trying for first driver are turned over to a sergeant assigned for the purpose of examination and rating. We are taken separately and asked a few oral questions. Whether the Fish had told the sergeant what to ask me, I didn't know, but they were the same thing the Fish had taught me and I remembered the answers. So far I was in with flying colors. The driving I wasn't worrying about. I felt pretty sure of my driving. It was the oral I was doubtful about.

So through a big door into another part of the building, and here I am sunk. Someone has gone nuts. They have a light beat-up automobile for the test. The car is one of the Henry Ford variety with a foot movement known to no human other than a Ford driver. We're given no explanation of what to do or why or that a Ford is different from a truck in the gear shift and other departments. The mechanics' building has big cement pillars about one hundred feet apart with a cement floor smooth as glass. To stop, a fellow can choose his own pillars. This I know because up against one of these is where I stop when my driving examination is over.

The sarge is a brave man. "Take the wheel, Libby. It will soon be over." The guy didn't know how right he was. When I asked where the hell is the gear shift, he brushed me off with, "Everything is done with your feet. All you do is push the pedal down, give her gas and you're off!"

He was absolutely right. We are off, like a wild man with the itch. We fly past one post, make a fast turn on two wheels and are gaining speed when I want to stop, ducking another pillar. Old Sarge turns the ignition off as we hit the next pillar square in the face. The old Ford gives a cough, her radiator spouts water, someone yells, "Ride 'em cowboy," and I have been examined.

No one is killed, not even hurt except the sarge. He don't feel so good and is about to give me a zero rating when the Fish shows up. He was the joker who yelled, "Ride 'em cowboy." The examining sergeant is only human. When the Fish explains to him what a lousy way to examine a truck driver, and goes so far as to say I have been his driver on a truck for two days, this more than satisfies the sarge, who has a lot of respect for my friend's ability.

So without any more worries until I get a truck, I am supposedly one of the best, at least that is what the rating shows. What happened to the Ford we never learn, the junk pile perchance.

We have been in training six months, which has paid off. We are the best dressed, best drilled unit in the Exposition Park. The man in Calgary said this would be our first stop, how long he didn't say. We all expected just to change cars here in Toronto, and then to France without any training. From all we can hear, the more training the better, as what started out to be a small battle is a real crisis and the first Canadians to go in action have taken an awful beating with horrible losses.*

These Canadian people are wonderful. They never cry, they

---

*This is undoubtedly a reference to the Canadian divisions that helped stem the German advance during the fighting in the Ypres salient in Flanders in November 1914. The Germans, in their sweep through Belgium at the outset of the war, were rushing to capture ports on the English Channel at the northernmost point of what would soon become the Western Front. They were stopped at the small town of Ypres by a combination of British, Canadian, Indian, and French forces, but at a terrible cost.

are back of England with everything. I'm real glad I didn't quit and return to the U.S.A. True, I've lost my citizenship, but America isn't going to finance me in the Peace River country. So the boys in Washington can go sit on a tack. I'm for the Canadians through this thing, right or wrong, and they speak my language, so they must be right.

It's April 1915, and we are away in a cloud of dust, the great day has arrived. There is no doubt about France. We are loading out and on our way for Halifax, then the boat to somewhere over there. Everyone is more than ready to be moving. It is a thrill in itself.

From Halifax we sail in a passenger boat, the HMCS *Metagama*, where we go first class, with dining room and service complete. We spend several days ducking around to avoid submarines and such, which gives my young pal Coapman time to get into trouble. This lad can stir up a row with the least effort of any human I have ever known. It is not done to give anyone trouble, just to have fun, which often boomerangs. This is one of those occasions. Some of the birds who have it in for him were about to throw him in the drink for giving the impression he was a German spy. It seems to be my painful duty to fight for this bird the rest of my life. At least while we are together in this man's war, I don't intend to let anyone push either of us around too much.

Liverpool at night. We couldn't arrive in daylight, when a fellow could see what he was doing. It's always night with nobody knowing what it was all about. Our officers are trying to find out where we go from here, so all we can do is wait.

We are finally aboard a train for a trip across England to our new quarters in tents on a spot where mud was first discovered. Here we are supposed to be equipped with trucks for use in France. Evidently the honeymoon is over and we are down to business.

I have been wanting to travel, so here I am in Good Old England on Dibgate Plains, near the city of Folkestone. Our tents are large with a center pole and a wooden floor and sleep six, everyone with their feet toward the pole. Everybody crabs. The quarters in Toronto were too good. We were all spoiled with too much comfort. We have always been paid promptly and far too much for what we are doing, especially when one thinks and remembers that thousands died of exposure this winter in the trenches, to say nothing of the wounded and killed.

While we have had the best clothes in the Canadian Army, with top pay, the poor guys in the trenches were dying for one-ten per day. We were to be paid before leaving Toronto, but due to some mix up and our hasty departure we were not and are on our seventh week in England without pay. From the crabbing and bellyaching, it is a major crisis, which might not have happened had our commanding officer, Major Harris, been with us, but he was too ill to leave Canada and had not joined us, although it was rumored he would in a few days.

What followed was not the fault of our officers. It was a spoiled group of trained men who thought they were soldiers but weren't. Of these I was one, and am entirely responsible for my part with no alibis for my actions because, while I was younger in years than many, I had lived a rugged life and was fully conscious that we were wrong, dead wrong.

Who was our guiding light in this dumb show I don't rightfully know, but somehow, some way, it was agreed upon by two hundred and seventy men that when the bugle blew for our morning parade, no one would leave their tent until paid, or until some agreement had been reached.

Imagine if one can, in time of war, a small group of would-be soldiers of every kind, where at an order we could all be shot for not obeying a command. When I think of this, I still get sick at my stomach. It was the one blight on my record, and the one thing I have always been ashamed of. The mutiny for a few lousy dollars was so wrong, and I knew how wrong, which doesn't excuse me, only makes it worse.

Out of the two hundred and seventy there was only one corporal who appeared on the parade ground with our officers. This fellow I have always admired. Here we were, a unit who had been given more than any other group, letting our officers down and disgracing the entire Canadian Army without any thought of the fellows fighting and dying in France. That we were not all shot or given hard labor the rest of our life was due to the protection given us by our officers. Among our officers was Captain McKinnon, who sent word to every tent that if we would carry on and parade, he would personally see that we would be paid the following day.

True to his word, we were all paid in full, including our back pay, so everyone was loaded, and here again trouble started. Those who could get passes hit for London. Those who didn't have passes left anyway, so the camp was almost deserted. In a very short time they were picking some of our soldiers up all over England. With all this, our officers protected us, and our major finally showed up from Canada just in time to see us equipped with new trucks in preparation for France. Soon our entire unit was complete with new Pierce Arrows, Locomobiles and Peerless and Packard trucks, all fresh from America. Also, we acquired some light English Daimlers and Leylands, with special motorcycles for our non-coms. The Second Division supply column was ready for service at the front. With a few days getting our trucks adjusted and the personnel assigned to each truck, we took off across England for Southampton, where we loaded our trucks aboard ship for the Seine River, destination Rouen, France.

I had joined the Canadians at Calgary on the spur of the moment with a wish, as the recruiting sergeant said, to see the world, with no expectation of ever getting into a battle. While our chances of getting in the fighting end of the war were still questionable, at least we were coming closer. This we realized after leaving Rouen and heading toward the lines, where we could hear the roar of the big guns and meet ambulances on their way back to a hospital with their sick and wounded. Then the observation balloons began to show up and we met thousands of troops on the march, both going and coming. The ones coming had just left hell, those going were just entering hell, some for the first time, many never to return.

This war, which many optimists thought would be over quick, had the appearance of just starting, and the Canadian troops had suffered terrible losses, with replacements filling the gap in all regiments. The Western Front stretched from the North Sea at Nieuport, Belgium, nearly four hundred miles southeast to the Swiss Alps. The trenches in the eighty-five-mile-long British sector were held by nearly half a million of our men. Our motor transport was to haul supplies to the boys in the trenches from a loading base in

Hazebrouck. We were parked on both sides of the road out of the town of Météren, and from here we loaded our trucks in the day-time with every known ration, together with a very special ration of rum in two-gallon stone jugs. This particular rum saved more lives from respiratory disease than all the medicine. To a boy soaked with rain for days, the ration of rum was a Godsend. It stimulated the cir-culation and warmed the insides so a fellow could digest the cold food, and when necessary an extra portion of rum would take the place of food.

For sleeping quarters, we were billeted out with French fami-lies. Whenever away from our trucks, we were in some chateau out of the rain. For our food we had the best, naturally, hauling the ra-tions. We always had corned meat with canned butter from Sweden. With this butter, French bread and a bottle of *vin rouge*, which was the French standard drink of ordinary red table wine, along with a couple jiggers of rum, no one was undernourished. I shared a billet with three of my closest friends — Coapman, Robinson and Cornell. We stuck close together on all occasions and shared our food and bed, good or bad, but with our gang there was very little bad. Every-one was on the alert to help the other fellow.

The winter of 1915 is upon us. Such rain I have never seen. Where we are located, it is always wet. To keep the big truck in the center of these cobblestone French roads is not too bad. It is when you pass, or meet someone, that the big babies gently slide in the ditch which lines these roads on each side.

Running at night you have just a small front light, from the lower part of one headlamp, for the purpose of seeing the truck in front with its very dim taillight. When a fellow makes the round trip up to the depot near the trenches, from which the load is then packed by horse transport in to the trenches, and returns to his base, he has had a full night. If a truck hits the ditch, he is left to be picked up by an emergency empty truck for that purpose and the convoy goes on.

If we think we have trouble, we always try to remember the poor devils living in the trenches. With water everywhere, it is im-possible to keep dry, and along with the weather there are the damned rats, cooties and, just a rock's throw away, our enemy, the

Hun. The Germans seized the high (and dry) ground on a long chalk ridge, while our boys are dug in across from them in what had once been swamplands.

Anytime I start feeling sorry for myself, I always think, but for the grace of God I could be an infantryman. I didn't know any better. It was just luck being in a motor transport. It's a cinch that if the Calgary sergeant had been recruiting infantrymen at the time he nailed me with his line, I would have joined anything to see the world. I was overripe for picking, regardless of what the boy was recruiting.

Always I have been told of the wonderful French girls. I know somewhere the sun must be shining and there are girls with time for pleasure. But where we are there are the young things who work in the bakery at Météren, whose parents see them home. Poor kids, I know they don't want to go home, but father knows best. Then there are a few who work in the stores and drinking establishments, who are overstocked with applications. For girls, this is a hell of a place. They are pretty wonderful to carry on with a pursuing male at every turn. If they stand still they are ruined. If they run they might break a leg. So who wants to break a leg? After all, these gals are all for France, *vive la France*. *Vivent les Canadiens*, a few million strong. It is *la Guerre*, who cares? The girls are wonderful. They have done their bit to make the world safe for democracy.

In our sector where there are so few girls, a medal should be issued reading Far and Beyond the Call of Duty, for a public relations job well done. Everyone is talking about leave and where to go. If they start alphabetically, I will be a real old man before I go and the rain will be over. The first place I will go if it happens is somewhere there is sun, any place out of this damned rain. Water in any form disgusts me. It isn't even good to drink. It's habit forming. Tonight, thank God for our billet. I don't have to drive, so shall fold up out of this cockeyed rain with a crock of rum. Tomorrow it may be worse. It's a bitch of a night for man or beast and the boys in the trenches will suffer. There is no way to keep dry. I've seen prairie dogs with better places to go than the trenches.

How anything like this could happen in a civilized world — it's unbelievable that millions could be buried in the ground just to

hold a front or stop an advance. The folks at home will never understand or believe it. Certainly they will never understand the
hardship. It is so impossible. Those who survive will live in a world
of their own, isolated in thought from families and others to whom
they seem unreal. The few infantrymen who survive the trenches
will not be able to talk to anyone other than their own kind, as the
civilian chatter will never be their dish. They will always think and
remember things no one believes who wasn't there.

17

I Join the Royal Air Force
to Get out of the Rain

O<small>N ONE OF THE BLEAKEST RAINY AND MISERABLE MORNINGS</small> while in France, I took a look at the bulletin board in the orderly room of my motor unit. Why, I will never know, for as a full-fledged private any orders I might receive came direct from some non-commissioned officer. Certainly this look changed the war for me in a way I didn't expect, and with a speed I didn't anticipate. From what happened to me, if one doesn't believe in fate one should never look at a bulletin board, especially during a war.

The notice which attracted my attention was from the Royal Flying Corps headquarters, stating that anyone who wished to become an officer in the Royal Flying Corps might, regardless of present rank, apply through their commanding officer with recommendation of a general, and would be given a thirty days' trial as an observer on probation, at the end of which time if service was satisfactory he would be given a commission as second lieutenant in the RFC, or return to his original unit at former status.

True, I know nothing about aeroplanes or what an observer is supposed to do — but one thing I do know, they don't fly in the rain, and we have been living in rain for months. One can reach up and get a handful of water anytime, it just stands in the sky. The only question is how high is up.

Me, I'm not thinking of flying, but it might be a nice way out of this damn rain. I have no desire to be a hero either, living or dead, though if fate is kind, being a second lieutenant would be good, as all second lieutenants I knew seemed to have it easy.

So without consulting any of my buddies, I find Sergeant O'Brien and ask him to take me to our commanding officer, Major Red Harris. Sarge objects that this is going over the captain's head. All of this I know, and I also know if I don't get direct to the major, my chances are not too good, as up to now I haven't been associating with any generals, and it appears one is necessary or at least his blessings are, and I know this can all be arranged if the Old Man is interested.

So, with much arguing, Sarge gives in and we head for the orderly room where the major is working.

The Old Man is busy with some people when we arrive, but upon seeing O'Brien, he inquires what he wants. After O'Brien tells him (with not too much glee) that I have requested an interview, we are told to wait. This I know is good news, and in a very few minutes my faith is justified, for we are called over to the major's desk, where he dismisses O'Brien. Then to my utter surprise he says, "Libby, I would like you to be in the Royal Flying Corps and have given it much thought, especially since the bulletin has come out — they need men badly and I will do everything I can for you. Be at the officers' mess at one P.M. and we will go see General Lindsay and I will ask him to sign your papers, also to write a special letter of recommendation, because I am sure you will be a credit to us and the RFC. Libby, when did you see the notice on our bulletin board?" When I reply, "About twenty minutes ago," he remarks, "That bulletin has been there for two weeks and you are the first to apply. Will Captain Parmalee be surprised, as I predicted you would be the first, although this is much later than I expected."

This reception and kindness from the Old Man are more than I expected, so with many thanks and a big salute I proceed to make myself as presentable as possible for my meeting with General Lindsay.

We have been, we have seen, we have conquered. General Lindsay signed my papers and wrote the letter requested by Major Harris, all of which goes in Canadian headquarters mail tonight.

This is much faster than I hoped for, but true to army routine I was quite sure we wouldn't hear from the RFC for at least thirty days, which was usual unless it was leave — then you could depend on a sixty days' wait.

On my way back from General Lindsay's headquarters, I thought of my buddies with the big trucks and particularly three of my closest, Coap, Baldy and Cornell, the four of us sticking together whatever the occasion might be since we were thrown together in October 1914. Most of our unit had certainly seen us drive away down the cobblestone road between the big lorries parked on each side, me in the front seat of the big Daimler with the driver, the Old Man in the back seat taking the salutes, and unless O'Brien had opened his big mouth the entire column would be dying of curiosity. Of one thing I was certain, that right or wrong they would be with me to a man.

I thought I was sure of at least a thirty days' wait before any action would be taken by the RFC, and if accepted, I would have thirty days' training by RFC to become a second lieutenant, which in itself wouldn't be too bad. Certainly there would be no flying without a great deal of training.

Of flying I knew nothing, plus having never even been near a plane, even on the ground. As I was coming out of my dream of what was to be and not to be, we reached headquarters, where I gave the major my best salute and unfortunately ran into Sergeant O'Brien. The first thing to come out of his Irish mouth was, How did our hero make out? He was a good sergeant, tough as hell at times but always for his men.

So I gave him all the information with my own opinion as to the length of time we would have before hearing from RFC — if ever.

The old boy was direct and to the point. "You are always willing to bet on anything. I'll give you odds you hear in less than a week with orders to report for duty. And something else, you won't go back to sit on your royal American for training to be a second louie. You will be up in the clouds the first day you start. They are so short of pilots and observers, that is why the bulletin. Man, did you ever see any of our guys win a fight? The Hun has more ships, more men, more everything, that is why they are scraping the bottom of the barrel for flyers. This rain can't last forever. Spring and summer are coming and it will be tough for all combat troops. Our flying corps will be up there and you will be up there. If I had the guts I would go with you, but I have several little O'Briens in Canada, so unless I break my neck with a motorcycle or a stray bomb gets me, I will come through. But you can bet on one thing for sure, you will have every one of our motor transport pulling for you. I'll even offer up an Irish prayer occasionally. And will still bet you on the time if you want some." Oh God, if I could only tell a bum of a sergeant to go to hell!

To say that this conversation slowed me down would be an understatement, he was so sure of what he was talking about. I was beginning to think I had moved too fast. I wasn't mad at anyone, life was good, even in the rain, and there were many places in the world I wanted to see, none of them in France.

By the time I reached the billet where my three pals were, I wasn't too dissatisfied with myself, and here, as I expected, I received a royal welcome. They had pinched a gallon of Jamaica rum from the rum truck, French bread, canned butter with a couple bottles of *vin rouge,* the good red wine which makes bread taste like cake. They all agreed that Sergeant O'Brien was not only nuts but didn't know from nothing. That no outfit would let you go into combat without training. So with good food, good friends, the rain outside, we four settled the question to our satisfaction at least for the night. It was the end of a perfect day.

The next three days were the usual routine, clean our trucks, load and at night deliver our load as close to the lines as we could go, where the horse transport would take over. On the third day after my trip to General Lindsay's headquarters, I hear O'Brien outside of my truck. Upon sticking my head out from under the canvas top to see what the battling Irishman might want, I am greeted with the remark, "Boy, you owe me some dough. How much did we bet? All right, so we didn't bet — but I was right, they must be hungry for men. Three days today and I have orders and transportation to RFC headquarters where you are to report to a Colonel Bennett for an interview. Major Harris has ordered his driver to pick you up at seven

A.M. and drive you to the depot, where the train leaves at seven-thirty. After the interview you return to us. Evidently the interview decides your fate. Maybe if you don't look too good you won't get the job, but boy you better or the Old Man will never be the same, and you can't let the Old Man down. Good luck!"

Catching the early morning train back toward the base as per orders, I arrive at eleven-thirty, where I am met by a driver of an RFC Crosley tender and we take off for general headquarters. Here Colonel Bennett's quarters are pointed out to me. The colonel is a fine looking man with the RFC wings on his chest together with several ribbons which are significant of service or decorations, I don't know which as none are familiar to me.

The colonel gives me the kind of welcome which makes one feel good, not stiff or formal, but puts me perfectly at ease with the remark, "Libby, we are glad to see you. This won't take long, it is only routine. We will take your weight and height first." This being done by his Sergeant Collins, there are a few questions.

Do you know anything about aeroplanes? Absolutely nothing, I answered. What makes you think you can fly? I don't know, I have never been near a plane. Can you ride a horse? Now, what a horse had to do with flying I didn't know, as horses don't fly, but here I was on safe ground, so I assured the colonel I was an expert with horses. This pleased him more than I expected, as he was the owner of several polo ponies, and we had a nice discussion about horses in general.

Our interview was evidently over, as he instructed Sergeant Collins to take me to the sergeants' mess for lunch and see that I had transportation to the railroad station for my return trip. His last remark was, "You will hear from us." Good or bad, he didn't say.

Going to the sergeants' mess seemed very unusual to me, as in our Canadian Army privates didn't eat with the sergeants, nor did sergeants eat with the officers. There was a mess for everyone according to his rank, and me, I'm plenty rank, which is nothing. So I ask Collins about it. He says that circumstances alter cases, that while I was now a private, I was making application to become an officer and would, when I reported to active duty with some squadron during my probation period, eat with the sergeants and share their quarters until receiving a commission or being sent home.

"And I might tell you that you will soon be in the RFC, because you have passed the Old Man with flying colors, and at staff meeting in the morning he will recommend you and a decision will be made as to which squadron needs you the most, as we are awfully short of observers, especially in the fighter squadrons. So, before you are back to your own base forty-eight hours, you will receive orders where to report.

"The thirty day probation will be up to you. Yours will be a highly specialized service with many responsibilities, where more fail than succeed, but to succeed is wonderful. To have earned the observer's wing is a mark of distinction and combat service.

"Here we are at the mess. Let's meet the others. Every one of us would give our eyeteeth to be an observer in our RFC. And every one will be watching your future with interest."

I lunched with as nice a bunch as I have ever met, then to my train back to the only place I know as home in France — my motor unit.

It is a funny world here. I have been wet to the gills for months. Today the sun is out. Don't look like it will ever rain again. Me, who was looking for a dry job, looks like I have it, all right, because I am told the Old Man wants to see me. This can mean only one thing, he has news from the RFC with orders for me to report somewhere some place in France. Too bad it had to stop raining. Also too bad they didn't lose the orders for a few days, this is faster action than I am used to. At the present moment I am not mad at the Heinies or anyone. Boy, if I can believe the two smart sergeants, O'Brien and Collins, I am about to engage in a fighting war where the boys are using real bullets. Me, who wanted to travel. Looks like I am going in the wrong direction. At least I'll have a look at how high is up. Oh well, I know what my big brother would say, "Move easy and take it in stride."

So up to the major's quarters, where I receive my orders together with much advice. Bidding farewell to major and staff, I make the rounds, bidding goodbye to all my friends, and if a guy ever had a lot of good luck thrown his way, I am the boy. Going back on the same seven-thirty train I had so recently traveled, my destination was not so far. I would be met at Le Hameau station, again by an RFC tender, only this time I would be headed for active duty in Twenty-third Squadron, RFC. With this information under my belt, I and my three pals Coap, Baldy and Cornell decide to do a little celebrating. This relieves all pressure, so that when morning comes along and with it the seven-thirty train, I feel no pain. In fact, I'm almost happy about the whole thing. When the conductor gives me a shake to prepare me for my departure at my station, I gently feel my head to be sure it is mine. I step off the train almost into the arms of my escort with the tender, and climb up in the front seat where there is more air, hoping for a long ride as I am in no hurry to do any more moving than necessary. It just isn't to be. In a very short five miles, we drive through a clump of trees into an opening and, whether I like it or not, this will be my home for thirty days or less.

The driver has completed his mission, turning me over to a sergeant major who instructs said driver to put my bag in the orderly room temporarily. He slips me the sad news that his instructions are to bring me out to the hangars to meet our commanding officer immediately I have arrived. As we move toward what appears to be an abandoned field, I spot nine big, highly colored heavy canvas structures, three in a row on three sides, with the fourth, open side facing the field, which was, I found very soon, the landing field for the planes. In each hangar were two ships, which made a complete squadron of eighteen planes. Standing out a short distance from the hangars in the field were three men engaged in apparent serious conversation, so we came to attention and the sergeant gave a salute.

The senior of the three, Major Ross Hume, says, "Welcome to the Twenty-third Squadron, Libby." This before the sergeant could open his mouth. "Libby, we need observers. This is Lieutenant Price and Lieutenant Hicks, both of whom are in need of a good observer. What do you know about a machine gun?" Up to now no one has ever mentioned machine guns, so, when I assure the major I know nothing, he shows no shock, but immediately tells the sergeant major to take me to the gunnery sergeant for a half hour of instruction and shooting on the gun range, then to bring me back and Lieutenant Price would take me up for twenty minutes practice shooting at a gallon petrol can on the field. "Libby will eat with the sergeants and share quarters with Sergeant Chapman."

This doesn't seem possible. I left my base at seven-thirty, it is now ten-thirty, and if his orders work out, hell, I could well be dead by noon. While I don't feel so good, I am real glad of our party last night, for the way things look, I may never have another. So away to the gunnery but not in high spirits. Here I am taken over by another sergeant to coach me with the Lewis gun, which comes very easy, possibly because I have been used to other guns most of my life.

At this time the Lewis used only a drum of forty-seven rounds, later ninety-seven, and to a fellow who could shoot at all, even forty-seven rounds was a lot of firepower, something I never dreamed of shooting. Evidently my performance on the range is satisfactory, for back we go to the hangars. The major's first words are "How did he do?"

"Wonderful, sir, I think he will be fine." What a blow!

"Very well, Sergeant, put a gun on the front mounting of Lieutenant Price's plane, have it wheeled out for practice at ground. Show Libby how to get in the ship and use the gun when in flight. Notify Lieutenant Price when ready."

The ship which was rolled out was the pusher type, with the propeller in the rear. The pilot was in front of the motor in the middle of the ship and the observer in front of the pilot. When you stood, all of you from the knees up was exposed to the world. There was no belt and nothing to hold on to except the gun and sides of the nacelle. Fastened to the bottom and toward the front of the nacelle was a hollow steel rod with a specially fitted swivel mount for anchoring the machine gun, which could be swung from side to side or to the front as the occasion demanded, giving it a wonderful field of fire.

Between the observer and pilot was another gun, which was for the purpose of fighting a rear-run action over the top wing to protect your tail. The mounting consisted of a hollow steel rod, into which a solid steel rod was fitted to work up and down with the machine gun on the top. To operate this you simply pull the gun up as high as possible, where it locks into the fitting, then you step out of the nacelle and stand with a foot on each side. From this position you have nothing to worry about except being blown out of the ship or being tossed out if the pilot makes a wrong move. This gun, I know, I am not going to like much. Brother, no wonder they need observers! All this I learn from the sergeant while waiting for Price to arrive. Who does, as nonchalant as a hog on ice. The engine starts, much to my sorrow, and we taxi out to the far end of the field, where we are to take off toward the woods where the entire squadron is hidden, with the hangars nestling against the woods' outer edge. My instructions are, when we turn back toward the field and come within range of a red petrol tin which Lieutenant Price shows me on the way out to take off, to shoot the tin in bursts from the gun, then to change drums and repeat the performance once more, then land.

All this is old hat to the lieutenant, but not to me, who one hour before had never had my hand on a plane, and have had my first contact with a machine gun a few minutes previous. I'm flat on my bottom for the take-off, then I am supposed to either stand or get on my knees to be in position to shoot on our way back. This I am preparing to do, when he throws the ship in a steep bank to turn. I almost swallow my tongue, and my eyes are full of tears, for I have no goggles, so we fly over and past the target, which I don't even see.

This I know is very bad, a very poor showing on my part. Something must be done. Sure I can't disgrace my old friend Major Harris with such a rotten show. As Price makes his second trip toward the target, I am in position with the gun pointed where I think the target will show up. This it does and I press the trigger and can see the petrol tin bounce and roll over — how could one miss with forty-seven rounds? — as I forget and let the whole works go. Now to change drums for one more shot. When I release the clip which holds the empty drum in place, it is caught in the wind and flies out of my hand, just missing the propeller and my pilot's head with no damage, but this could have ended our careers forever. Again I know I have done something very wrong. So slipping the full drum in place on the Lewis, I wait again for the target to appear in sight, and again the entire forty-seven go and I see the petrol tin this time really roll. We are past the target in position to land. My pilot throws the ship into what I learn later is a steep bank, turns and lands, taxies up to the petrol tin to see what happened to our target. If there were no holes when the tin was put out, there were now plenty. And in front of our hangar stood the major and two sergeants. His remark of "Good show, Libby" helped a lot. I felt terrible about losing the drum, so mentioned it to Lieutenant Price, whereupon he called the gunnery sergeant, asking him if he had explained how to change drums in the air. He immediately said he hadn't. Was told to always do so in the future. Asked to show me my quarters which were with a Sergeant Chapman, the sergeant accompanied me over to a pup tent well back in the woods which contained two cots, my bag and Chapman's personal flying things, with a mirror hanging on the pole for shaving, together with a couple of beautiful flying coats.

In a few minutes Chapman arrived. He was a fine looking fellow, about my size and build, and was one of the three sergeant pilots in the RFC. Was attached to the Twenty-third on special duty, flying a single-seater Martinsyde Scout used for reconnaissance and photographic work. He was an old timer and a top pilot although just a boy. After a few minutes of visiting, he said, "Libby, let's go to the mess." Then he stopped. "I just heard you are quite handy with a machine gun. I also know you had a busy morning. Suppose we refresh before eating." With this he reached in a pocket of one of his flying coats and came up with a flask, pouring a couple of large portions, and handing me one with the remark, "This may not cure you, but it will never hurt," which was too true, as it was the British ration rum of which there is none richer.

This is God's gift to man, and is issued by the British wherever they have combat troops. Three swallows and you never have any pain, either mentally or physically. The British should know, it has been a standard with them for years. Chapman didn't know that a few hours previous three characters — Coap, Baldy and Cornell — would have told you that the British ration of rum would cure gout, leprosy, smallpox or what have you, and while they weren't trying to cure me of anything, it was certain they were trying to preserve me in a state known only to embalmers, and now after my refresher with the good sergeant, I am alive, I think.

To lunch, and if the flying corps is willing I will catch a little rest. This seems in order, so both stretch out on our cots while Chapman is giving me some much needed advice about the entire flying corps and our squadron in particular, many things which would be of help to me in the future. And one thing he told me — which relieved my mind of any doubt that, without even trying, I had gotten myself into one hell of a mess — was his explanation of our squadron's purpose and activities:

"You know, Libby, all F.E.2b squadrons are all-purpose squadrons. While being primarily a fighting squadron, they can do anything, such as reconnaissance or bombing, and while the Hun is faster and more maneuverable, the F.E.2b in the hands of a good pilot and observer is hard to defeat.

"In fact, it is so solid that unless they hit the pilot or engine, the ship will keep afloat and limp home, often riddled with bullets, and here is where you come in. The observer is the most essential part of the team. You do all the shooting, all the photography, all the bomb dropping, if bombs are used. And you're entirely responsible for your pilot's life. True, the pilot flies the ship. He gets you there and back, and a good pilot will put you in a position to shoot and will not get panicky, tossing the ship around, throwing you out of position to shoot or defend yourself. If you're lucky, you can be with Price, Hicks or Captain Gray until you are used to the air. After that, even with a green pilot your chances are good so long as you can shoot. I am not telling you this to get your wind up, but to help if I can, because anyone on their first time in the air who shoots like you did will be one surprise to the Hun."

18

First Flight over German Lines, One Enemy Plane Confirmed

THROUGH ALL OF THIS I HAVE REMAINED QUIET, but finally come alive enough to inquire what is so wonderful in hitting a can where you have forty-seven shots and let the works go, which was quite contrary to what I was told, and I don't feel too cockeyed good about my showing, even if everyone seems to think it wasn't bad.

"Libby, the point is you did shoot. I have seen them freeze and never shoot. After two or three attempts they go back to their unit. This is one reason we are so short of observers. Shooting from the air, where you are all exposed, with nothing but your gun to keep you steady, is why so many men fail as observers the first two or three times."

Our conversation is interrupted by the entrance of a buck private with flying coat, helmet, boots and gloves, which is a squadron issue and fits like it. Asked by Chapman if there isn't something better in the coat department, he says, Possibly, but there is not time for that. He's flying at three and is to be on field at two-thirty. "All right, son, you may go, and take your junk with you. I'll fit Libby out with one of my outfits. Try this helmet, it fits like a helmet should, doesn't drop down over your eyes. The coat is just right and, if I were you, I would put on a heavier pair of socks as your shoes are good and won't be awkward like boots. Now for a pair of gloves and goggles and you look the part, which will please our Old

Man, who you can bet will be out to see the flight leave. So while you are here, wear these clothes for good luck. You will soon be buying some for yourself."

What a chap. You would almost think I couldn't miss. All I could say was thanks. I at least looked like a flyer, regardless of how ignorant or green I might be. So with my new flying coat over my arm I am in front of the hangar at two-thirty promptly, where I find my pilot is Lieutenant Hicks. We have thirty minutes before flight time, as his ship is not out of the hangar. I wander over to wait, where I am assured by one of the mechanics that he is a top pilot, which is sweet music to my ears. Now, if I can just do my part and not let him down. In a few minutes I see him approaching from around one of the hangars, his leather flying coat hanging over his arm, helmet cocked on one side of his head, perfectly at ease and as carefree as a school girl headed for an ice cream parlor.

His first words were, "Stout show this morning, glad to have you with me." Whether he really meant it or was just trying to build up my courage, I didn't know. Still, he didn't think it was anything to worry about when I explained that if I didn't see the insignia, I couldn't tell our planes from the enemy. "This, Libby, you will learn, but be on the safe side, have a roving eye, don't let any ship get in a position to shoot us down. If he is friendly, he will show his colors. Unless he does, let him have it. And tomorrow, if you will go to the adjutant's office, he will show you silhouettes of all ships, both the enemy and ours. I suggest you study three of our enemy ships, the Fokker, Roland and Albatros. These are the most deadly the Germans have at present. They are faster and have much more maneuverability than our ships, unless it is our Nieuport. And of these we don't have many. As for our F.E.2b, the enemy have a wholesome respect for it. A good observer can shoot from any angle and has a wonderful range of vision with the front gun. The rear gun is to keep Fritz off your tail when returning home from across the lines, when you can't turn and fight with the front gun unless forced to. If this happens, you lose your formation back of the lines and have to fight your way home alone. This is tough and is just what the Hun is after. A lone ship they all jump on, so we try to keep formation at any cost if possible. Fighting your way home in a single

ship, the odds are all in favor of your enemy. The wind is almost always against you because it blows from the west off the sea — this
they know and they can wait. Remember, we are taking off in a few
minutes. Shoot at anything you see and don't know. Here comes
Price with orders for this show. I'll give you the information in a few
minutes."

Upon his return to our plane, I am told we are on a three-hour
reconnaissance mission. Will dash over into Hun Land below Arras,
making a wide circle down toward the Somme River and crossing
back into our own front at Albert. Our flight formation is: Captain
Gray leading with two streamers on the tail of his ship to denote
leadership. Direct on Captain Gray's right is Price, with one streamer
denoting second leader, and on Captain Gray's left another ship
known as left escort. Back and slightly higher would be two more
ships, and directly back and higher, our ship which was known as
upper back escort and considered to be the toughest spot in the formation.

This I didn't know, which was just as well, as finding out the
hard way might be the right way. It would at least save a fellow considerable worry. Before taking off for the blue sky above, my pilot
said there would be nothing for me to do for the next hour except
relax and enjoy the ride. Each pilot would climb on his own to gain
altitude of ten thousand feet, where we would rendezvous and pick
up formation over our own aerodrome, then head for the lines for
our dash across and beyond. He suggested that during our climb it
would be well if I familiarized myself with the ground, picking out
landmarks which would be easily recognized from the air in the
event your pilot got lost and you had to direct him home. "It will not
be necessary to be alert for the enemy until we pick up formation
and start for the lines, which I will point out to you, so for an hour
I'm on my own."

With this bit of information — nothing to do and one hour to
do it in — I take my pilot's advice and study my map, where I see
many things I have never seen before. I am able to spot La Basse
Canal, woods, roads all having different shapes and sizes. There are
the two main roads leading to Arras, one from Saint-Pol, the other
from Doullens. Both are straight as a string with a line of trees on

each side, something one could never miss from the air. And from Arras, where these roads come together, extending back from our lines to the above-mentioned villages, are several air fields, including our own, which is hidden in a woods on the Arras-Doullens road. This much I have learned, so how could one miss? If lost, pick up the road and follow it home. These roads, together with a few special woods, proved my guiding light in the next months, and while I did not know it at the time, these first few minutes would in days to come be responsible for my safe return many times. With this aerial observation complete, I have plenty of time before the rendezvous to think. So what does one think about your second time in a plane, sitting like a bottle of water in the nacelle of an F.E.2b, with a machine gun on either side with whom you have just a slight acquaintance, headed for God knows where? My mind turns to my favorite people, Father, Brother Bud and my darling Aunt Jo, the home in Colorado where Father and Brother are or should be. Aunt Jo in Boston, none of whom have had a line from me. I can just hear Father say, My God, that boy didn't even learn to write! I think of my favorite horses which meant so much. I think of all my many friends in the Canadian Army, and particularly the three I left this morning, Coap, Baldy and Cornell, and how they would get a kick out of me up here in the sky with a pilot and machine guns going somewhere.

Somewhere I know nothing and care less about, though when we return I am supposed to report where we have been and what I have observed. Why, when I had started to Tahiti, did I go to Canada? Tahiti, where your breakfast falls out of a tree in your lap, where they grow grass with girls in it who have a shake which has nothing to do with machine guns, and best of all where one never worked. How the hell had I taken the wrong direction and the wrong boat? This ends my dreams, goodbye Tahiti. For Captain Gray just sailed past with the streamers on his tail and the rendezvous is on. There is no time wasted. The big ships fall into formation with no effort and we are on our way toward Arras, where the trenches are well in view, and I can see in every direction for miles as the sky is exceptionally clear. One can see into Hunland, far as the eye can reach. What is to happen is in the lap of the Gods, but I am now alert on my knees, hoping for the best. I remember the advice given me by my big brother, who, while I was growing to the ripe old age of nineteen, had helped me more and had been closer than any other human. "Say, Pard, take it easy, don't be tense and if trouble comes, your muscles will tighten up fast enough in action," so maybe I don't have too much to worry about. It's possible the enemy may have someone as green as me. After all, they are only human.

Practically all the towns below us are piles of brick and rubble. About this time Lieutenant Hicks points down to row upon row of trenches zig-zagging every way, with a blank spot of blown-up dirt splintered with trees in between, separating the German trenches from ours. This strip, wide at some spots and narrow at others, is the famous No Man's Land. But I am ten or twelve thousand feet up, which I don't know as the observer has no altimeter, so I quickly lose interest in trenches and look around and concentrate on our own problem.

Our formation is slightly forward and below us, when out of the blue and to our right making directly for us, only slightly higher, is an enemy ship out of which is coming what I take to be puffs of smoke, but which I learn later is tracer ammunition. Instantly I grab the Lewis which is resting in a clip on the left of my nacelle, to throw it over so I can get into action. In doing so I fall back with the gun on top, having missed the clip where I was supposed to anchor the Lewis. When I have kicked the gun off and into position to shoot, the Hun is almost directly in front of us and has gone into a vertical bank. There are two big iron crosses, one on each wing, with the body of the ship in between. Again I press the trigger of my Lewis and let the forty-seven rounds go, no aim, no nothing. I just shoot. I am not thinking, everything I did was automatic, as the Hun disappears from my view, going along about his business.

I gather myself together and change the empty drum to a full one in case the guy comes back, which I hope he won't. Our formation was somewhat split up but is quickly back in place. What has happened with the others I don't know. The thought occurs to me that Mr. Hun was a rather bad shot or we would be out of circulation, though I did notice some holes in our wings that were not there when we left our field. The guy must be as green as I am.

The remainder of the trip down toward the Somme and crossing back into our territory is uneventful. I have seen nothing on the ground which meant anything to me when Captain Gray fires the white light, signaling we can go home on our own, the formation is over. Lieutenant Hicks raps me gently over the head with his glove, sticks out his hand to shake. It's okay with me, I'm just as happy to be alive as he is, the flight is over. My first flight, over in nothing flat. Nobody hurt, but I should be dead, certainly. The Hun had beat me to the first shot, but my pilot didn't seem to mind, and why he was so pleased I couldn't understand. The boy is sure a great pilot. He never changed direction from the second we were in action, nor did he toss the big ship around. I hoped he would be mine for the duration, which wouldn't be long if I didn't move quicker and shoot faster.

Being dumb is no handicap if you are lucky and keep your mouth shut. When we landed Captain Gray and Lieutenant Price had landed ahead of us. Having never landed from a flight before, several people by the hangars meant nothing to me, and I was quite unprepared for what happened. Climbing out of the plane, which I am doing like a veteran as this is my second time, I hear the sergeant major say, "Colonel Shephard is on the field and wishes to speak to you. I'll take you over, and by the way, congratulations," which surprises me, but then my pilot says, "Go ahead. I'll wait because I want to help make out the report of your victory."

The colonel is more definite, giving me a hearty handshake, with the remarks, "First flight, first fight, keep up the good work, because when they go down in flames they don't come back." And I didn't even know. I wasn't even sure I had hit the machine. Must have hit the petrol tank with the entire burst of forty-seven. I know now I have much to learn, as this was pure luck. But for the grace of God it could have been the team of Hicks and Libby.

And here am I getting credit for something I didn't even see happen because I had been changing the magazine on the Lewis gun. At least I will tell Chapman the real truth about the entire affair, also how lucky his clothes have been. Going to my quarters with Chapman, it is now past six o'clock. I find him more pleased than any of the others except my pilot. He tells me the fight was reported back to our squadron from one of our artillery observers' posts almost before the fight was over. That is why the colonel and others were on the field when we landed. "Old man, while you wash up, I will report to our mess that we won't be in for dinner, and I will take you to a place I know at the edge of our woods where there lives a French lady and her daughters. Her husband and sons are away at war, and she is having a tough time. She will cook us some eggs and potatoes, and serve a rare bottle of champagne, all this at practically nothing. The food is good, the champagne better and the few francs help her live. Then we will return and give the bulletin board the once-over for tomorrow's orders, for we are both a cinch to be up once if not twice. So let's celebrate. Tomorrow is something else."

Losing no time with my washing, with a quick lick at the hair, we dash through the woods on a trail known well to Chapman. We are quickly at the chateau, where my friend is more than welcome. I know he is giving me a build-up, as at the word American they are bubbling all over the place. As I spoke no French, my conversation was limited to what little English they spoke. The food was good, the champagne wonderful and, as Chapman says, a change from the sergeant's mess, with a chance to visit over a bottle without a crowd. "The change from scotch and rum is good once in a while, and the lady appreciates the francs, so if I am not around, come over by yourself, as she only takes people she knows well into her home, owing to her two small daughters."

Back at our quarters in the tent waiting for orders to be posted, I tell my friend all about the fight, the fact I had not seen the Hun go down in flames, how awkward I was in shooting and that, had it not been for pure luck, both Hicks and myself would be a couple of dead ducks. His reaction is marvelous and gives me just the help I need. Handshakes and congratulations are fine if you are through flying, but me I'm just starting. What I need is help and I get it.

"Libby, what you tell me is good news. You remember every-thing you did which you think was wrong. Hell, man, you were

Captain Frederick Libby, M.C., in the full
dress uniform of the Royal Flying Corps.

Me on wild horse I broke to ride. My home town, 1911.

"Me on wild horse I broke to ride. My home town, 1911."

Below: In His Majesty's service in France with a motor transport unit of the Canadian Army.

Right: "Coap" Coapland, a close friend in motor transport who shared a billet with Libby.

The F.E.2b (Farman Experimental 2b), the RFC's all-purpose fighter, bomber, and reconnaissance plane in 1916. In this "pusher" plane the propeller was in the rear. The observer—the gunner—sat in the front cockpit, ahead of the pilot's, and fired a Lewis gun positioned forward or another mounted over the top wing for rear action. *NASM, SI negative 83-7382*. Inset: *TheAerodrome.com.*

Captain Stephen Price *(right)* and Lieutenant Libby *(center)* emerging from Buckingham Palace on December 13, 1916, after having been decorated with the Military Cross by King George V.

Above: Price and Libby in their F.E.2b at 8,000 feet over Bapaume on September 23, 1916. The discoloration on the right wing reveals fast work to repair damage suffered in a crash the previous day.

Left: Eleven Squadron, winter 1916. An aerial view of No Man's Land taken by Libby, showing enemy lines at top.

"Heading for Hun Land!" Captain Libby and his observer, Lieutenant
Pritchard, in a Strut-and-a-Half Sopwith in Forty-third Squadron,
July 1917. In this tractor-type plane, the propeller was in the front.
The pilot, armed with a forward-firing machine gun synchronized
with the propeller, sat in the front, and the observer was in the rear.

The men of B Flight of Forty-third Squadron, May 1917.

Left: Albert Ball, the friend and ace whom Libby credited with saving his life many times. Not yet twenty years old when he scored his first five victories, Ball shot down thirty planes in four months over the Somme. *History of Aviation Collection, University of Texas at Dallas.*

Hauptmann Boelcke.

Right: Oswald Boelcke, the German ace, "was a fine gentle-man and a great fighter, who . . . had the respect of all the RFC fighters and was a good enemy." *History of Aviation Collection, University of Texas at Dallas.*

Left: Manfred von Richthofen, the Red Baron, who became Germany's top ace, was judged by Libby to be a step down in gallantry. *History of Aviation Collection, University of Texas at Dallas.*

Some of the enemy planes faced by Libby: *(top to bottom)*
Fokker EI monoplane, Halberstadt D.II., Roland, Albatros
D.I. *History of Aviation Collection, University of Texas at Dallas.*

Me, France / Flight Comman. / 43 rgd RF (/ May 1917 —

Libby in front of Forty-third Squadron barracks, May 1917.
The man at the left may be Flight Commander Sam Collier.

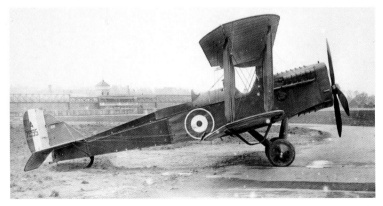

The Airco D.H.4, longer, heavier, and with more speed and climb
than the Sopwith, was flown by Libby in Twenty-fifth Squadron,
his last assignment in France. *NASM, SI negative 78-6157.*

working automatically, faster than you could think. If a flyer stops to think every time he is in trouble, he is in real trouble. A good flyer does things instinctively, not after thinking it out. The main thing, you didn't freeze when in trouble but came up shooting. As for taking your finger off the trigger to shoot in bursts, forget it. This was the proper time to shoot the works. It did the trick where a burst might not, and you might not have time for a second burst. As I told you after lunch today, an observer in our F.E.2b does everything but fly the plane. It is the toughest job in the air today. That is why headquarters are trying for observers all over the place. We have in this squadron at the present time all officers, some of them like you are, on probation, trying to make good so they will rank in the RFC as second lieutenants where in their own units they may have the rank of captain, even majors, and will return with this rank to their old unit if they fail with us or if during the thirty-day training period they feel flying is not for them. Today we are three observers short in our squadron, with you the first private to try since I have been attached to the Twenty-third, and your success today, call it luck if you wish, is something every observer in this squadron would give his eyeteeth to have done. So I predict you will be flying with top pilots like Price, Hicks, Captain Gray, and not the green ones, especially over the lines. And I have a feeling that one of the best pilots, Lieutenant Price, will come up with you as his regular observer. Wait and see."

So while my friend goes to the bulletin board to see who does what to who, I have time to meditate and wonder what it is all about. From seven-thirty this morning I have left my motor lorries, which were as close to the front as motor lorries can go, have made the trip to Twenty-third Squadron, have been up twice and in contact once with the elusive Hun and have had nothing but luck. So tomorrow I promise myself to do something which will give old Lady Luck some help by studying all planes, both ours and the enemy, and the machine gun will be my baby. I want to live, and now that I am in this scrap and can't back out, me and the machine gun will be as one. My mistakes of today I shall remedy tomorrow, so the next Hun who ties onto me will get shot loose from his underwear and it won't be just luck!

Perfectly relaxed and satisfied now that I know what is necessary, I find I am not on the early flight but my friend is up for early
photography, and other orders will be on the board later. With his
advice to sleep in and have a good breakfast and don't worry, if they
want you they will find you, we hit the cots for the night. At seven-
thirty I am up and shaved, so to the mess for breakfast. As I am finishing, Chapman comes in, having just landed from his early flight
with the news, as he puts it, a very uneventful flight. True to my decision of last night, I go to the adjutant's office where I study the silhouettes of planes, which will be a big help in recognizing the
enemy. Then to the gunnery where I work with the Lewis until
lunch, and am told by an orderly I am up for the one-thirty flight
with Price as pilot.

What could be sweeter? Price or Hicks, not one of the new
boys who have never been near the lines. In Price's ship I steady the
machine gun mounting, especially the back one between pilot and
observer. This gun is a nightmare, nothing to hang on to except the
gun, sticking up in air, anchored to a steel rod. A quick sideslip by
your pilot would toss you so clear of the machine you would never
get back. With a steady pilot it might not be too bad. At least better
to be trying, rather than be shot down from the rear by some playful
Hun.

The flight was an easy one. Price in his usual place as second
leader, we spent three and one-half hours in the air as a defensive
patrol for the purpose of protecting the helpless artillery planes directing artillery fire, poor guys that can't defend themselves and are
utterly dependent upon protection from either the F.E.2b fighters
or scouts and are always a prey for some enemy flyer trying to build
a reputation as a great fighter by picking on the lone, defenseless
ships. No enemies were seen, except far back in Hun Land, which
gave me a chance to experiment with the Lewis in bursts of from
five to ten rounds. The back Lewis I didn't try, first because it had
not been necessary, and second, I wanted to become a little more
sure of myself before waving around in the breeze with nothing but
a steel rod for support.

The next few days were uneventful from a standpoint of combat. I learned to use the camera and also to dispose of the ten

twenty-pound bombs that are arranged five on a side under the wings. When ordered, we carry these for use against artillery emplacements or anything moving on the ground. But I learned to dispose of them quickly if it appeared we were going to engage in a fight, for if just one enemy bullet hit one bomb, our careers would end abruptly. Regardless of where we might be, so long as we were in enemy territory, at the sight of a Hun coming our way or even close I pulled the gadget which released the bombs. This was always a relief and put us on more or less equal terms, except we were always on their side of the trenches, with nowhere to go with engine trouble but down. We have had several brushes with the enemy. No one hurt. On our side a few holes through our wings . . . It begins to look like the Twenty-third is in for a quiet war. I am on my tenth day, have only been over the lines with Price and Hicks, although up a couple of times with green pilots just to show them the lines and landmarks from our side of the trenches. Beginning to feel like an old timer, being told by Chapman and Price that I am a cinch for my commission, which is at least encouraging. The first step toward an observer's wing, something I now want to earn. It is a mark of distinction respected by all flyers and, in my case, will be earned the hard way.

The enemy must have gotten a new barrel of brew or some other stimulant, for today we had just crossed into their territory when they came from all directions, breaking up our formation. Price and I are surrounded by them, and one beautiful Fokker monoplane expecting to make a sneak attack slips by and under us, but the Kaiser's boy gets a big surprise because, when he makes a quick turn to pick us off, Price has the big F.E.2b half turned and this time I am not excited and have control of myself. A quick burst of ten does it. His war is over, ours is just beginning.

We fight our way back across our lines. Holes everywhere, and most serious of all, one of the struts between our wings is shot through and is dangling in the breeze, but our flying wires are intact, so we are okay. Home to report, we have lost one ship with pilot and observer, down out of control. Hicks came through but his plane was badly damaged. We have one plane to our credit, confirmed for sure. Price says we have two, but of one I am definite, so report one, other results unknown. The poor mechanics and riggers will have to work all night as the five ships that returned have been hard hit. Another ship to replace our loss will be flown up from the base.

This was my second real engagement with the enemy and my first real dogfight, where there are unknown numbers milling around in enemy territory. We're greatly outnumbered by the enemy. Here I learn the true value of a cool, experienced pilot like Price, who is alert and able to maneuver so the observer can keep the front gun in action, as in a dogfight the back gun is useless for the quick action necessary to keep the enemy from shooting you loose from your tail.

This boy Price is a honey. The grin on his face would give anyone confidence, and his apparent lack of fear I would learn more about in days to come. Back in my quarters I review the show to my friend Chapman. I am of the mind we have done rather poorly. We go over with six ships and lose one with two officers, and only Price and I have one single-seater Fokker to offset our loss. My friend tells me we are damn lucky to get back with anyone, as there were over fifty Huns in the air and we caught only the front end. What saved our skins was a flight of our own scouts coming to our rescue. This I didn't see or report. While I'm not doing too badly with the gun, I must learn to see everything going on around me, even while handling the Lewis. I feel pretty cheap and wonder how my report of our flight will affect my promotion. I have as good a pair of eyes as anyone flying, only I was concentrating too much at close range. I am now on my twentieth day with the squadron and in Price's ship, trying to figure some way of improving my shooting, when the major climbs up on the edge of our ship. "I have today sent through your recommendation to headquarters for your promotion as second lieutenant in the RFC, and very soon you will receive orders with six days leave for England to get your uniforms." This is the news I have been working for and didn't expect quite so soon. I could have fallen on the Old Man's neck if he hadn't been hanging on the side of the ship, I was so pleased.

19

Recommended for My Commission
and Trying to Live,
I Have a Great Idea

THIS I WANT MY FRIEND CHAPMAN TO KNOW FIRST. I thank the major and start for my quarters. On the way I meet Lieutenant Price and give him the good news. Evidently my report of our fight has not done me any harm, as Price says, "Libby, when you return from England as a commissioned officer, I will be in Number Eleven Squadron as a captain and flight commander. Number Eleven Squadron is F.E.2b, same as we have here, under the command of Major Hubbard, a good friend of mine. I will ask to have you assigned to Eleven as my observer. I am sure we will make a good team, and before you leave here there will be orders to report to Number Eleven on Savoy Air Field, which we have flown over many times. We will still be in Thirteenth Wing under Colonel Shephard, which is good. I knew your promotion was coming. All my best wishes and congratulations for a remarkable record. When you leave for England, I will give you a letter to my tailor, who will relieve you of a world of trouble. In fact, I shall write it immediately. Will see you in our plane this afternoon." It has been just twenty days and my papers have gone to headquarters, where I have a feeling they will be acted upon immediately. During the twenty days, I have worked hard to learn under my own power as much as possible. One reason, possibly, is I have become used to living and like

it that way and have concentrated on the machine gun more than
any other part of observing such as map reading, bombing, or all the
other parts. As I figure, the little Lewis is and has been my lifesaver.
I have become so efficient that I can clear a jam in nothing flat,
should it occur, which it hasn't in action, only when I force it on the
ground just for practice. One thing important is bothering me,
though, so important I'm afraid to say anything to anyone, for after
all I am only a private on probation. There are hundreds of gunnery
sergeants who know the Lewis gun backwards, to say nothing of
many senior officers, so I decided to say nothing until I had passed
or failed my probation period. Then I would pass my idea on to
someone, and now that I am almost a second lieutenant, I decide
Price is my boy. With this decision made, I search the hangars and
find him in C Flight with our staff sergeant. With his "Wait a minute,
I'll be with you," I walk outside and wait because I want him alone.

Price joins me in a few minutes. We walk toward our ship in B
Flight. On our way I tell him what has been on my mind for several
days. I explain how well I like the Lewis, but of one thing I am sure,
that it could be a more effective weapon if it could be held firm and
not allowed to bounce when in action, which could be accomplished
by the fellow shooting having his left hand free to hold on with,
whereas now it takes both hands to shoot the gun and you don't
have a true or steady arm. Where the handle of the Lewis is, there is
a clip that holds the gun together. That's what you take off to break
it apart, and that's what you fasten on to hold it together. It locks all
parts. This clip could be removed from the handle and attached to a
short buttstock like a shotgun has, which would serve the same role
as the handle and give the operator of the gun an opportunity to
hold it in place with his shoulder against the buttstock, leaving the
left hand completely free to hold on while he operates the pistol
grip with the right hand. As it now is, both hands are occupied, the
left hand ahold of the handle and the pistol grip in the right. By having a buttstock on the backgun, I am sure an observer would have a
real chance and give his enemy the Hun one hell of a surprise. All of
this Price takes in to the end and inquires if I have talked to anyone.
Upon being assured I haven't, and my reason for not doing so, he
says, "Libby, when we get to Eleven Squadron, I will ask Major

Hubbard to appoint you gunnery officer, which will give you authority and opportunity to try your idea out on our ship. To me it sounds terrific. Why it hasn't been done before I don't know, but if it works we shall be the first to know, except Major Hubbard, who will give us all his support."

London, wonderful London, a place I learned to love even with no lights, everything rationed, a shortage of petrol except for the military, all windows and doors and entrances curtained so no light could escape. London, a place of as near total darkness as possible, and the only large city in the world where I was never lonesome.

Here am I, through the courtesy of His Majesty, to become an officer and a gentleman with the rank of second lieutenant and a full six days to get the job done and return to France. Having been allowed to leave one day early, I have a full five days here and one left for travel.

Now, thanks to Lieutenant Price, I know where to go for my uniforms. I have to be measured and fitted. This I decide will be my first call. Except there is a little matter of money. I don't know how much is needed, but I do know it is more than I am holding. So when the bank, any bank, opens in the morning, I shall help them open to see if they can help *me* with a few dollars I have in the Bank of Montreal in Toronto, which I had assigned there from the Canadian Army. Why I will never know, unless I was saving for my old age, and in this game they just don't grow that old. This is a matter I should have thought of in France during my probation period. If I did think of it, though, I probably reasoned that, if I fail, I won't need any money, and if I pass, something will show up. So now in my hour of need if the bank won't help, I'll talk to said tailor and see what happens.

When the bank opens, I'm the first customer and undoubtedly discouraged the banker for the rest of his day, as I wasn't sure how much was in Canada. But the old boy bore up nobly, taking down all information I could supply as to what I thought was there and how much I wanted. He agreed to cable at my expense, and if I would return tomorrow they would try to help. This was a beginning. So to Price's tailor by taxi, as time is important and up to now I only have prospects. Had I read Price's letter, which was unsealed, I could have saved myself some worry. Somehow I didn't feel right about reading it, so saved it for the tailor. No one in this world had ever received me more gracious, making inquiries about Price and about me being an American, which Price must have mentioned, unless it was showing all over me. They assured me they would take care of everything, including bed roll, caps and four nice uniforms, my flying coat, helmet and boots — I am to send to their place to save time. Taking my measure now, they will have one uniform ready by tomorrow afternoon. I am to come by at lunchtime for a try on, as they know I am anxious to get into my officer's uniform soon as possible, to enjoy London better. I could tell them that I could enjoy London with or without uniform, but I don't. Now for the sad and gloomy part. No money! These boys can really take a shock, as I talk in my best American about money I don't have but there are prospects from Canada tomorrow, so if they will try and tell me what the works might be, for there has been mention of several items a gentleman was supposed to have which I didn't have and hadn't thought of having.

While I am trying to plead my poor financial condition, one of the partners who has been a quiet observer to my effort speaks up with the remark, "You have plenty of money. You just don't know it." Turning to one of his employees, he asks for the *Morning Gazette.* "Here you are, gazetted second lieutenant RFC as of the day before yesterday. You have been an officer for two days. You are rolling in money. Take a cab down to Cox and Company on the Strand. Every cabbie knows where they are and all you will have to do is sign a signature card, because the day you were gazetted they automatically opened up an account with sixty pounds for uniforms and one month's pay in advance."

This is done so a young officer will not be embarrassed or have trouble getting the original uniforms which are required. All your allowances, including so much each month to drink to His Majesty's health, are included in your account at Cox & Co., the official bank of the Royal Flying Corps. After your first signature card you won't have to sign anything, except checks when you need money. All of this was a great shock, but the kind one can take without too much fortitude. Why someone had not told me sooner, even the banker, I didn't know. Without more ado I head for Cox & Co., feeling pretty certain the gentleman knew what he was talking about. It just wasn't possible to have that kind of information and not be right — so Mr. Cox., you have a new baby!

My tailor was right. He is now my tailor after what he did for me, otherwise I would have found some old police sergeant to shoot me. Instead, I have a nice thin checkbook so it won't bulge my pocket. With money in one bank and prospects of another, fate, you have been good. Buying my flying coat, which is just like Chapman's, I wind up with officer's boots and a flying helmet, which completes one day's work before lunch. The rest of the day I think I shall just sit in the nice plush lobby at my hotel and be grateful. While watching the parade go by, maybe I'll see some Canadian I know and can share the joy of my being a millionaire. I don't even have to hurry in the morning about my Canadian money. Lunchtime will be soon enough. Then my uniform — life is sure wonderful. All one has to do is stay alive to enjoy it. I must be awfully old; here I am with nothing to do and all kinds of time to do it. With money besides, and I don't feel like playing. I'm just content.

I am now in my new uniform, the fit is perfect, the goods of the same material as Price's uniforms, and he is the best dressed officer in the squadron. Wow! But I feel so new and green. The Sam Browne belt is dark and flexible, not stiff like I have seen on so many new officers. Again a copy from the Price wardrobe.

The bank this morning gave me my money from Canada. I am now the richest, newest, greenest officer in His Majesty's service. Before leaving the tailor shop in all my glory, I was asked by the same gentleman who had made my life so happy with his good news to come up to his private office, where he assured me all my uniforms would be ready together with any other necessities. This was the day before I was to leave for the boat train to Folkestone. No one had ever before taken so much interest in my problems or relieved me of so much responsibility as had this gentleman. Now that I'm leaving, he hands me a note, saying, "Libby, this is an introduction to Jimmy at the Savoy bar, which opens at six every night for two hours. If you have time, run over, he is just across from your hotel. I would like you fellows to know each other. The Savoy, you know, is where you will see everyone in the RFC sometime or other. It seems to be the gathering place for all pilots and observers. Do give it a look." So back to my hotel, which is the Strand Palace on the Strand angling across from the Savoy.

Now to give the hotel clerk a peek at my new uniform. With the change from private to second lieutenant, I expect him to at least register surprise. His total lack of interest amazes me. Taking a look around the lobby I find no one even giving me the once-over, so decide that new and green I might be but no one gives a damn!

In the privacy of my own room I look myself over in the mirror and try adjusting my cap to an angle like Price, when I remember last night, returning from a show, there wasn't a drink or sandwich to be had in the joint. So, before going over to the Savoy, I decide to do something about this matter. Ringing for a bellboy, I am about to give up when there is a rap on my door, which I have left un-locked, and in bounces a very pretty young girl with the salutation, "Did you ring, sir?"

This I had, but for a bellboy. "Sir, I am the bellboy." At my look of amazement she continues, "I am taking the place of a man in service. There are girls answering bells in this and many other ho-tels. May I do something for you?" For sure she could, but what is in my mind is not her cup of tea. . . .

The gal is all business, so I tell her my troubles, which she agrees to remedy with a bottle of scotch and some sandwiches. Be-fore I return, which will unquestionably be late if my meeting with Jimmy is what I expect. To my utter surprise, my young lady refuses a tip — won't even collect for my order. Will have it charged to my account. This war has certainly upset the applecart. From now on I shall keep my door locked. Suppose I had been in the bathtub when my bellboy or girl bounced into my room. She might think I was Venus. No, she probably wouldn't — too many arms. To hell with it. I am not running the hotel or the war. I'm only a visitor with things to do. I have found out, by becoming an officer and supposedly a gentleman in His Majesty's service, that I have a very serious duty to perform every Thursday evening at dinner, namely drink to His Majesty's health. Each month there will be credited to my bank of

Cox & Co. funds for this purpose. These boys think of everything, so I will do my part to see that His Majesty never has a sick day during my service, and indeed shall not just wait for a particular day but will devote some of my time and funds between regulation dinners to this very worthy cause. And believe it or not, through my three years on the Western Front, His Majesty would never have a sick day. Of this fact I had two wonderful opportunities to tell him personally of my stout effort in his behalf, once when he inspected Number Eleven Squadron in France and the other when I was decorated at Buckingham Palace. Somehow I didn't. It was a question of what was doing who the most good. *Gentlemen, the King!*

I wander over to the Savoy, full of curiosity, to present my note to Jimmy. The Savoy sits back off the Strand. There's a horseshoe-shaped driveway to the entrance. On the right hand of the entrance and downstairs is the Savoy Theatre, where *HMS Pinafore* is playing. A large door leads to the spacious hotel lobby with reception desk and office to one's right, with many people moving around both in the lobby and far back to a large dining room. To my very left from the entrance is another wide door, through which one enters a spacious lounge, and directly back and to the left is a bar with two busy barmaids. The place is packed, with only a few vacant seats. While I am surveying this picture, a voice says, "May I help you, sir?" This is my boy Jimmy. He is about my height, I would judge in his early thirties, with a personality plus. Upon reading the note, I am welcomed like a long lost brother returning with a couple tons of gold. He introduces me to three RFC men at a table with a vacant chair, and before I know it, without asking he appears with a double scotch and soda. As I reach for my bank roll, am told "not this time." This brings inquiries from my three companions as to how long I have known my host. Upon learning that I am new in the picture, they bring me up to date on some of my host's history. He had wanted to be one of the RFC, but because of some difficulty with his eyes just couldn't make the grade, so devotes his time to helping his country in every way possible as a civilian. And from six to eight each evening, when the Savoy bar is open, serves as maitre d' where he can mix with the men he likes best, the officers of the Royal Flying Corps, many of whom he has helped when help was needed most. No one who ever asked for help was turned down. He is known and loved by all the RFC gang and never forgets a face or name. He will become my very good friend in the months to come. As closing time for the place begins to approach, I am invited to many parties, as it seems everyone is throwing one, some immediately after the close of the bar, others to start after twelve o'clock when all the showgirls are free and ready to play and entertain the boys "for King and Country" until morning or past. Boy, what a life, only I'm a total loss. Just want to do what comes easy without an effort and am in no mood for play. So back to my hotel, where I hear a piano being played in the lounge, so drift in and spend two hours listening to a Canadian in a private's uniform playing the music I like best in a way no one else could. He is the famous Getz Rice, later to become an officer and professional entertainer for the troops, swell fellow, and in time one of my very best friends.

My last day of leave. Everything is ready at my tailor shop. All I have to carry is my British warmer, my bag with shaving kit and a few undergarments, shirts and etc. Everything else will be checked at Charing Cross Station, from where the boat train leaves for Folkestone. So to settle up with my tailor without whose help becoming an officer would have been, to say the least, very difficult. I am expecting a tremendous bill, because they have done everything, even paid for my bed roll, cot, etc. And I'm not certain if it will take all my newfound wealth or not. But I expect the worst. So what happens, to me, a perfect stranger? The boss asks where they may send their statement as it isn't made up. Here I am leaving for a shooting war where the boys are using real bullets, and I can't possibly return to London before three months (which I understand is the usual time allowed for officers of RFC to go on leave), and these babies are insisting on sending me a statement! They are either the world's greatest optimists or just plain nuts. If me and my new clothes get knocked off, who will pay the bill? I don't know, but they're not worried. So I give them Eleven Squadron RFC "somewhere in France." When I tell them I will be with Price, this they know, smart people, and there is nothing to do except say goodbye. This I do, thanking my new friends for their great kindness to a strange Yankee who knows he don't know too much, and one who has just had his first real contact with the English people. They certainly are different from what my schoolbook said, Boston Tea Party and all. I like everyone I have met. Their graciousness I shall never forget.

While I made many friends in my few short days, my heart hasn't been in having fun. I find myself thinking of Price, Chapman, Hicks and the others, but most of all my idea of a buttstock for the Lewis, which I feel will help Price and me to stay alive, for I must have a full hundred hours of combat as an observer before I am qualified to wear the observer's wing which will fill up the vacant spot on my left chest. If I am allowed my hours with the Twenty-third, it won't be too long. Everywhere one hears of the big push this summer, in our sector. Even green as I am, I know we will be in for plenty of flying, which means the enemy will be out in all his glory. This doesn't worry me too much. With Price, one of the best pilots in the RFC, I feel we will do well, and if my buttstock works for the Lewis in our F.E.2b, the Hun may have a real surprise. So goodbye London for now, and when I return I will be a full observer, with a flying wing on my chest and a lot of experience under my Sam Browne belt.

20

Back to France as an Officer, Where I Meet and Become Friends with the Royal Flying Corps' Greatest Fighting Ace, Lieutenant Albert Ball

The seventeen-mile boat trip from Folkestone to Boulogne across the English Channel is always interesting. There are days when you know you should have stayed in bed or at least left your stomach there, for when the Channel is in one of her moods, even the strong get weak.

Today the weather is perfect. It is approaching summer 1916. The water is calm, and for the time being I can size up the crowd of fellow passengers. Most of them are old timers returning from leave. On their faces there is no doubt, no expression of uncertainty. They know what is ahead. It is just a question of how long their luck will hold out.

The faces of the inexperienced and new express wonder, doubt and expectancy. They are on their way for the first time to join some combat unit, and for them tomorrow is almost here. There are Indians and Hindus in their colorful uniforms. Ministers of the gospel. Canadian nurses, very snappy and beautiful in their officers' uniforms. Many RFC pilots and observers. But the most outstanding are the infantrymen going back to a hell on earth, the trenches, with their cooties, rats, mud, water and filth. These boys have no illusions. Every day for them is just another day and tomorrow, if it comes, just another of the same. They are the poorest paid, the poorest clothed, the poorest fed, but are the backbone of the entire army and always fight under the poorest conditions. Thank God for the infantry.

For myself I have no illusions. I am reporting to Number Eleven Squadron, where my only friend is Captain Price. I know we are in for a big push. This was the general conversation on the boat. This will mean many casualties, and to survive will mean a lot of luck.

Arriving at Savoy Air Field, which is Eleven Squadron head-quarters, I find almost the same kind of a field as at Twenty-third. Our quarters are in the woods and there is a hedge around and in front of the hangars. To reach the landing field the ships are wheeled out through an opening in the hedge. Coming through the opening toward the headquarters to report, I am spotted by three fellows beating a shuttlecock attached by a long string to a pole. They are in shirt sleeves and really giving themselves a work-out. Quitting their game, they give me a welcome greeting, telling me they are glad I am to be a member of Number Eleven and that Major Hubbard is expecting me, that Price is in the air but will be back for dinner. They are Lieutenant Ball, Lieutenant Foot and Captain Quested.

Quested, being the officer of the day, insisted on taking me to my quarters, then to Major Hubbard to report. Here I receive the most hearty welcome. "Glad you are with us, Libby. Price will be very pleased, as he has been telling me all about your work in the Twenty-third, so in the morning we three will have a talk about something Captain Price has mentioned pertaining to our Lewis machine gun."

I am again in a pup tent very close to Price and very nice. Arranging my new clothes and bed roll, I wander over to the mess to kill time until Price shows up. And here are several fellows playing cards. Everyone wanting to give me a drink, all at the same time. This crowd I am going to like. There is a spirit here which speaks of good fellowship and teamwork so essential to a squadron.

My first dinner in our officers' mess at Number Eleven

Squadron is a very enjoyable one. Everyone is in high spirits and congenial. As I'm standing around having cocktails with Captain Price and several others, our commanding officer, Major Hubbard, comes in and joins us for one cocktail, then takes his place at the head of the long table, with Captain Price on his right and Captain Quested at his left, while down at our end of the table is the third flight commander, Captain Dowling.

The dinner is excellent, everything from soup to nuts or cheese, if you prefer. When the liqueurs are served, the commanding officer says, "Gentlemen, you may smoke." This is what many have been waiting for, either his permission to be excused or to light a cigarette. It is a nice custom practiced in all British officers' messes and protects the non-smoker from suffering through a haze of smoke while eating his dinner. When the commanding officer leaves the table, dinner is over, and you may do anything you wish, but during dinner no one leaves the table, unless first going to your ranking officer and asking permission. This is a tradition with the British and is a deference of respect to your commanding officer. After dinner, Price and I go to my tent where he inspects my new uniforms, which have his hearty approval. He is delighted when I relate all my experiences with his tailor. We are not scheduled for the morning show and agree to have breakfast together, as breakfast is served anytime up to ten o'clock, the only formal meal being dinner. We agree to see Major Hubbard immediately after breakfast.

When we arrive at headquarters, the major wastes no time getting down to business. It is evident he and Price have talked our business over, only our major wants to hear my idea direct before giving his approval, so I explain what advantage I think attaching a buttstock to the Lewis will offer the observer. We have his entire support. I am made gunnery officer, which gives me opportunity and authority to work with the crew of five responsible for the forty Lewis guns used every day, thirty-six on the F.E.2b and one for each of the Nieuport scouts attached to us for escort protection. The gunnery sergeant is an expert and very understanding. He quickly sees the advantage this will give an observer and is personally going to design the buttstock and promises to have one for testing tomorrow.

My quick appointment over many older and experienced men is worrying me. I am not a fully qualified observer with enough hours in the air to have earned my wings, and am wondering if there might be some resentment from these older and more experienced observers. So, to my friend and pilot Captain Price, who quickly straightens me out, explaining, "Libby, no one will ever resent anything that can be done to improve our strength and firepower. If we're successful, all observers will be using your idea, because to go through this coming push the RFC will take the offensive, which means our casualties are going to be terrible, and the better all observers can shoot, the better chance we have to live. Working as a team, if your idea improves your shooting over what you did at the Twenty-third, I feel with reasonable luck we will be a match for any Hun."

I am more than anxious to try it out, so tomorrow if the sergeant has it ready, we will try the range first, then in our first show over the lines try it for real on some live target. Our squadron has the usual eighteen F.E.2b. All of these ships have been donated to the RFC by the heads of Indian provinces and bear names evoking their donors, such as the Sultan of Keds, Punjab, Rajah. We have two Baby Nieuports* flown by Foot† and Ball.‡ Foot is the damnedest stunt pilot I have ever seen, while Ball is just the opposite, very young, very quiet, but does his stuff on the end of some enemy's tail. He is a hell of a fighting pilot who wastes no energy, except where it will bring results. These two fellows are reinforcements for our squadron of F.E.2b and are supposed to pick us up on our way back from Hun Land when the going is at its worst. They can't carry

---

*The Nieuport was a fast and maneuverable French-built single-seat fighter. The Bébé or Baby Nieuport was armed with a Lewis gun fired over the wing, whereas the larger Superbébé, flown by Ball and Foot later, was equipped with a Vickers machine gun synchronized to fire through the propeller, a significant improvement.

†Major Ernest L. "Feets" Foot, an English ace with five victories, survived the war but died in an aviation accident in 1923.

‡Albert Ball became one of the most distinguished British aviators in the war, scoring, as a rookie, thirty victories in just four months over the Somme battlefield.

enough petrol to make the trip with us, but can meet and escort us home.

Sergeant Maxwell has the Lewis ready, so without any delay we try it on the ground range, where it is even better than I expect. On my reporting this to Price, we give it a trial from the air, where I am more than pleased, as it gives me the support I need and leaves my left hand free to maneuver the gun and hang on. All we want now is a crack at Fritz. This will come fast enough because our activities are stepping up.

We will have no trouble finding Fritz. Just cross over his lines and the battle is on. Without waiting for a battle, I ask the sergeant to make a buttstock for our back gun. Here it is needed most. With a free left hand to hang on with and one's right shoulder to hold your gun in place, your back gun can be a real defense weapon when returning home. But what the hell Fritz is waiting for I don't know. We have been over three times and have never been in shooting distance. A and C Flights have both had a battle with one loss on our side, but our B Flight has never been close. Our day will come when least expected. Several of the observers have asked for the buttstock and it won't be long until Eleven will be completely equipped, and if we don't knock the Hun on his rear end I will be surprised.

We have just returned from my first big show, we along with some sixty other fighter ships acting as escort to thirty-six bombers. The bombers are converted artillery B.E.2c, which have no observer so they can carry more bombs, and are completely dependent on their escorts for protection. The escort consists of F.E.2b, D.H.2, single-seater scouts, Nieuports, a few Martinsydes and F.E.8, the escorts outnumbering the bombers two to one. Our targets are the Douai and Cambrai air fields. The bombers going over are strung out in tandem, one following the other, their mission to drop the bombs and back for home as fast as possible. Their altitude is approximately seven thousand. We of the escort range from eight to ten thousand. Our A and B Flights of Eleven Squadron catch the front end of the bombers going over, where we escort them to their target, then return with the last bombers leaving the target, which gives the Hun ample time to get altitude and catch us going back.

Throwing everything they have in the air from all their other fields, the Huns fill the sky between us and our home by the time we start for our lines.

Dropping down to a thousand feet above our last two bombers, we are in a position to see anyone attacking and set quick, if necessary. Our flight is in perfect formation, when a flight of Huns splits up and attacks from different directions. This is ideal for us, as we simply nestle down close to our lonesome bombers and pick the Hun off when they come in, and here is where my buttstock proves itself. A Hun making a pass at one of our bombers might be too far for a good shot with an unsteady gun but is like shooting fish with the front gun held firm by the shoulder. Two bursts and he is upside down, then into a spin. I thought Price would jump out of our ship, he was so happy, but this was nothing. Almost to our lines, I catch a Fokker moving to come up under the tail of our upper back F.E.2b. Using the back gun with a firm grip with my left hand on the gun mounting, giving a signal to Price to pull the ship's nose up a little and holding the gun solid with my shoulder, I empty all forty-seven in his middle. Two chances, two wins, two confirmed. Price and Major Hubbard are the happiest men in the squadron, unless it is the sergeant who made the buttstocks — to him should go a hell of a lot of credit. His work and understanding made it possible.

We now have four ships to our credit. Price says we got a couple more at Twenty-third, but four we have official, so to hell with it. The ones we shot stay shot, which is the main thing. There is no guessing. When we are sure, we're sure. I have quit being sorry for them. If we don't get them, they get us, so I'm going to be glad about the whole thing.

Out of the entire show, with over a hundred of our ships on the raid, we lose two fighters and no bombers while the Hun lose eight, and two of their best aerodromes take a hell of a bombing. How many ships were destroyed in the hangars was not confirmed. This was one of the first quick raids and was considered a big success. But as Price says, this was a surprise to the Hun. The others may not be so easy.

Others there will be, as all hell is going to break loose in the trenches at some particular sector very soon. Where we don't know, but think it is in the vicinity of the Somme.

For the boys in the trenches, I have nothing but admiration. They live like damned prairie dogs, buried in the ground, while we of the RFC have the best of everything when on the ground. We may not live forever in the air, but the hours not flying can be very pleasant, providing you don't worry about tomorrow. If one can get into the mood, take things as they come and just be prepared to do your best when necessary, it is quite a life with never a dull moment. Even if you don't last too long, you are never bored with time on your hands. True, the odds are heavy against anyone in a combat unit living to a ripe old age, but we only have to fight the enemy in the air, while the boys on the ground have to fight to live — against sickness, pests, cold, muck — even if there is no human enemy.* Me, I'd rather be bumped off in the air than be buried under several tons of dirt.

Ball slipped away quietly this evening just before dusk and picked off a couple of ships annoying our artillery machines. This boy is a swell kid. I like him better every day. He is so unassuming, don't talk much, but has a habit of slipping up under Fritz with his Baby Nieuport and using the Lewis, which is mounted on the top plane, by pulling it down in its mounting with the right hand and shooting like a pistol. The Hun is usually a dead duck. This boy is one hot fighter pilot. This makes four for him in the last three days, as in the raid where Price and I had two confirmations, Ball also had two, which gave our squadron four enemy ships of the eight destroyed that day.

We are doing a great deal of defensive patrol for the purpose of keeping enemy ships from crossing our lines to observe the accumulation of troops and equipment back from the Somme front. There is every form of motor vehicle, including hundreds of new equipment which look like armored cars only more so. They are the first new tanks to reach the front and have never been in action, but are expected to play a big part in the push coming up.

Sure the Hun knows all this, for from a ten-thousand-foot alti-

*But there is, and even when there is no big push, the poor infantrymen have to endure constant sniping and artillery fire, mines and trench raids.

tude back of their own lines one can see a big movement of troops, trucks and supplies far back in our territory for many miles. Today, A and B Flights are to be inspected by some dignitaries from India, including a sultan, a rajah and what have you. They are the donors of all our F.E.2b, so we will all be in front of our ships when they arrive. Price and I are flying Punjab the Second. What ever happened to Punjab the First, I don't know. It probably is somewhere over in Hun Land, for as fast as one "goes west," as they say, another is flown in from the base before you can turn around. Certainly when we lose a ship it is lost for good, as all fighting is done back of the enemy lines. If one of our ships has engine trouble, even if not shot down, it's lost, while with the Hun it is different. They never engage in a fight with us where the odds are even and on our side of the lines. Always our fights are when we just cross their lines or they wait until we are far back, then attack so we have a headwind to buck, as the wind is against us coming home ninety percent of the time. This, plus a flock of enemy planes . . . Here is where little Albert Ball comes in. He can pick us up with his Baby Nieuport about twenty miles back in Hun Land when we need him the most, especially when we're getting low on petrol and ammunition. God, but he is a welcome sight moving over your backside to knock the tail off some enemy plane who thinks he has you for sure. Then escort you to your lines and go back for more. He always seems to be where one is in the most trouble. Stout fellow!

Where the devil they coined the expression "he went west" for when a poor soul is knocked off back of the enemy lines, I don't know. When one crosses into Hun Land, one is always flying east. Yet, whenever a fellow is finished back of the enemy lines, east or not, he has somehow gone west. Somewhere someone became confused, and east is west whether I like it or not.

The big push is at the Somme River and begins on July 1, 1916. Artillery has turned loose everything they have, from both their old and new emplacements, and when they raise their fire to hit farther back to the Hun's rear, our infantry will go over the top. Our planes are everywhere, protecting our artillery. Planes beetle back and forth across the lines directing their batteries' fire, watch all roads coming up to the front from Hun Land, and engage in low strafing of troops or trucks moving on the enemy side, together with dog-fight after dogfight.

The days are never long enough. Price and I with B Flight have been flying four to seven hours, always back of the enemy lines and always mixed up with the enemy. Our casualties are bad. We have Boelcke and his squadrons opposite us with a new and faster plane. Also the Roland seems to be improved. We are still flying the F.E.2b with the one-hundred-and-sixty Beardmore engine, with the D.H.2 pusher our principal scout, while our Baby Nieuport is giving Boelcke his real competition only we have too few.

Every night at dinner there are always new flyers in our mess, taking the place of our lost ones who have been killed in action or are prisoners of war. Every week Boelcke has one of his pilots drop over a list of our fellows who are prisoners and also the names of the ones who are wounded or killed. Damn decent chap, this Boelcke. The German Air Corps treat all our pilots and observers with re-spect. They have good quarters, good food and are even allowed a batman from some of our soldiers that have been taken prisoner.

To be shot down and captured by the German Air Corps is not too bad, but to come down close to the lines where the German in-fantry can get their hands on you is curtains. They shoot you quick and find a reason later. This is owing to the fact that the RFC often give the infantry a bad time by emptying their machine guns in the trenches on the way home, peppering the boys down there and of-ten dropping a few twenty-pound bombs just for practice. Since the RFC are always back of the German lines, while the German flyers never come over ours, the drill is that if one of our planes is out of commission and can't make it across our lines they are supposed to glide as far away from the trenches as possible, hoping to be picked up by the German flying corps.

The Somme battle still goes on with not much gain by our side, at least from what I can tell from the air. We hear that fifty or sixty thousand of our boys became casualties on the first day alone.

I now have a new job training our observers with the machine gun. This I am glad to do, and any help I can give I am more than willing, for it hasn't been long since the day I first appeared at

Twenty-third Squadron. My own pilot, Captain Price, goes on leave tomorrow for two weeks, for which I am real glad. He needs it very badly, and for two weeks I shall miss that grin of confidence he wears when the going is the toughest. So for two weeks I fly with Captain Quested of A Flight — another stout flyer.

21

In a Drinking Bout, Price and I
Lose a Battle to Our Own Artillery

POSTED ON OUR BULLETIN BOARD IS THE GOOD NEWS that I am fully qualified and entitled to wear the single wing with the "O" which denotes observer. This wing I shall always be proud of, prouder than I shall even be of my pilot's wings, whenever I qualify for them. When I think of all the observers who have "gone west" that were flying when I started, I have indeed been awfully lucky. Today I know my luck is in. I have been flying with Lieutenant Russell of A Flight, substituting for Captain Quested. We are over Bapaume, where we are engaged by a flight of Albatros and are in good position to win our battle, when all of a sudden my pilot goes into a sideslip and then a big dive down to fifteen hundred feet where there is really a dogfight. He damn near loses me over the side with his sudden move and no warning. Without any chance to recover, we are in the midst of Fokkers, Rolands and the Germans' pet Albatros. All seem to take a poke at us. I am only able to get a shot at one Albatros with my front gun. My pilot seems to have gone wild. We are all over the skies, with lead hitting our F.E.2b from every direction. At five hundred feet we cross our lines and land in the first vacant space. As neither of us has been hit, I survey the situation. Our upper, emergency petrol tank in the top plane has been hit and petrol has been flowing out of it, two struts are shot and broken, the top wing is drooping. The pilot's altimeter, peter tube* and compass have been ruined, and my back Lewis gun has been hit. Also there are holes everywhere, except in us and our engine. I am reminded of Sergeant Chapman's remark: If the Hun doesn't get the pilot or engine, the old F.E.2b will stagger home. It is almost impossible to break one up in the air. Nothing truer was ever said, because here was a ship that the Hun rated as shot down. Still we were down on our side of the lines, with a plane completely out of commission other than the motor and propeller. This has been Lieutenant Russell's first time to lead a formation. What happened to the other five ships of our formation, I don't know. What to say, I likewise don't know, so I keep still.

Out of a small hill about one hundred yards from us emerges an officer of the artillery. The hump of what looks like a hill is an artillery emplacement. With his greeting, "Are you boys in trouble, and can we help?" I want to say, "No, Major, we just stopped to pick wild flowers," but settle for asking him if we could notify our squadron of our location. He very graciously says, "Certainly, come into our quarters. We will relay a message back to your headquarters."

The artillery quarters are all underground and very good in comparison with the underground quarters of the infantry. Here we park, enjoying some scotch and soda until the CO's private car arrives to take Russell and me to our squadron, leaving the poor old F.E.2b to wait for our crew, who are following with truck and trailer. On the way back Russell is very nervous and asks me what I am going to report. Who am I too condemn anyone? So, setting his mind at ease, I tell Russell he is a hell of a flyer and should be on single-seater scout, but as long as he is flying a pusher ship with an observer he will have to learn to rely on his observer and his Lewis gun for some protection, or he may not be so lucky next time. My report was brief and to the point: Engaged enemy aircraft at eight thousand, then dropped to fifteen hundred to assist Forty Squadron in

---

*The peter tube was a crude arrangement that allowed the pilot, who might be in the air for several hours, to relieve himself when necessary.

dogfight. Results of combat unknown. Our ship disabled, causing us to land back of our lines. When I show my report to Russell, he is very pleased and grateful. What the three who returned report I don't know. We lost two of our best pilots and observers, as only four of our formation of six were able to make it back.

Next morning our rigger sergeant gives me a report on the condition of our plane. He and his crew count one hundred and eighty-six holes in the ship, with two bursts hitting the leading edge of the bottom plane. Also, one of the tail booms was clipped. The ship is a complete write-off, except the engine and propeller. How any two fellows can be so lucky with that much lead from every direction, where it only takes one bullet to do the job — our guardian angel must have really worked overtime. Tomorrow Price returns from leave, thank God. I'm sorry he has to get in this mess, but as he does I'm glad he's my pilot.

The last few days would be a horrible shock to Father. He never expected me to survive too long. He was sure if I didn't get killed accidentally, I would die of consumption. That I won't, not here. I may die of lead poisoning, but after what just happened with Russell, I seem to be on the crest of the wave. I have been trying to write, but why worry Father? If he knew, every day would be a nightmare. If anything happens to me he will know soon enough. I would surely like to tell him that I am a man without a country and see what he has to say about that. I lost my citizenship by joining the Canadian Army. So, after this war, I shall join the Tahiti folks and grow bananas or something, because they tell me this war is going to make the world safe for Democracy. It doesn't matter if you are a participant or not, everything will be safe for everyone. All we have to do is crucify the kaiser and his flying corps, and Democracy reigns forever. Whatever Democracy is I don't know. If it takes this war to make it safe, it couldn't have been much to start with. Over here, I am sort of a curiosity. Everyone treats me wonderful, but still wonder why I am here. If I could answer that one, I would be a world champion. Certainly, it has nothing to do with making anything safe for anyone, except for Price and me when we get in a fight. If we come out safe, I am satisfied for the present.

Every few days I am asked about a guy by the name of Ford,[*] who had some idea of having the boys out of the trenches by Christmas. What Christmas, I don't think he said. He must have a lot of guts to try and kid the British, who have lost so much and seem to be fighting everyone's battle that any such comedy is a complete loss at this time. All I know about the bird is he invented some kind of a contraption which runs and scares all animals to death. I wonder if he lost his citizenship, messing around the edges of this safety business?

I have decided to write all my family when I go back to England for my pilot's wings, which will be after this Somme affair is over or slows down on account of weather. This is what I call being a real optimist. Price is back and brought me six new observer's wings, one for each uniform and one extra. He is a peach and knew my confirmation was coming through, so his batman, who is in civilian life a tailor, is sewing them on. Good old Price. It's good to have him back. Tonight is Thursday, our night to drink His Majesty's health. With Price back, I shall endeavor to do more than my share, because in matters of this kind I don't want to be backward. Someone might think I am just another American, or not interested. I am now senior observer of the squadron, which means I have lived longer than the others. I have six enemy planes confirmed. Next to me is my good friend Lieutenant Allen, who flies with a South African by the name of Turk who is a wonderful pilot. We have lost Ball and Foot. Both have been promoted to captain and are off to England for leave and then will return with a complete squadron of Nieuports. Eleven Squadron will depend on help from Twenty-four and Forty Squadrons with their D.H.2s and other Nieuports that are attached to our wing. We never cross the lines without one or two

---

[*]Henry Ford, the automobile manufacturer, was a vocal non-interventionist, as were many Americans, especially in the Midwest. But with the sinking of the *Lusitania* and consequent loss of American lives and the revelation of the sinister Zimmermann Telegram, in which Germany tried to intrigue Mexico to start a war with the U.S. in exchange for the promise of the return of Texas, New Mexico and Arizona, American isolationism began to waver.

brushes with the Hun. They are very foxy, take no chance on the front end of our F.E.2b but try and get our formation split. Then, working three or four together on a lone ship, they attack from back and under, which is a tough spot for a lone F.E. This method has accounted for many of our losses, while Price and I have worked out a plan to offset their advantage. Others are not so successful, mostly because the other pilots don't work as close with their observer and can't handle the big F.E. like Price does. God, we need new and faster ships bad. Price says there will be several faster and better squadrons of our ship out this fall with a gun synchronized and shooting through the propeller, which will take the place of our pushers. Everyone knows the folks in England are working as fast as possible to give us new ships, but if they don't hurry, who in hell is going to fly them?

Every day we are taking a licking, but every day we go back for more. One has to admire these English boys. With barely enough experience to fly a ship, they sail into Boelcke and his gang like a bunch of old timers. They are short on experience but long on courage. I'm real proud to be one of them.

This damn war is just one thing after another. You don't only have to fight Fritz, but you might die with the hiccups, or an overdose of alcohol. Socially, Price and I are not such a success. Every so often some artillery unit that goes back for a rest period and to delouse has a couple of our officers as guests for dinner. It is usually an occasion for much hilarity and drinking, then a little more drinking. On one such occasion, Price and I were chosen by our commanding officer to represent Eleven Squadron. This was fine, only we had no time or warning. So we started with a large handicap — we did a morning show, then caught an afternoon patrol and didn't land until five o'clock where we were met by our major at the hangar, giving us the news we were to attend a dinner with Twenty-sixth Battery as his representatives. We were to take his big Crosley car and sergeant driver and were due there at seven, so if we hurried and changed we wouldn't be too late. This was sad news, for I had other plans such as enjoying a good dinner at our mess and going to bed early. We don't even have time to snatch a quick drink.

The sergeant driver tells us he knows where we are going quite well. They are billeted in a chateau in a woods twelve miles back of us. We leave everything to said sergeant, until we discover the guy is lost. He is completely lost, on some side road covered with trees, dark as a black cat, with only a lousy flashlight and a poor map. Price wisecracks, "Glad I have my own observer. No need to worry." That's what he thinks. In the air we can both find our way anyplace; here on the ground at night is different. I figure we are far past our destination, so turning back to another crossroad we find a dimly lit chateau where we are put on our way in the right direction. Arriving late, we find everyone going strong. While dinner is waiting, the cocktails are flowing, so in nothing flat we are separated and given the old rush act of one cocktail after the other.

Their billet is in a chateau slightly off the road, with the usual high fence and back yard where there are pigs, chickens, a cow and the standard manure pile square against the back door. The table is set in a long room which could have been used for anything in peacetime, but has been converted into their dining room, at least for their rest period. Having had too many cocktails too fast, Price and I are seated as honored guests to the right and left of our host, the commanding officer, and directly opposite each other. When the cream of tomato soup arrives, taking possibly as much as three spoons of soup, I am deathly ill. Up come the soup and cocktails, hitting right in the center of the table in the general direction of Price. Here is the world's most embarrassing moment. You know you can't die, but you have to move, and move you do, out the back door with soup and cocktails flying every way. You just want air. Air you have on a big dead log up against the manure pile, with pigs running around grunting and giving you the once-over. You've finally reached your proper environment, sick and with the pigs. Then the back door flies open and out comes your pal and pilot. If I thought I was sick, he is sicker, sharing my log but too ill to talk. He is having a heaving good time.

Here are two of Eleven Squadron's best in a manure heap with pigs, while inside I can hear much hilarity. They are having a swell time while we are in disgrace. Which doesn't appear to be troubling Price, for he is trying to die like a man, sitting up and weaving on our mutual log, while a curious pig gives him a sniff every once in a while just to see if he is human or some new kind of a pig. Finally an orderly shows up with two glasses of water, asking us if we would care for some. Price hasn't yet reached the talking stage, so I take care of the orderly with a few well chosen words and tell him to find our sergeant and send him to us immediately. I am going to load my sick pilot in the big Crosley and head for home — to hell with those guys, they won the battle without even a struggle. But there will be other days, I hope. A short while ago I didn't care, but now life is returning. This must be true with Price, for he just kicked a pig in the ribs that was trying to eat his shoe. The squeal that came out of Mr. Pig convinces me my pilot has returned to the living.

The blooming sergeant finally puts in an appearance, so without any fond farewells we leave our manure heap and our pigs. Putting my pilot in the big roomy back seat, where he immediately falls asleep, we cover him up with a robe and I climb in the front seat with the sergeant. Every time we would make a quick stop, there would be a thump in the back where our passenger had fallen off, and we would rearrange him although he didn't give a damn. So, the sergeant having been cautioned to take the stops a little easier, we arrive at our castle in the woods, our pup tents. It is not really late, as our stay at the battery dinner was brief, if dirty. Neither one of us is in any condition to report to Major Hubbard, even if he should be up. I'm just getting nicely settled in my sleeping bag when there is a scratching on the flap of my tent. It is Price's batman. He has tried to awaken Price to notify us we have the early morning show. This means five o'clock. Neither of us has enjoyed any food since lunch. We both missed afternoon tea, and our dinner was a sad affair. Telling the batman to be sure and call us plenty early and have a good hot pot of tea to help wake us up, I am asleep but fast.

Morning comes, bringing the batman with our tea and a couple of big drinks of rum, which will cure anything. All you have to do is swallow it. This Price can't do. While he sips his tea, I drink the rum and then sip a little tea. It's surprising how quick I am revived even before we take off. I am feeling better, and with the first whiff of fresh air blowing on my face I am back to normal and hungry. The Huns this morning are very friendly. No one bothers us except the usual archie or anti-aircraft shells bursting around. This is always par for the course. The minute you near their lines, if there are no enemy ships in the air they are always poking at you with the anti-aircraft guns, and do occasionally score a hit, but the average is practically nil. At least they have a lot of practice, and are always trying.

Before lunch, even before we have a chance to report to Major Hubbard about our recent dinner engagement, all pilots and observers are called to the mess hall for a meeting, which is very unusual. The meeting only lasted a few minutes. The major explained that GHQ wanted and asked for volunteers. It seemed they were desperate to establish some kind of ground communications, so some swivel-chair pilot had evidently worked out the brilliant plan to stretch a line between two poles about twenty feet high and about twenty feet apart and attach the message to the line, then have the observer catch the line with a hook secured to a light cable, which could be reeled in fast, complete with message. This was to be tried on our air field. All that was needed was a pilot and observer to volunteer. Major Hubbard asked everyone to think it over before volunteering and to let him know by evening, as tomorrow would be the day. Some of the general headquarters officers would be on our field to watch the stunt.

Of one thing I am damn sure: I don't want any part of this business. But I keep still, waiting for Price to say something. Which he finally does, asking what I think and should we give it a whirl. Price is the senior pilot of our squadron. His work or action carries a great deal of authority. So I tell him that, in my opinion, with one of our F.E.2b ships, the stunt they are contemplating is rank suicide. If they would use a tractor ship, like the artillery planes where the engine and propeller are in front, they might have a chance, as all these planes are equipped with a wire cable on which they let down a piece of lead to conduct their Morse code with their artillery battery. I feel sure that, with our pushers, where the engine and propeller are in the back between a set of tail booms, what with the speed and wind, the message and cable will be whipped into the propeller and cut off the tail.

All this my friend and pilot takes in, then asks, "Do you mind if I tell the major what you have just told me, and I shall tell him we are not volunteering."

"Sold America, and also tell him about our stout effort last night, and don't overlook the damned pigs. This he will enjoy."

Lunch is over. I feel a little disturbed. Certainly our wing commander will expect Price and me to be the first to volunteer. I know, or think I know, that Colonel Shephard has not had anything to do with the new idea. It must have come from the boys higher up. Certainly, if it works, whoever does the flying will be a very popular team, but me, I would rather take my chances with a Hun in the air. What we need is some fast machines, or at least something more, as the boys from Hun Land are flying all over and around us. To live you have to be fast and lucky. Meeting Price at tea, I tell him I hope that my feeling has not caused any reflection on his rating in the squadron. His reply is typical of his thinking. "Libby, if you are wrong and Allen and Turk are fortunate, that will be good. They are two of the best. But right or wrong, we stick together, regardless of what anyone thinks." This is the first I have heard of Allen and Turk volunteering. They are both my good friends and two of our best flyers. Allen is a top observer, devoid of fear, and is at his height with the old Lewis and a Hun to work on. God, I hope I am wrong. These boys deserve to live, or at least go down fighting. The rest of the day I will stay to myself, because everyone is wondering why Price and I are not doing the stunt and have not even volunteered. This I don't want to talk about, because I could be wrong. Certainly, if no one had volunteered it would have been rather embarrassing to our major. So tomorrow will tell. I only hope we are in the air when they make the test. I just haven't the heart to watch, I am so sure of disaster. The minute dinner is over, Price and I hit for bed. After last night and a lot of good natured kidding, we are sadly in need of rest. Before retiring, we find we are up for the twelve o'clock show, which pleases me mightily, as I don't want to be around at two o'clock when the fireworks comes off.

22

Boelcke, the Great German Ace, and His Boys Cause Us Our Greatest Loss in Any Single Engagement

I WISH I KNEW HOW TO REALLY PRAY. I would try and help my friends, so please, O Lord, do your best.

Our mission is over Bapaume, and here we always run into difficulties — just far enough over that, if crippled, it's hard to get back, and for some reason the Hun defends this area at any cost. They evidently have a project going which they are trying to keep secret. With an early lunch we are on our way for three and a half hours. While we are both alert to our own business, our minds are active with what is going on back on our own air field. For once we take pictures of the Bapaume area without being jumped by a bunch of Boelcke's boys. They must be up to something; it's far too quiet to be natural. We make a complete half circle into Hunland and out over the Somme without firing a shot. Sure, some of their ships were in the air, but they don't attack us, and we don't bother them, a very friendly and unusual occurrence.

At three-twenty Price fires the white light, and we head for home with but one thing in our minds. Coming in from three thousand and getting in position to land, we both see the nacelle of the F.E. in one part of our field and the tail in another, which confirms my worst fear — that the tail would be cut off. Upon landing we find everyone out of sight except the mechanics and riggers cleaning up the mess, and we are given the ghastly detail by one of the sergeants. Turk came in fast and good. Allen let down the hook, which caught the message and cross rope. With the speed forward and jerk when contact is made, the line and hook are thrown up and into the propeller, cutting the tail booms square off. Allen was thrown clear and Turk came down with the engine on top of him. Both were killed instantly, without a chance. It is not the way any flyer wants to finish. Price says nothing, just reaches out and shakes my hand, which expresses more than words. I feel terrible, two of our stoutest boys. I know our major must be sick. We are all used to death but not in this form. Our major won't preside at our dinner tonight. He is over to wing headquarters, so Price, being senior officer, is at the head of the table.

Tomorrow is the day we have been waiting for. It is another push on the Somme, and we will get to see our tanks go into action. This will mean two shows a day, four hours and three hours, low flying, strafing the infantry and roadways and also providing a cover for the tanks. It will be the very first time this kind of equipment has ever been used in warfare. We sure as hell need something to help the poor infantry. This may be it, and probably why our major is at wing headquarters for dinner, working out our flying programs for tomorrow.

September 15, 1916: The tanks are in action. We have been on top of them for four hours, and I am supposed to make a report of their progress. I only counted forty. How many there are supposed to be I don't know. To say that they are something new would be very accurate. They were not only new to the German infantry but to ours as well, and very new to some of the poor guys driving them. I saw one jumping along like an ant on a hot rock. He flopped from one trench to the other until free of the trenches, then started spinning around in a circle like something was wrong with his steering apparatus. Poor guy was in Hun Land going around in a circle. What happened I don't know. I saw another flopped over in a trench sidewise, going nowhere. Another hit a mine crater on his nose and stayed there. He couldn't back up or go ahead. He needed someone with a cable to lift him out of his hole. I am told later that forty-nine tanks attacked, and one-half were put out of action for one reason or another. But also that the other half broke through and took some ground. Tanks may become a big success, they may be the weapon of the future, but this first bunch I don't think could have done much to bolster the infantry morale.

We have done seven hours today, all in enemy territory from five hundred to five thousand with no combat for our flight, although C Flight picked off a couple of the Kaiser's pets this morning. This was the day we expected the worst. No savvy. Why the powers to be sent in only a few tanks puzzles me, unless they were just for a trial, because there must be at least a thousand parked back of our lines. If they are ever going to use them, now is the time for the infantry, and our air corps needs something to give us a boost too.[*]

September 17, 1916: We now know where Boelcke and his squadron have been. They have been changing over to new Albatros D.I and Halberstadt D.II scouts. This morning Boelcke and his crew went into action on our C Flight. Just as they crossed the lines, we lost our entire flight of twelve men and six ships, plus two of our D.H.2s. It is the worst defeat we have ever suffered. We have lost three out of a flight before, but a complete loss of all six ships is horrible, and two of our best scouts on one show seems almost impossible. I knew it was too good to last, for the last few times we have been over, Price and I have had no action. Now with Mr. Boelcke in his new and faster machines, we will really catch hell. The bad news was given us at breakfast. As it was our early flight that has been wiped out, we are to catch the nine o'clock offensive patrol, which means we are going over strictly to do battle. This loss will upset all the boys commanding and may hurry up the delivery of some new and faster ships we need so badly. They sure won't get here in time to do B Flight any good, so we have to do the best with what we have. We are told there will be F.E.8s and D.H.2 scouts to help us in

---

[*]Winston Churchill, who was instrumental in having the concept of the "tank" developed, had literally begged Prime Minister David Lloyd George not to give away the secret that the British had tanks by employing them in a piecemeal fashion. He argued instead to wait and use them in concentrated strength on a decisive push, but his pleas fell on deaf ears.

our coming battle, for come it will. With Boelcke and his boys full of success, they will be hard to live with. Price calls our flight together before climbing in our planes, tells everyone regardless of what happens to stay as much in formation as possible, and to protect each other's tail, and if anyone is hit get as close under our ship as possible without colliding.

We are only scheduled for a three-hour flight, which can be over much quicker if we are contacted by the Hun. Hurt by the morning defeat, our wing commander has thrown all our F.E.8s and D.H.2s, a few Nieuports, with many F.E.2b into the air. Price leads his formation into what should be the Hun's favorite hunting ground. While there are enemies everywhere and our scouts are seeing plenty of action, we don't get close enough to shoot. The Hun don't even make one pass at us. Whether they were satisfied with their morning's kill of F.E.2b, I don't know, but Price, who is spoiling for a fight, stays over until we are almost out of petrol, then home without firing a shot.

Tonight there will be twelve new faces at our dinner, and there should be six new machines in the hangars. All the flyers will undoubtedly be new and green. It just isn't possible to have any old timers. There can't be any left. Price and I are the only originals of Eleven except our major, who I know has suffered terrible with our losses. He is a wonderful commanding officer and a good pilot, but commanding officers are not allowed to fly. They are too important to lose. Dinner tonight will not be much, but the twelve new boys will have to be made welcome, for certain they are not going to be enthused with their future.

Among our new officers are four very interesting chaps each in his own way. One is Captain Mitchell, formerly of the infantry, where he was wounded and invalided back to Blighty via Boulogne clearing hospital. While in England recuperating, he applied to be an observer in the RFC and, like all observers, he is on the usual thirty days probation. If he makes good, he stays with the RFC; otherwise back to his infantry with his present rank. He is just as inexperienced as I was several months ago, only he has one advantage: he has been in action and knows all about a machine gun. Him I am going to give all the help possible, for I shall never forget how green

I was and how badly I needed help and advice. He told me a story which I'm sure is true and shows how sportsman-like the British are and how they play the game, even in war.

There are under the British command troops from every place where the Union Jack flies — Australians, Canadians, Indians, South Africans, New Zealanders and one particular detachment of Gurkhas. The Gurkhas, who speak no English, were put in the trenches under British commanding officers, using their own non-commissioned officer with an interpreter. These boys the Gurkhas are no marvels with firearms, but with a very special knife, similar to a bowie, they have no equal. The first night in the trenches is quiet. There is no movement from the Germans, and the Gurkhas are becoming familiar with their new home. Their British commanding officers are satisfied they have some good fresh troops. This they have, only how fresh they don't know. At about midnight of the second night, when the officer or officers commanding are in some other part of the trenches, the Gurkhas disappear quietly through the barbed wire fence in front of their trenches. And on their bellies, with nothing except two beautiful knives, slip into the German listening post in No Man's Land, where they play "Home Sweet Home" on the Heinie's throat with a real sharp knife before the gentleman knows his throat is being cut. Then on down to the communication trench to the main trench, where a lot of nice fat boys are dreaming about their Fatherland. The sad part for these boys, they are awakened with a nice friendly Gurkha whittling on their throat. After this successful operation, just for souvenirs or keepsakes, they whittle off a pair of ears, then return to their trenches as quietly as they left.

How many of the enemy the friendly Gurkhas butchered was never made official, but there was so much hell raised by the German high command as to a very unethical warfare that the Gurkhas were immediately pulled out of the trenches. But if the Gurkha who was wounded and in the same ward with Captain Mitchell is a fair example, they did quite an operation. This fellow had a very overripe smell and wouldn't let anyone touch or bathe him. Until they gave the boy a hypo, and from a wire tied around his waist they extracted twenty-two pair of ears. It sounded not bad to me after our loss in Eleven, but with the British it wasn't cricket, so the poor Gurkhas are out of a job.

Among our new members is Norman Read, an American, the first I have me in the RFC. He is a Yale man, a traitor to Harvard as he comes from Boston, Massachusetts, and paid his own way over to join the American Escadrille with Bill Thaw, Bert Hall, Norman Prince and Victor Chapman, all original members of this French Air Service squadron made up entirely of Americans and under French command.* But he changed his mind and qualified as a pilot with the RFC as a lieutenant and is with us for his first action. He is a wonderful chap and will be a wonderful addition to our squadron, unless his back, which he hurt in a bad accident while learning to fly, gives out. There is another very new pilot, Tommy Malloy, quite young, a typical English pink cheeked boy who I have taken a great liking to. There is another observer by the name of Bogart Rogers from Winnipeg, Canada. He's new but alert and, if lucky the first two times across the lines, will make a great observer, as with a machine gun he is a real good one, and after all, that is what keeps a pilot and observer alive.

Tomorrow we have new orders. Eleven is to do patrol duty fifteen miles back of our lines at a height of eleven thousand. Our mission is to fly back and forth for four hours to keep any German planes from coming over. This we do for four days, not knowing what it is all about, except there must be some conference or important people we are supposed to protect. On our fourth day of this very boresome warfare, we of B Flight are asked to be in our best field uniform and in front of our ships at two o'clock. Without any warning, and while we're hoping to hell it isn't any more of the Indian dignitaries, His Majesty and escort come around the corner from one of the hangars. We are inspected; he shakes our hand and thanks us for our splendid service. Here is the fellow I have been doing my best to keep well all these months on Thursday evenings and other days as well. He looks healthier than I. Anyway it has

---

*Formed by the French government in April 1916, the Escadrille Américaine first saw battle in May of that year. For political reasons having to do with America's neutrality, the squadron was renamed the Escadrille Lafayette in December 1916.

been fun, so will keep up the good work just in case he might have a relapse. After all, don't Cox & Co. have some dough for that purpose? This was the person we were flying a protective patrol for. Price is thrilled to his ears. It is evidently an honor not accorded everyone, and quite unexpected.

With our four days off for patrol duty, we have missed the fighting at the front, where our casualties in the air have been very bad. The Germans with their new ships are making the best of their superiority. Today has been B Flight's first contact with Mr. Boelcke's new ships, and we came out rather well. There were at least one hundred ships, both ours and the Germans', in a dogfight over Cambrai. Our formation is split so it's every man for himself. We have no chance to regroup. It is up to everyone to fight their own way home. Our scouts are marvelous. Until one has seen one of our single-seater pushers fall out of the sky on a Hun's tail, you haven't seen anything. When a trail of smoke from the rotary hits the sky and the machine gun goes to work, it is a sight to thrill anyone. Although not so fast as the Germans' new ships, on the level they are magnificent in combat. With a top pilot like Hawker or Green at the controls, the Hun is still in for a bad time. Price and I have credit for two, which were confirmed by Twenty-four Squadron, and three we put down as results unknown, although Price is pretty sure of them. In a dogfight of this kind, one is lucky to come out safe. To hell with who did what to who.

There are some rumors that Price will be sent back to England for a rest period. We have both been out all summer on the F.E.2b, which with due respect to all our scouts has been the savior of the Somme. If Eleven could have the new F.E.2 with the Rolls Royce engine, we would give the Hun a hell of a battle. Why they gave Number Twenty Squadron the first ones, where they are north of us and don't have the activities of the Somme, I'll never know, especially when Eleven has, with the Huns brought down by Albert Ball, the greatest number of enemy planes destroyed by any RFC squadron. And without my friend Ball's, we are the third. This includes all scouts and combat squadrons on the Western Front.

Norman Read has been sent back for hospitalization with his back. Lucky stiff, I'm glad. What is going to happen to me I don't know, though I understand I am past due for England and my pilot's training, which will be just a rest, for to fly as a pilot will be easy, thanks to Price who has taken a special interest in teaching me the F.E.2b. This I could solo on without any training. I started on this show from Canada, just for the trip and to see the world, with no thought of their so-called Democracy. With good pay, good clothes, no responsibility and no place to spend my money except girls, life was sweet. Girls weren't expensive, all of them trying to do their bit for King and Country. What more could a fellow ask?

The Canadian girls were not quite up to standard when we left Canada, but most likely quickly got into the mood. But the English girls had been at war longer. If you were in uniform, you deserved the best. The French mademoiselles are all for winning the war. They are with you down to their last chemise. As a blooming private I had more time for play with no responsibilities and plenty of money, which wasn't too necessary. And my chances of living were one hundred to one in my favor. Now what happens? There are still girls, but who the hell can romance with Fritz breathing down your neck and every day getting worse? Father, you sure raised a simple son.

Tonight I was going out and raise hell, but when I send Price's batman to Major Hubbard with my compliments, asking if I may be excused from dinner, I get a message back with the major's compliments, stating he would appreciate my presence at dinner and to please notify Captain Price. What the deuce goes on? This is the first time he ever refused me anything, and his wish is a command. So what is in my mind will have to wait. It can't have anything to do with flying, for business is never discussed at dinner. I suppose we have guests, and I hope it is the damned artillery. I would like another crack at them. Whatever it is, my major, I will be there, for you I will do most anything.

Price comes into my tent, and I tell him we are both requested to stay in for dinner. He is just as much in the dark as I am, except he thinks Colonel Shephard may be our guest, as he is our wing commander. This could well be the occasion for some special, important information, such as the announcement of new ships.

Dressing for dinner with the usual slacks and tunic and leaving the Sam Browne in our tent (as the only person wearing a Sam Browne at dinner in a British mess is the officer of the day), we go early to our mess to partake of a cocktail or two before the major shows up. This is just a practice run to get in condition for the evening's festivities, as we are both expecting Eleven Squadron to have guests. Price and I are standing off to one side with Bogart and Tommy Malloy, when our major appears. He is alone with no guests and joins us for one cocktail. Then the usual seating and dinner, which is always of the best. With nothing apparently happening, evidently something has misfired. Dinner is almost over — they are serving the demitasse and liqueurs to those who partake — when Major Hubbard stands up, saying, "Gentlemen, may I have your attention for a few minutes?" Everyone is quiet, as this is very unusual. "Gentlemen, I have a duty to perform which is for me a great honor and privilege. I have for months had under my command two officers whose performance in the line of duty has been of the highest. Working as a team they are unparalleled, with so many stout efforts to their credit I hesitate to mention just one. To these officers the RFC and Eleven Squadron owe a debt of gratitude, and it is my honor to announce to Eleven Squadron that His Majesty has awarded the Military Cross to Captain Stephen Price and Lieutenant Frederick Libby for conspicuous gallantry while engaging and destroying enemy aircraft."

Then all hell breaks loose. I am completely taken by surprise. Everyone yelling "stout fellows," everyone shaking hands. I don't move. This I never expected in a thousand years. Price is down at my end of the table congratulating me, when I should be up at his end. He is my senior, but I do come out of the haze long enough to thank my major, and the sincere pleasure expressed in his handshake and congratulations mean as much as my decoration. To be called worthy of this honor was all I asked. The decoration I never expected. As a former American who has lost his citizenship, I wonder how Congress would like them apples.

I have been in Eleven Squadron for months, and this is the first award or decoration given to any member, although I understand my friend Albert Ball has been awarded the Military Cross since his return to England. If there ever was a boy who deserved a

decoration, this boy does. Price is more than happy. He tells me the
MC is only given to officers and is only given for combat, which
means anyone with the Military Cross ribbon has earned it in battle.
He also tells me that when we return to England, we will be decorated at Buckingham Palace by His Majesty. I wonder what Father
will think. He has always had a warm spot in his heart for the English. I shall write when I get to England. Here I just can't write.
Everything is too uncertain. My darling Aunt Jo in Boston will be as
happy as Price, and will she be surprised when she finds her boy is
mixed up in something America doesn't think important. They
could be wrong.

23

Captain Price Returns to England
— I Follow Shortly —
We Are Both Decorated at Buckingham
Palace by His Majesty King George V

Today, October 3, 1916, has been the toughest and most difficult assignment since Price and I have been together in B Flight. General Headquarters ordered a photographic and reconnaissance report on Valenciennes, which is the greatest distance back of the lines an F.E.2b has ever been. It is a German railroad and shipping center, where there is evidently something going on that is essential to our headquarters. We were instructed to take photographs and report on all rolling stock in the railroad yards, movement of troops or anything unusual and to avoid a fight at any cost, if possible, but to concentrate on our photographing in and around Valenciennes. At the best, with no opposition, the F.E.2b carries enough fuel for four and one-half hours. Using the emergency tank on the top wing, with just an ordinary wind against us returning, we will have petrol enough, as we carry no bombs but all the ammunition and petrol possible. None of our scouts can carry enough fuel to escort us, so they have been ordered to pick us up on our return — just as far back as a scout can reach with safety. Why the hell B Flight always draws the tough ones I don't know. It must be because Price is such a cool flight commander. We have almost a complete squadron of inexperienced pilots and observers. In our flight we have only one old timer, Captain Adams, who will be second leader on our right with a new but excellent observer, Lieutenant Bogart Rogers. The other four ships of B Flight are all new pilots and observers with not too much experience. This is the first time in our many months together that I have known Price to be so serious. He gave strict orders to the pilots of our five other ships to follow him close in their respective positions, and if attacked to draw in close and not to break formation at any cost. The cameras are carried by the lead ships, Price and Adams with Bogart and me doing the photographing. To save petrol Price has ordered a rendezvous at three thousand feet over our aerodrome, where we will pick up formation and gain altitude while crossing the lines in the direction of our destination.

The trip over is easy, as there is a solid mass of white clouds at six thousand which we climb through, and far as the eye can see are nothing except clouds between us and the ground, with sunshine and space above. While the enemy will hear our motors, they can only spot us by sound, and they don't expect we are going so far back, so all we have to do is stay well above the clouds and catch a break if possible over Valenciennes and be prepared to catch hell on the way back because the Hun will be up in force to pick us off on our return with plenty of time. Their fast scouts, lightly loaded, can gain altitude quickly.

We run out of clouds before reaching our destination with plenty of sun at an altitude of eleven thousand. We do a good job of photography and reconnaissance. All we have to do is avoid the Hun and any combat, if possible. If our scouts are alert, it may be an easy show. But this is only wishful thinking. We are sitting ducks well back of enemy lines. What pilot could miss such an opportunity? I would give anything just once to be in such a position, with my prey over on our side where I could get to him at my leisure, knowing if anything happened to us, all we would have to do would be to break off the fight and go home. This never happens to us during our months of combat. We have never had a fight back of our lines. The enemy just don't work that way.

We are in the vicinity of our clouds again, only they are on the move coming our way, and we are in a headwind which is doing us no good, so Price is losing some altitude with our nose slightly down to maintain our speed. We both know this is taking extra petrol. Off in the distance to our right and higher, I can see a formation of ships which are our D.H.2 scouts, while to our left in the vicinity of Bapaume are several single ships, which are Albatros scouts. The clouds underneath us are spotty, so Price keeps high enough over these that we won't be subject to a sneak attack without any chance of defense. The way the air between us and the lines is filling with ships, we are sure in for a battle.

To try and avoid one by going right or left will cost us too much petrol, so Price keeps a straight line, hoping for the best from our scouts. The Hun evidently has orders to get us at any cost, because they are now appearing everywhere with three Rolands coming up fast behind. With none of our scouts close enough to take care of these, the back guns will have to do the job, because we can't turn and fight with our front guns, which would mean a loss of petrol and possibly a loss of formation. There are now three Albatros flying parallel to us only higher. When the attack comes, Bogart on our right and a new observer to our back each get one of the diving Hun ships. I think I crippled the third, but one of our back escorts is hit in the petrol tanks and is aflame. There is nothing we can do but keep going. We are hit by another flight from higher up. This time I am sure of one and my friend Bogart gets another, and our scouts go into action. We have lost another of our back ships. It is going down in perfect control, which I am sure is motor trouble. If they will just let it land, the boys will be all right, as they are far enough from the infantry to be safe.

The old grin has returned to my pilot's face, which it always does when the going is the worst. With our scouts everywhere, Price is concentrating on getting the F.E.s across our lines with the pictures. Our nose is well down and the trenches are quite visible. If our scouts stay on our tail, all we need is a little luck and we may even make our squadron. Even if we don't and have a forced landing, their precious pictures are safe, which seemed to be the principal reason for our trip. Luck is with us and we cross our lines at Arras with enough petrol left to reach home. Our four returning ships show considerable damage, but we have four Huns for certain with three probables. Not a bad show, and everyone is congratulated by General Headquarters, but we lost two ships, which is always a blow. No matter how long you have been flying or how tough you are, there is always the knowledge it could have been you.

This had been Price's last show. His orders for England and a rest period came in before we took the air for Valenciennes. All our major could do was hope for the best. He didn't want to tell Price before the take-off. It didn't seem right to be going on the kind of a mission we have returned from with orders for his leave effective tomorrow, but now everything is good. My friend and pilot is out of action and will have a rest which is long past due. As to what is going to happen to me, even our major is in doubt. He sent a recommendation through at the same time for both of us to return to England, but the GHQ don't do things that way. We both need a rest as we are edgy, and thirty days with no action might be the answer. And to say I am glad that my pal is on his way is putting it mildly. No more early shows, no more combat for him. He has certainly earned it. I shall miss him terribly. We have become so accustomed to battling our enemy together that to fly with a new pilot is going to be very difficult.

We only have one old timer, Captain Adams, so I suppose we'll be together, for he is taking Price's place as flight commander of B Flight. While it has only been a few months since the day I came to Twenty-third Squadron as an observer on probation, it has been a lifetime for many. Of all the officers I first knew, only a few are now living. True, there are several that are prisoners of war, but our losses have been great. It hardly seems possible that Price and I should have lived, where so many have gone west. Today we are the only ones who have survived continuous service. I have my observer's wing and the Military Cross. Of both I am proud, but with the knowledge that so many have been lost while we have been so lucky, one wonders how long will it last. Of one thing I am sure, if I can just get back for my pilot's wings and fly a single-seater scout where the gun shoots through the propeller, I may have a new lease on life. Pilots like Price on an F.E.2b are very few, and with a single-seater fighter scout you are on your own. If possible, I would like to join my friend Ball when he returns.

October 28, 1916: My orders have come through for a rest in England, then my training for pilot's wings. The British have given me credit for ten enemy planes confirmed and eleven probables. This only means I have been lucky and am still alive. One true thing I have found about being a flyer with the RFC is the greatest feeling of good fellowship I have ever known. Just to be a member in any capacity is an honor, and being an American I am glad to be mixed up in this damn war, regardless of what the American Congress thinks. The Americans flying with the French under the name of the American Escadrille are a swell bunch, I understand. I'm going to contact them at my first opportunity, since in the RFC the only American I know is my friend Norman Read, who is now in a hospital in England. He'll be the first person I look up when I land in London.

The joy of being back in London is enhanced by complete freedom from anything to do for some time. I am on leave until the first of January before reporting for my pilot's training. No early morning show, no responsibilities, and I am at liberty to go where I wish. So my first night I go to visit Jimmy at the Savoy, where life is easy especially if there is no strenuous tomorrow. Jimmy is glad to see me with my observer's wing and MC ribbon — he is as proud as if I were his brother. Everyone and everything are more natural than on my first visit when I was so new in the RFC. Time either makes or kills you, it doesn't stand still. In a few minutes Mr. Grant, my tailor comes in. Jimmy has sent word I am with him. So for the rest of the evening my money is counterfeit. They make me feel just like I was home. Tomorrow I am invited to have lunch at Simpson's with Mr. Grant and his partner, which I am happy to do as I have an idea that I will see my old pilot and friend Captain Price.

The lunch is a big success. Price is present as I was sure he would be, even if it was supposed to be a surprise. Our hosts return to their business, while Price and I linger on until Price has to return to Gosport, where he is temporarily in command of a training squadron.

With my promise to come to Gosport for lunch in a couple of days, we complete a wonderful visit. When I do meet Price at Gosport, I'm introduced to an American also named Price. He is no relation, but is Raymond B. Price, vice president of the United States Rubber Company. This is November the fourth, 1916. Mr. Price is in England on a speaking tour, trying to bring the English-speaking nations closer together, and is one of the most interesting men I have ever known. He is not a large man physically but is a giant mentally. I am asked to drive back to London with him, as he has a driver and a car, so we have an opportunity to discuss many things. And one thing in particular: he thinks America should be in the war helping England and France. At Mr. Price's invitation, I go to our American embassy, where I am introduced to Mr. Page, our ambassador, and his military attaché, Captain Chapman. During the remainder of my service with the RFC, these gentlemen become two of my very best friends.

Thanks to them, and to Captain Chapman in particular, I met many wonderful people. Two of the most interesting and enjoyable Americans I was fortunate to meet were Lee White and Clay Smith. They owned and operated the Strand Theatre where, with a change of show every two weeks, they wrote all the songs and music and also did the directing, a most wonderful team. They were in England when the war started and just stayed. They are fellow Americans to be proud of, and through this pair I met many interesting people in and out of show business. Lee White was responsible for Gertrude Lawrence's early show business success, as the girls were great friends and anyone who was a friend of Lee's was always sure of help if needed.

One of the principal topics of conversation at the embassy was America's November election, so on the night of the seventh I agreed to have dinner with Mr. Raymond Price and Captain Chapman at the Savoy Hotel, where we would know the results before going to bed. This we did, but things are not always what they seem, for when we departed for bed Mr. Charles Evans Hughes was elected but in the morning at breakfast Mr. Woodrow Wilson was president. Some mistake in the count or communications, I don't know which. I only know that Mr. Price and Captain Chapman were two very unhappy men. There was talk of Mr. Wilson being too proud to fight, and they both felt that, with Mr. Hughes, America would be in the war soon. To me it made no difference who was elected. I had a job to do and was making friends doing it, and awfully glad I switched from trucks to the RFC. The pace is faster and a damned sight more interesting.

Today I order a couple more uniforms, not that they are needed, but I'd just as soon be the best dressed officer on leave. Captain Price had on a beauty at our last lunch, and I wanted one just like it. Quite the copy cat. But what's the difference? Clothes won't help a fellow in the air, though on the ground they do wonders for the old morale. I have taken an apartment in a gentleman's apartment house where they serve breakfast until eleven and tea in the afternoon. It is a nice two-room affair, with a large living room with a fireplace and closet space for all my uniforms and bed roll, and is only a little more expensive than my hotel. My new abode is on Jermyn Street not too far from my tailor, and without his influence I would never have made the grade, as there is always a waiting list for apartments.

Mr. Price is returning to America tomorrow. I have written my family, and he will mail the letters in America and look up Aunt Jo's only son in New York and give him firsthand information to be passed on to my darling aunt in Boston. We are going to have a farewell luncheon at Simpson's. I have become very attached to the gentleman. He is such a decent person and so sincere, no wonder the English admire him. If I ever go home again he will be one of the first people I hope to see.

The more I see of the English, the more I like them. Everyone takes the war in their stride. There is no crying or bellyaching. London is in a state of total darkness at night, not a peep of light showing. All entrances have double affairs, so there will be no light visible when entering or departing. All windows are heavily shaded, and there are no street lights. So if you're going anyplace, it helps to know your way. All taxis and cars have absolutely no lights except a small dim light showing from the bottom half of the right headlight. As everyone drives to the left, it is necessary to have some light from the right front.

The theaters are going strong, playing to capacity audiences.... George Robie knocking them dead at one theater... Beatrice Lillie a honey... Lee White and Clay Smith at the

Strand . . . Gabby d'les and Pilsnor just returned from America, where she is putting on a new girl show at the Gaiety with a bunch of the youngest undressed kids in the business. They are chaperoned to the teeth. The kids are willing, but they are handicapped with some thirty-year-old crows protecting their honor. The pubs are only open nights from six to eight. There is always a private party in some hotel where a bunch of flyers are whooping it up. A couple of nightclubs open after twelve, and an officer can go there if he has a gal who is a member and can sign the check, for he can't spend any money here, nor can he dance unless in mufti. The British have a rule which they encourage an officer on leave to follow: He is privileged to wear civilian clothes for the duration of his leave if he desires. This is so, in the event he wants to raise a lot of hell, he won't be conspicuous in uniform. There is no restriction on his dancing so long as he is in civilian clothes. I like the idea and am going to purchase an outfit tomorrow. Several months ago I couldn't get into my officer's uniform fast enough, now I think a change will be nice for a few days.

I have been back from the front a little over a month. Time has certainly flown. I have met so many nice people who have invited me to their home, where I have been treated like one of the family. Whatever we are fighting for, it is worth the effort if it helps these fine people in any way.

Returning to my apartment I have a note to call Price at his home tonight without fail. Before I can call, my phone rings and it is the gallant captain himself, all enthused with the news that tomorrow is the day we are to appear at Buckingham Palace to receive our decoration from His Majesty personally. This is rather sudden notice, but it is the way everything happens in this cockeyed war, so I tell my pal to "lead on, McDuffy," I'm ready. He gives me instructions on what to wear — of course, my best field uniform with Sam Browne and boots — and to meet him in front of the Savoy Hotel at nine A.M. as our date with His Majesty is for ten o'clock.

We meet as per his orders. His first words are, "Libby, let me give the cabbie instructions." With this we pile in, and Price says, "Buckingham Palace, James." He tells me he has been wanting to do just that for years but didn't really expect to have the opportunity.

If he thought he would upset the cabbie any, he must have been surprised, because the cabbie asks, "Do you want the big gate, sir?" This was evidently old hat to our driver, who had been through all this before, including the James business. Arriving at the big gates, we were held up just long enough for a guard to stick his head in and inquire our names and purpose. With no delay the big gate swings open, and we are driven up to the entrance where we dismiss our driver, and before we can touch the door it flies open and we are received by a man in a beautiful uniform with knee pants and a coat to match and a white wig. Our gloves, British warmer and cap are taken and we are turned over to a full colonel, who precedes us to an enormous room with beautiful drapes at the windows, thick carpets and extremely high ceilings. Here we are introduced to a brigadier general, who gives us our instructions as to formality and such and how to proceed when our name is called.

We are to be decorated separately. A very pompous individual has placed a curved pin immediately over our MC ribbon with an open end sticking up. When our name is called, we are to march through a large open doorway where His Majesty would be standing to the left. You go into the room until opposite where His Majesty is standing, stop and do a left turn and bow, then take three paces up to the King. Your decoration has been brought in on a plush pillow by another one of the boys with a white wig and gorgeous uniform. After placing the cross on the pin attached to your tunic, His Majesty may ask you a few questions but always shakes hands. With me, he thanks me for my services. I then step back three paces, bow, do a right turn and go out a door opposite the one I had entered, where my cross and pin are taken by another one of the gorgeous boys, with instructions to pick it up with my coat. It is a beautiful show, put on with all the pomp and splendor which the British do so well. It is something to be proud of and to always remember.

By the time I have reached the cloakroom entrance my cross is there in a beautiful case. Price is waiting, as he went first, so together we are let out once again through the big gates, only this time walking out to where we get a big salute from the guards and are hailed by the camera boys. It has been a wonderful morning, very impressive, and His Majesty more impressive than the entire show. He seemed very tired, much more so than when we met in France. This damned war must be hell for him.

It's lunchtime, so to the Savoy where Price blows the works on me. Then to my apartment, where we take a nap in preparation for the night. God, what a life. I'll be glad to get back into action, especially as a pilot, and on the first I report for school. As this is December the thirteenth, it won't be long.

Price's and my picture coming out of the Buckingham gate appeared in the *London Daily Mirror* the next morning, which has stirred up a commotion with many of my friends. I have an invitation to have lunch at the embassy, which I like very much, as Ambassador Page and Captain Chapman are sure one hell of a fine team to represent America. I hope they are appreciated.

I am getting fed up. Nothing to do was fine for a while and did I enjoy it! I could just sit and be happy. I'll soon have been idle two months with nothing to do except get up in time to go to lunch, then mess around until teatime and wait for the pubs to open, then a show and play all night. I know everyone in town I want to know. The civilians are all busy. Me, I have nothing to do but play. I just rested too fast, so now I need action, and I certainly hope this damn weather doesn't hold up my training, for with this kind of rain there is no flying, and the poor guys in the trenches are wet to their eyebrows. If the British had left the Gurkhas alone and put a few more in the front lines, the Germans would have surrendered by now or would have at least stopped hearing. I'm all for the Gurkhas, long may they live.

I have been in this war for two years on September the second. This Christmas coming up tomorrow is my third Christmas in service, the first in Toronto, Canada, my second in France in water everywhere and my third tomorrow here in London, where I shall have breakfast at the Strand Palace with Lieutenant Getz Rice and a bunch of Canadians. Then to the big lounge, where Getz will entertain everyone with the hotel piano for hours. When this boy entertains, the professionals come to hear.

Early Christmas Eve at the Savoy Hotel I join Bill Thaw and Bert Hall, two fellow Americans from the Lafayette Escadrille. While I have never met these boys, my friend Norman Read gave me their history. They are both stout fellows and Thaw is the commanding officer of the squadron, made up entirely of American boys who came over at their own expense to help France. I certainly can't claim this distinction, for I came just for the trip and a free trip at that, hoping never to get into battle. We are to have Christmas dinner at the Savoy, which promises to be quite a Christmas evening. I find they have just returned from America and are leaving for their squadron in France tomorrow. With these two chaps I spend one of the nicest Christmas evenings of my life. We have a table in the big dining room where we enjoy a good dinner, then just relax and watch the dancing till long past midnight. We part with a promise to visit their squadron when I return to France and call it a day.

24

Thank God for America's Ambassador Page and His Military Attaché, Captain Chapman

CHRISTMAS IS OVER, 1917 about to begin. I am starting my third year with the British, and where I shall spend my next Christmas is anyone's guess. I hope it is in good old London. . . . I love the big town, even in darkness. If they could ever turn on the lights, the place would go wild. My leave is almost a thing of the past. I have enjoyed a wonderful rest far away from the fighting front, but I continually think of the boys in the trenches and my old squadron and wonder how many have survived. It is impossible to have been one of them and not remember. I have ordered that once a week a couple of cakes be sent to Number Eleven for teatime — cakes are one thing our mess didn't provide, so always someone sends cakes, which were shipped and received in unfailingly good condition. I have been to Reading, a beautiful little city a short distance from London, and I have reported to the commanding officer at Wantage Hall, a famous peacetime school now taken over and operated by the ground training school for flyers, both pilots and observers. This is the kind of place I had expected to go for training when I joined the RFC, but evidently there was no such school then and I went direct to action, getting my training on active service.

Now that I'm a full observer, I'm to undergo training for the things I've been doing for months, such as map reading, machine guns, bombing, etc. However, these the commanding officer says I can skip, so will concentrate on engines and the new Vickers machine gun, which is the equipment the new ships are to use for the front gun shooting through the propeller. After all, this should be a very easy course for me. It will be more in the way of a rest, not that I need any more, but studying the things I haven't been using at the front will be interesting. I have my billet with two charming maiden ladies in their home, where I will have breakfast and dinner. My quarters consist of a den and bedroom. It is a luxury, all arranged by the staff of my training center. It seems, according to the adjutant, I am the only qualified observer to attend this school, which may have something to do with the attention I'm receiving.

As my term starts on January second, I have time for one more rendezvous with my friends in London where I shall spend New Year's Eve, and then my future in 1917 is in the lap of the Gods. If I am half as lucky as in 1916, everything will be just ducky. No one will be hurt except the Hun. Though it is hard to understand with all that has happened, I am not sore at our enemy, the German flying corps. I can honestly say all the planes I knocked out of the air have been downed out of self-preservation and protection. I don't even know what the hell it's all about — thousands being killed every day under the guise of Democracy — and I very much doubt if our enemy knows any more than we do, particularly the boys who do the fighting. My one contribution to this war of which I am the proudest is my introducing the buttstock to the Lewis machine gun. It was a lifesaver for Price and me and has become standard equipment on all Lewis guns for observers. If I get knocked off, they can just plant me with a Lewis buttstock on my chest. I'll be satisfied. Why the Lewis people or someone hadn't thought of it before I came along, I don't know, but think of it they had not.

Bogart is back from Eleven for his fourteen-day leave and has his observer's wing and five jolly Huns to his credit. He is a stout fellow but arrived here too late for me to spend any time with him. After New Year's Eve, then, I start class and will be back in France in plenty of time for the spring push. With the weather as it is, everything has slowed down at the front till spring, when hell will break loose again.

In the winter the poor infantry catch it from the continuous rain and mud, which causes trench feet, in many cases necessitating amputation, as well as pneumonia and every other disease stemming from exposure, while we of the flying corps have rather a soft time. No matter if his idea was good or bad, you have to give that fellow Ford from America credit: he at least was thinking right in wanting to get the boys out of the trenches.

I have taken my friend Bogart to the embassy to meet our ambassador and Captain Chapman as well as my two special friends in show business, Lee White and Clay Smith. While Bogart is a Canadian, I want him to know my American friends, as he is almost as green as I was when I first hit London. He is staying at my apartment, which I shall keep even when I go back to the front. It will be someplace to store my extra uniforms and things I don't want to take to France. I shall have a place in London to call home, and the fellows from my squadron who haven't a home in London can use the apartment when on leave. Last spring, when I went to France, everything I owned went with me. This spring, I shall take only a couple of uniforms, a bed roll and the essentials a fellow needs on active service. I have learned one lesson: to travel light is to travel easy and fast.

My first week of school is grand, no hurry, no worry. My billet is the finest in Reading. There are over a thousand fellows from everywhere taking this course: boys from India, Canada, New Zealand, Australia and naturally from England, all very young with absolutely no training, but the things they learn here will help in the future.

On my third morning when reporting to class, we were told to report on the parade grounds at ten o'clock. This will be my first time on a parade ground since transferring out of the Canadians. Why we should be forming up, I couldn't understand, and no one else had any idea of what it was all about, unless it was an inspection by some high ranking dignitary.

With the entire school membership assembled in a large square, leaving an opening on one end, a very young lieutenant was marched under guard out in the center of our square, where the crime of which he had been convicted was read, together with the punishment he was to receive. The punishment was to be drummed out of the British Army. His buttons were all cut off, the insignias of his

unit removed, and, with his tunic open and cap gone, the drums began to roll and he was marched ahead of our formation with the
drums continuing to roll to the outskirts of Reading. This was the
saddest and most heart-breaking parade of my military career. What
he did, I don't know, as I was too far away to hear the reading of his
crime, but whatever it was, one couldn't help but feel sorry for the
poor guy. The disgrace will be with him always.

The course here is two months. Those who qualify are assigned to different advanced schools for more training. By the beginning of my fourth week, I have divided my time with the Vickers
machine gun between the Rolls Royce and Beardmore stationary
engines and the Le Rhône and Clerget rotary engines.

One Monday morning I am called into our commander's office
and handed orders to report to Waddington Air Field for my flying
training for pilot's wings. For this I am grateful, even if I have been
having a wonderful time. It has rained continuously, which hasn't
bothered me any as I have my most comfortable billet since joining
the Canadians in 1914. This delightful existence is too good to last
and the RFC needs pilots for the spring offensive, so my playing
war is really over. I am once again faced with the real thing. Waddington being on the opposite side of London, I shall stop over just
to see Jimmy and a few others and sleep in my own apartment for
one night and report the next day to Waddington when the prelim-
inary flying begins. Here one does five hours solo, then on to an advanced field for five hours on faster and final training, then to
France to see my old enemy the Hun. The solo and flying my own
ship have no horror for me, thanks to my observing experiences.
Here at Waddington are a large group training to be pilots. Some
have had several hours of dual control flying, none have soloed. The
weather has been so miserable they have only had time to fly in between rains, which has retarded all progress. One of the principal
flying instructors, Darsy, is a former pilot from my first squadron, the
Twenty-third. He was invalided back to England with a throat condition and given an instructor's job. And what a hell of a job it is.
Much worse than fighting the Hun, considering the number of
dumb kids he has to train.

Have been here five days with no flying, just one hour of

ground school where we listen to the theory of flight, as it is a pre-
liminary school whose principal function is to solo their pupils, then
send them to a more advanced school.

Darsy has taken an interest in me and promised he will give me
priority on the first decent day, and it looks like this is it. For a
change the sun is out and it is real early. So to the hangars, hoping
for the best. True to his promise, they roll out an awful looking contraption, a Graham White pusher which actually flies. It has an
eighty-horse Gnome rotary, with dual control. On Darsy's invitation
to climb in, we finally take off, fly around the field, then land, then
take off again. This time after taking off I take over the controls.
There is no power to give a feeling of safety, just enough power that
if you don't pull the nose up too much you can stay afloat, but no
margin of safety between your power and your flying speed. So, in
the event your engine quits near the ground, you never try and turn,
but just keep straight and land. After we circle the field and land a
couple of times, Darsy says she's all yours, don't go far away from
the field, land as often as you want to and remember, don't try to
turn her near the ground. He steps out, giving me a wave. I am on
my own. My solo was easy, the air field was enormous. I could land
anytime, so practiced with the control awhile before trying my first
landing, which came off beautifully as I had no fear of the ship,
thanks to my many hours as an observer with Captain Price.

After two and one-half hours, Darsy flags me down, telling me
I can finish my solo hours in the afternoon while the weather is good
and he will okay my transfer to Lincoln for the better ships. This is
swell news to me, for the faster ships are what I want, especially the
tractors with the engine in front. I've had enough pushers for a lifetime. I want one of the fast babies where the gun shoots through the
propeller and the pilot does the shooting as well as fly the ship, with
a rotary engine preferred.

To say that my start as a pilot was lucky would be a true statement, for I finished my five hours of solo on the Graham White
pusher just as the downpour started, which made me eligible for
Lincoln. There it takes me twenty days to do what I did at Waddington in one day. It rained, then rained some more.

I got in one hour of solo on a beautiful little ship which was different in every way from any ship I had ever seen or dreamed of fly-ing — the Strut-and-a-Half Sopwith. This was a two-seater tractor with a one-hundred-thirty Clerget rotary. The minute you opened the throttle, you were in the air. It was easy to fly and a delight to land. It had no funny tricks, such as burning in the air on the take-off like the R.E.8 (another of the Lincoln training ships). How I should be so lucky as to draw the Sopwith for my training, I'll never know. The only thing to keep me from being a full pilot is the damned weather, and we are in the last of February. It can't last much longer. I suppose soon I'll be praying for rain when I get my belly full of the front, though right now this inactivity is driving me nuts.

The fifth of March I am a qualified pilot and have to do away with my observer's wing and put up the pilot's wings. Though this is what I have been working for, still the thought of not having my observer's wing when I have been so lucky doesn't seem right. While a fellow can't wear both, I'd carry mine in my pocket. Hell, my observer's wing was one hundred times tougher to get than the pilot's, and having been an observer has made the pilot training a breeze. I shall always try to be helpful to any observer that comes into my life, and if I go out on a two-seater, I will try to be as good to my observer as my pal Captain Price was to me.

My orders are for General Headquarters, Cecil Hotel, London, where I will receive transportation and orders for somewhere in France. So tonight I shall see as many of my friends as possible be-fore taking off for the front, where I am a cinch to be for at least three months. These senior officers of our RFC are all swell chaps. They're always glad to see you, as they have all had service and un-derstand flyers. I have never met a senior RFC officer that I didn't admire. Headquarters has assigned me to our southern pilots' pool in France, which means I shall be in some squadron in my old area, back of Arras and between the two famous landmarks, the Arras–Saint-Pol and the Arras-Doullens roads. This is good news, not only because I know the area, but also it means I will be in the Thirteenth Wing, where Colonel Shephard is now brigadier. It is al-most like coming home.

Regardless of what squadron I join, there won't be anyone that

I know, though, except for General Shephard of our wing. If they had me assigned to our northern pool, I would be in new territory as well, which wouldn't make much difference, only I like it best this way. What squadron I go to will depend on fate, as the pilots drawn from the pool take the place of some pilot that has gone west or is fortunate enough to be returned to England for a rest. My train for Folkestone and the early boat to Boulogne doesn't leave until evening, so I have most of the day to see my friends at the embassy and Captain Price at Gosport just to hear his cheerful greeting. Him I shall miss very much. My friend Lee White gave me a mascot for my plane. It is a duplicate of Bairnsfather's "Old Bill,"* made in cloth and stuffed with some soft material, which makes it light but durable. This I shall fasten on my plane where it will remain. It will be my good luck omen. The crowd at the embassy treated me like one of their official family. If their good luck wishes just work, I am in clover.

The boat for Boulogne has its usual interesting crowd, but something new has been added. A couple of beautiful silver-colored blimps are escorting our boat. They are flying at about five to seven hundred feet and slightly ahead as our protection from submarines, in the event that some ambitious enemy wants to commit suicide. There is the usual talk of a big push, as there was last spring on my way over, only this time the talk is of Arras and Messines. The Somme seems to be relegated to the ash heap, or just plain forgotten for the time being. I am rather anxious to see what has happened along the line while I have been living the life of Riley (whoever he is). The sun is out in all its glory. Spring is here. The boys in the trenches will be doing their spring cleaning, preparing to go nowhere except over the top to clean out the enemy. We of the flying corps will see action every day. All of the Western Front is coming alive with a bang. All casualty clearing stations are cleaned out and all who can move are being invalided to England to make room for the new crop of casualties. The same old routine is on.

---

*Bruce Bairnsfather's Old Bill was a cartoon character representing the typical British soldier in World War I much as Bill Mauldin's Willie and Joe did the GI in World War II. Old Bill was a popular figure with the British troops.

Many who are here will be gone tomorrow. This war should put all the celestial clairvoyants out of business. Anyone with guts enough to predict what will happen is crazy. I don't think they will find anything in the stars about this business, and up to now I haven't had any member of the cloth tell me the answer. They all seem to be in a shell, just doing their best for humanity and hoping for sanity to return to the world.

I have been in the pool two days and am first up for a scout rotary or the Sopwith two-seater, in which I finished and qualified for my pilot's wings. Today I have been assigned to Forty-third Squadron, as they need two pilots. Another pilot named Kirby is scheduled to the same squadron, and the usual tender will pick us up in the morning. This squadron is equipped with Sopwith two-seaters powered by a rotary one-hundred-thirty engine. They have their front gun firing through the air screw and the back gun mounted on a Scarf ring. The pilot is in a very comfortable seat between the wings, directly back of his engine, with the Vickers gun and control directly in front in alignment with the ship. The observer is directly back of the pilot, close enough so they can talk to each other. The Forty-third is commanded by Major Sholto-Douglas, to whom Kirby and I report. Here is a typical British commanding officer, only more so. He has the sincerity and the graciousness of all RFC commanding officers, only this fellow has had a lot of service. On his chest are the flying wings with the Military Cross ribbon, which I learn later he acquired as an observer. This puts us in the same category, both having been observers and both having the MC. This fellow I like immediately. He has dignity, with kindness and experience, which go to make up a wonderful commanding officer.

I am assigned to B Flight, which is flying this evening's show at three P.M. under the command of Captain Collier, who will become one of my best friends. As it is eleven-thirty, almost lunchtime, my major asks me if I would like to take a flight before lunch and make a landing or two. I am glad, so climbing into my new Sopwith, I take off with no uncertainty and all the confidence in the world.

The flying was beautiful. The ship performed grand. I even took a short look at the lines, then came in for a landing. Seeing that I was coming in too fast and overshooting my field, I began to realize that this wasn't Waddington where I had all of England to land but a very small field with no distance for a runway, and that when you touched the ground, you should be down.

After three attempts to land and having to take off again, I remembered how Price used to sideslip to lose height and speed, so on the fourth attempt I am in. I haven't been worried but know I have to do some practice landings on a small field. In the F.E.2b I was only an observer and didn't realize what the small landing fields meant to a pilot. Price used to make them so easy. After lunch we make our first reconnaissance over the same territory I had traveled last spring, with nothing different except that I am a pilot.

Forty-third Squadron has the usual eighteen ships in three flights, A, B and C. A Flight is commanded by Captain Harold Balfour, B Flight by Collier, while C Flight is commanded by Major Stanley Dore. Here are possibly three of the best and stoutest flight commanders of any squadron in France. My old luck is sure holding once again. I am in a top squadron with top commanding officers. I have been assigned an observer by the name of Pritchard. Pritchard is a typical Englishman, with a great personality and sense of humor. With this fellow, in the days to come, I have many experiences. Things are most the same as last spring. There hasn't been much change in the trenches; we have gained some ground at the Somme. The salient has been straightened out some, but at an awful cost. There are only a few of the old flyers left. Ball is back in action and going strong with Fifty-six Squadron in Nieuports, and thank God the kid is in our wing. It's good to know he is close, because I consider him the best fighting pilot in the RFC.

I am beginning to get the feel of my little ship. It is such a pleasure after the big F.E. When nestled down in the pilot's seat, I am not exposed to any wind. The change is marvelous, and my observer has a wonderful gun mounting. With some experience, we should do well.

Forty-third has an excellent mess. With a caterer from one of London's best hotels as mess sergeant, how could we miss? The lounging room has a flock of easy chairs with couch and piano, and we have a boy who is a natural on the piano. With my whiskey tenor, everything will be noisy, if not good. Today a great enemy fighter,

Boelcke,* was killed in a collision while fighting some of our F.E.2b back of the enemy lines. He was a fine gentleman and a great fighter, who didn't build his reputation by picking on cripples. He had the respect of all the RFC fighters and was a good enemy. One of our squadrons is dropping a wreath of flowers over the line as a courtesy to our respected friend and enemy. Many of our RFC boys who are prisoners of war have written home many nice things about Boelcke and his kindness to our flyers. The only courtesy or respect by any combat units on either side seems to be between the two flying corps.

Today Kirby, who came with me from the pool to Forty-third, made his first flight and is missing. No one knows what happened, as the weather was bad. He could have been lost in a cloud and landed safely back of the lines. While Boelcke was alive, we always had reports of our boys if killed or landed safely. With this new gang opposite our front, I don't know. They seem to be all out for a show. With their highly colored paint job on all their planes, they are called the Flying Circus, commanded by a Baron von Richthofen.[†] If these babies think the RFC scare at paint, they have a surprise coming. This so-called circus hasn't a chance. They stay back of their lines. Hell, if the RFC didn't go over, there would never be a battle, but the British always take the offensive, which does wonders for the infantry morale. Now, with Boelcke and Immelmann[‡] both gone, I have a feeling the new German flying corps

---

*Oswald Boelcke at the time of his death had become Germany's most revered pilot, having chalked up forty British kills. He died in a midair collision with another German pilot. Germany's first air ace, Boelcke had been awarded the coveted Blue Max and before his death composed the still famous "Seven Rules of Aerial Combat."

[†]Manfred von Richthofen (the Red Baron) became Germany's most famous fighter ace, shooting down eighty Allied planes before himself being shot down and killed in 1918. It remains disputed whether he was downed by a rookie Canadian flyer or by rifle fire from the trenches.

[‡]Hans Immelmann, also a Blue Max recipient, was a German ace with only six kills to his credit before being shot down and killed, but he immortalized his name in the aviation world by devising the Immelmann turn. Known simply as an Immelmann, it was an upside-down-inside-out loop which all fighter pilots eventually employed and which has delighted fans at air shows ever since.

will be different. With the loss of their two sportsmen, the standard set by these two great airmen through 1915 and 1916 may exist no longer.

When one thinks that these two great German aces lost their lives fighting F.E.2b, Immelmann having the wings shot off his monoplane by Second Lieutenant McCubbin and Corporal Waller of Twenty-fifth Squadron and Boelcke losing his life in a collision with one of his own ships while fighting a flight of F.E.2b from Twenty-third Squadron over Bapaume, one realizes what a fighting ship the F.E.2b has been for the RFC. Without this group of combat planes in the Somme push of 1916, the RFC would have been in a bad way. The Hun is out with a new Albatros, much faster and better than their 1916 Albatros scout, which caused us such great losses. We have some real competition for them with our Spads and Sopwith Pups, only we don't have enough. We at Forty-third are holding our own, although the going is tough and our losses are too many. It is rumored that Fifty-six is to be equipped with S.E.5s, our new ship with the Hispano-Suiza motor, which is considered very fast. This may help us against our enemy's new Albatros. It is also rumored that Bishop is coming back into action with Sixty Squadron equipped with all S.E.5s. Bishop* has been trying to catch up with Ball in number of ships destroyed, with some distance to go, and unless Ball is injured no one will come close.

We of Forty-third have suffered a terrible loss caused by an accident to Major Douglas. He was seriously hurt in my plane, which makes me feel doubly bad. He is a great commanding officer. To lose him in an unnecessary accident is an awful blow to the RFC. We have been standing by to take some photographs of a particular sector that our wing headquarters needs, and the weather has been bad and makes it impossible to do any flying, when suddenly at

---

*William A. "Billy" Bishop was Canada's most cherished flying ace, having shot down seventy-two German aircraft. A recipient of the Victoria Cross, Bishop was one of the few big-time aces to survive the war. He died in Palm Beach, Florida, in 1956. After his death, his flying career in France became the subject of a popular book and a Broadway play.

about three o'clock it starts to clear, we hope enough to do the job before dark. Since the leader of B Flight, Captain Collier, is on leave, I am acting flight commander. The major orders us to try and take the pictures. Out of a flight of six ships only three of us are able to take off. While the three of us who do take to the air are climbing for altitude and hoping the others will get off of the ground, my ship is not flying right. The wires to my stick control seem to be slack. As the ship is sliding and slipping and is in no way answering to my control, I decide to make a quick landing to give the rigger a chance to check my plane.

Landing close to the edge of our field and leaving plenty of distance for a quick take-off, I call the rigger sergeant over to check, when our major comes running out and wants to try the ship for a flight around the field. Leaving my observer in his place, he opens up the engine and starts across the field into the wind for a perfect take-off. Only it didn't take off. Square in front of where the major is bouncing across the ground at full speed and coming toward the ship is a big Belgian horse weighing at least two thousand pounds, led by a Frenchman, with a plow and another Frenchman on the other end. The horse is so petrified, he squats and stands still, while both Frenchmen jump, just in time to keep from being killed. With the horse standing braced and the plane traveling full-out, the propeller kissed the horse square on. Poor Doug and my observer and the horse are all mixed up together. It was a horrible sight. Landing on the side with their hands waving and their mouths opening and shutting with nothing coming out were two of the most frightened Frenchmen in all of France. Forty-third has lost a good commanding officer, but fortunately both officers will live, although they will be months recovering. Major Dore, our senior flight commander, is now in command of Forty-third. He is a great friend of Major Douglas and an old timer in the RFC.

We have lost Albert Ball, killed in action back of the enemy lines, where it always happens, never on our side. It was a dogfight near the ground. Everyone in the Richthofen circus is claiming victory. We were not in the fight, so have no definite knowledge. I only know that one of the best will be missed by the RFC, and I owed

him many a favor, for when we were together in the early days in
Eleven Squadron, he and his little Nieuport helped Price and me
out of many a tight spot. I shall never forget this boy as long as I live.
I wish that Captain Price and I could have been there in the old
F.E.2b to give him some help when needed.[*]

---

[*]Captain Ball had been credited with forty-seven victories before his death.
He was fighting the enemy in a thunderstorm and there is controversy over
whether he was shot down by the Germans or his crash was due to mechanical fail-
ure or the weather.

25

A Great Major, a Sick Observer
and a Forced Landing in Our Trenches

EVERYONE IS KIDDING ME now that America has declared war on Germany, with good natured gibes such as, How did you get here so soon? It is time America came in, if they ever were going to. England and France have been carrying the load for the world over two years, and before America can give any real help here I'll be old and gray.

I have been helping all observers as much as possible at the request of Major Dore. We are getting our share of them on probation, and to the new ones I'm devoting a lot of time, both on the range and in practice from my ship shooting at a ground target. Among my pupils is a second lieutenant out of the trenches. He is a fine looking blond boy whose family want him to be a flyer, which is why the lad is with us as an observer on probation. He has been nicknamed Babe because he has such a good complexion, but this boy is no babe. He has seen action in the trenches, in and out for the past year, and has acquired the Military Cross. Cattell is an excellent shot with the machine gun on the range, but the minute he is in the air he becomes deathly ill. He vomits all over the ship and loses interest in target and machine gun and the world in general. Then his one ambition is to land. I have tried three different days at the target from my machine, without him firing a shot. He is just too damn sick. This has been necessary to report to the major, but I have

recommended that he be sent on some patrol duty where he won't
see any action, which on a three-hour trip will give our lad a chance
to become accustomed to the air. This the major tries twice, but our
boy is so sick that the pilot brings him back, for when he is ill, he
just don't care anymore. About this I am very unhappy, for Cattell
has told me all about his family and how they want him out of the
trenches. With the war as it is, I know the major will have to send
him back to the infantry, which is a shame, for he has had one year
of rats, cooties and German infantry. I wish I could help. At dinner I
learn from the major he has told Cattell the bad news. So my boy
isn't at mess. Immediately after dinner, I head for his quarters. Here
is a boy with all the guts in the world, afraid of nothing, which is
shown by the MC ribbon on his chest, about to go back to something of which he has a big belly full — the trenches. And not only
going back to the trenches, but to his family. He feels that not making good at flying is letting them down. All this is too much for me,
so I stick my American neck way out, tell him to slip over to the
mess and have himself a few drinks and a sandwich as he didn't join
us at dinner, and I will take care of our major.

To interrupt the major when he is just starting a bridge game,
where he is about to take three flight commanders into his camp,
isn't done. When I explain I wish he would give me permission to
give Cattell another chance, that I will take him with me as my observer tomorrow as I am up for what promises to be an easy show,
the good major says, "Certainly, Libby, this is very commendable,
go to it and good luck."

When I find my boy, he's half tight, so I join him and we finish
the job. For all I know, this may be the proper treatment for his
trouble. My plan is to take him with me on our show over the line,
regardless of how sick the said stomach is and no matter how bad.
All he has to do, if worse comes to worse, is fold up in the bottom of
our ship, where time will tell. Of all things, he isn't to worry. Having
done my best for the day with the aid of much scotch support, I put
a future flyer to bed without a worry in the world. At least he is
happy for tonight. Tomorrow I am in trouble. I tell my friend what
the score is and assure him it will be an easy flight, that if his stomach gives the old heave-ho, just let her rip, curl up in the bottom un-

til we finish our show. True to his past, the old boy is sick before we have reached any height and disappears from view. And from the rear comes no sound and I know he hasn't fallen out, so concentrate on my flying.

It always happens when least expected. A flight of Albatros and Rolands tie into us, and me without an observer, at least one that is conscious. The fight don't last long. Our leader and flight commander, Captain Collier, knocks one over quick, and I am able to nail one by simply pulling up the nose and pressing the control. The Hun had misjudged and pulled up over me, making himself a sitting duck. Through all of this, I have forgotten my boy and am throwing my plane around through the sky when from someplace, I don't know where, my engine is hit and propeller split. Shutting off my ignition to avoid any chance of fire, I figure I have altitude enough to make our lines if the Hun don't get me on the way down. I know that if it is necessary to outmaneuver the Hun without a motor, my loss of altitude will cause me to land back of their lines in the lap of the infantry.

Our formation is completely broken up but, fortunate for me, Captain Collier sees something is wrong and stays on my tail for an escort. Through all of this, I haven't had any sign of life from my observer. We just clear the trenches and land in between some old reserve trenches without any injury to our plane. Waving to Captain Collier, who is circling overhead, that we are all right, I take a look at my boy, who is a mess but alive, though deathly pale. He climbs out of the plane and flops down on his back, saying, "Oh Mother, oh Mother, I made it." He is game to the core. Soon as his feeling of equilibrium has returned, he shakes my hand and insists on thanking me as though he had received a Christmas present. Babe and I only made one more trip together. Though he was ill, he was able to use the machine gun when we had a brush with the enemy, not too effectively but at least he was conscious, and after our two flights he continued to do better each trip. He was admired by everyone of our squadron and made good his ambition to be an observer with the RFC.

When Babe returned from leave on May 28, 1917, he brought me a large American flag and a beautiful pair of boots for a present.

Major Dore, upon seeing the flag, suggested I use it as a streamer or streamers just to show the Hun that America had a flyer in action. This I did — from May 28 until my return to America. During this period, there were always one or two streamers of an American flag over the German lines. With two streamers on the struts, it denoted leader of our formation. When only one, it denoted second leader. This was not done with any idea of a stunt to be first with anything. It was in the line of duty and at the suggestion of my squadron commander, Major Dore. These streamers were later auctioned off to the highest bidder on a Liberty Loan drive at Carnegie Hall, New York.

Now I know we are in for a big push or battle. Every time we have a big push, we don't seem to go anywhere except to advance maybe a trench or two. I think it is more to keep the Heinie awake, but it also puts a hell of a lot to sleep, permanently, as both sides take a terrific loss. We of the air corps will be very much in the middle of the whole affair. Today we have orders to move our entire squadron close to the lines. When we take off for the morning show, we are told to land at Auchel, which is just eight miles from the trenches.

Our new home is all ready for us, having been built and completed by prisoners of war, even to a tennis court. The hangars are large wooden structures and look like part of the town. We have separate sleeping quarters for each flight, with a special and separate quarters for our commanding officer and a mess hall and lounge, very spacious and nice. This affair is the swankiest I have occupied since joining the RFC. Our landing field is very small, as usual. It's an abandoned farmer's field, where in taking off you have only one side where it is safe to land if your engine conks. The other three sides are slag heaps, two woods and the town of Auchel. With the new pilots we're getting, we can expect the worst. If it doesn't happen we're lucky. Our little Sopwith ships can be landed on a dime after a fellow learns to fly, they are so easy and light to handle. Still, to a green pilot the small field is frightening.

I like our new home very much. This is war at its best, with tennis court and even two saddle horses for the use of our pilots and observers who like to ride. Major Dore has given me charge of these horses and I have been assigned a groom to take care of them. They are a couple of typical English saddle horses with English saddles complete. The war today is looking better. In our new location close to the lines, I am real close to my old motor lorry unit, so, with the major's permission, I take my little plane and land near their headquarters. They are a wonderful bunch of fellows, my old pals Coap, Baldy and Cornell, with whom I was billeted in our early days in France, and I have a grand visit with my old major and his staff. With such a sincere welcome, it was just like coming home. It is good to know that one has such friends. I have signed papers recommending twelve of my old unit to be given a trial as observers on probation. I only hope they will be as lucky as I have been. At least they will have a trial, and the rest is up to them.

In the future, when I have an early show, I shall dress to the teeth. This morning, we are called early. The weather is dull and cold, with a slight mist in the air. My batman says it's sure to rain and we won't have to take off. Still, the ships are out and ready. We have to be there to go if our major says to go. So, though I believe my batman and so does Pritchard, my observer, we hastily put our uniforms over our pajamas. Climbing into our big flying boots, with our helmet and flying coat over our shoulders, we are standing by our ship expecting a washout word from the major. We're all prepared to hit the bed again, when our adjutant tells us to take off.

I'm sure we won't be gone long as it's already misting. With a ceiling less than a thousand feet, we are directly over our lines when the rain begins to pour and my beautiful little rotary gives a cough and is dead. We don't have a thousand feet altitude. We have no time to go anywhere but down. If we must go down, it's better to crash in our trenches than in the Germans', so away we go through rain and lousy visibility. We just miss our back trench and bounce a slight distance, with no harm to our ship. Now it's raining like hell. We take a look at our surroundings. After a hasty once-over, I decide that if we can get some help with our motor, by clearing a short runway and having a couple of strong fellows hold the ship down until I hit the peak engine speed, we can bounce out of this spot and won't have to notify our squadron.

As it is as light as it will ever be and raining hard, we head for an artillery repair unit for help and breakfast. Me, I'm hungry and the odd egg will make the world right. Nuts to the ship, she can't get any wetter than she is now, and these birds are just getting up. Until they have food, I know we won't have any assistance, so to the officers' mess and mess it is. These birds certainly don't live like we do. They think we're crazy, wanting a shot of rum at this time of the day. We get around that nicely by explaining this is just a continuation of the same day, but when they see the pajamas under our uniforms, they are quite sure we're nuts. I still haven't made any attempt to notify our squadron, as this outfit has a mechanic who knows something about rotary engines, and I think we can fly out of our spot with help.

After about an hour and most of their rum, and some breakfast, we're ready to stagger back to our plane and, if their mechanic is any good, make an attempt to take off. I tell my pal and observer, Pritchard, it will be awful close, it might be well for me to try alone and if I make it I will send a tender back for him. "What, and be left here in my pajamas with nothing to drink? Damn, I'm going with you." We hope. Our new mechanic turns the rotary over two or three times, does nothing to it. Suggests we give it a try. So, having one big fat boy sit on the tail and two men hold each wing with instructions to jump clear when I wave, we suck some petrol in our engine. At a signal from our mechanic, I throw on the switch. With no hesitation it starts on our first try. Immediately moving the throttle up to our peak, I wave my boys away. The ship makes a jump, hits the ground once more, then bounces off, misses a sunken road and a shell hole and I start to pull her up when again the rotary quits cold. We hop across another sunken road and under a communication wire and wind up on a flat bank. Again, we and our ship are not hurt.

By this time, my boy Pritchard has had enough. He doesn't think we should repeat. His expression and comments damn near kill me. He is for the time being fed up with the flying corps, so nothing to do but report to the Old Man where we are and why. They are so damned glad to hear from us that nothing is said about reporting late. They were afraid we had gone west for sure.

We can wait for our own mechanic and then fly home, because this spot is much better than our previous landing and, with our own men, it will be a cinch. This I explain to my pal, who isn't interested. He's going back to the squadron in the tender. When I explain that I will be home having a nice highball and lunch before he gets started, he still isn't interested. Twice in one day, he has had enough. He doesn't mind when we are up in the air with the Hun, but flying around in the trenches with boulders and rocks has no appeal for my observer. And while he don't know it, I have had more than enough for one day myself. When our mechanic arrives, he works on our ignition a few minutes and, with the help of his crew and Pritchard holding down my machine until my motor hits its peak, I am bounced off of the ground and into the air and am home in two shakes. I am having a wonderful time in Forty-third. I love the little Sopwith after the big F.E. They are so light and easy to fly and can be landed anyplace, so different from my first days in the RFC.

In our squadron I have a very good friend, an Irish boy by the name of Cathey. His home is close to Dublin, and since our acquaintance he has been after me to visit his home on my first leave. He is a wonderful chap and loves horses. In fact, he is the only one I go riding with, because he knows horses and is always talking about his Irish hunter. My leave of fourteen days is coming up soon, so I have promised to visit his home. At the same time, I'll visit my friend Carruthers' family. Bob Carruthers is an old buddy of mine out of our motor unit and has tried every time I'm on leave to have me visit Ireland. So, on the one coming up I have promised. They have both written their families. I am honored and delighted, only Ireland is so far from London and I just have a few days. Perdie, our adjutant, with the permission of Major Dore, has worked out a deal to save a full day of travel to London. We will be driven to Saint-Omer, our base for condemned planes going back to England. These are planes that are out of service, are not good for active duty but can still fly if handled carefully and are scheduled to be dismantled for their parts. From Saint-Omer to Folkestone, our field is approximately twenty-five miles across the English Channel. By flying one of these ships over in place of taking the boat, we will gain the one day. All we have to do is climb to enough altitude. If our engine quits, we can glide the rest of the distance. The night before our leave is to start, the major has his driver take us to Saint-Omer, where we arrange to take off early in the morning. There is only one trouble — Perdie has half of France for souvenirs, including a German helmet, a couple of Lugers, some shells and everything a fellow shouldn't have, especially with a dud ship such as we are sure to get.

The first plane they gave us was impossible. With our load, I could just get off of the ground, make one circle and land. They gave us another. Transferring all Perdie's junk to our new ship, plus his suitcase tied to the underneath, we again take off. It is a B.E.2e, but I am able to coax it up to one thousand where we should be at least six thousand, ten preferred. We both want to get it over with, so over we go. At the very far edge of Folkestone Air Field, we land with no motor, where a tender picks us up. I register the ship in and leave it where we landed. God is good to some people, why we will never know.

In my little apartment on Jermyn Street, I have made a decision. I don't like to go to Ireland; I don't know anyone there, but I have promised the boys I will visit their families. I should be flattered that they want me to go, but Ireland is so far away and I have such a short time. I know if I go to the Savoy tonight, I'm sunk, so I shall get aboard the first train for Wales and the first boat over, stay two days, then back to London. This will keep my promise and not spoil my entire leave.

Without calling anyone or going to the old familiar places, I catch a night train and next morning am on my way on the boat, headed for Dublin. The place I am going to is Killacon, in Kilkenny near Dublin. Here reside the families of both of my friends. They have no warning of the day I shall arrive, only a letter telling them that I will be over to see them when I go on leave. Going to the Carruthers' address first, I am amazed at the size of the place. It is an enormous castle on magnificent grounds, and I am damn sure I have the wrong address. But what the hell, this is the bunk, so I give the knocker a wallop. After a reasonable wait, the door opens quietly on a very dignified butler with a "Welcome sir, we are expecting you. His Lordship has gone to the city, he will see you at dinner. I will show you to your room, then your lunch will be served. I have a paper with a clipping which concerns you. I shall bring it to your room."

Slowly, I begin to piece the picture together. I am in the home of Lord Wrench, and my friend Bob is one of the family. Lord Wrench is a member of the nobility, and here am I. If my other friend turns out this way, I won't be surprised.

Corbet, the gentleman who let me in, is a very dignified butler, didn't know the Catheys, but he had a newspaper in which Cathey's sisters had inserted a notice with their phone number and street address, just in case I was too dumb to find their home, knowing someone would see the notice and tell me.

I'm beginning to like the place. The country is beautiful. The rolling hills surrounding the village, with the sheep grazing about, is like a lovely picture. Calling Cathey's sisters after lunch, I am told I can't ever go anywhere unless I stay at their house a week. This is embarrassing, as I have promised myself I will return to London after two days. Sure, I can't run out on Bob's family, so I make a date to have dinner with them tomorrow and talk things over. With my usual luck I had stumbled into a haven for tired soldiers. Between the Bob Carruthers family and the Cathey family, I had the time of my life. The Cathey sisters knew everyone and every place. They showed me the famous Phoenix Park in Dublin and the Guinness brewery, which took a full half day to go through. I kissed the Blarney Stone, which is accomplished by hanging with your head down in a sort of well. I divided my time fifty-fifty and just caught the last boat that would get me back to France at the end of my fourteen days.

I have been many places and met many people, but never any place or any people where I had such a sincere welcome as the twelve days I spent in Ireland among the families of my two friends, Carruthers and Cathey. With these folks, things were wonderful, but there was another side to Ireland which I observed, and it shocked me. The Seinfinners* have just raised hell in Dublin, wreck-

---

*In 1916 there was a fierce uprising in Ireland against continued British rule of the country, with rebel attacks on British outposts. This ultimately led, a decade later, to the partition of the Irish Republic from Northern Ireland, which today remains under British control. The Sinn Féin and its Irish Republican Army courted aid from, and cooperated with, the Germans during World War I, in hopes of overthrowing British domination.

ing many places, and have a great hatred for anything British. The feeling is so strong that the Cathey sisters outfitted me with some of their brother's clothes. I didn't put my uniform back on until the day my boat sailed. It is hard to understand thousands of Irish over in France fighting for Britain, while at home in Ireland thousands were fighting their own people. The thing that caused me to take my uniform off and wear mufti was getting into a compartment of a train with two gentlemen. They took one look at me and promptly left for another part of the train. When I told Lord Wrench about this, he told me they were Seinfinners and would not even ride in the same compartment with a British officer, and suggested that I should wear mufti to keep from having trouble, as someone might really insult the uniform and I would take exception and the fight would be on. Lord Wrench did his best to explain the cause to me, but no part of it makes sense, so I can only feel sorry that such a beautiful country should have this kind of trouble. I had only twelve short days in this lovely spot. I could stay forever, but there is a damned war, which by the time I return will be in full swing. With a push at both Arras and Messines, July will be a hell of a month.

Arriving in London on the morning of July 7, 1917, I am due back in France on the morning of the eighth. Going down Piccadilly with a cabbie to pick up a new helmet I had ordered and a few things to take back to my squadron, I notice people hurrying down tube entrances and buildings. Then I begin to hear a wonk, like anti-aircraft guns. About this time, my driver drives up to the curb, bounces out without saying anything and runs into the first store entrance available. By now I realize something unusual is taking place. Climbing out of said cab and looking up, I see twenty-two German Gothas at about ten thousand with their engines throttled back, coming in over London in a gentle glide, getting in a position to drop their bombs. They have come in and around back of London at a high altitude and are now heading for Charing Cross Station, Buckingham Palace and then for home across the Channel. I am more amazed than even my cabbie for these big babies to be over London in broad daylight, where over at the front we can't coax them across our lines. It just didn't seem possible, but real it is, for here come the bombs.

It was all over in a very few minutes. The bombs did some harm; nothing hit the palace. One bomb hit the edge of Charing Cross Station, but not enough to affect the boat train. The main damage was to the civilians' morale at home. The idea of twenty-two big Gothas, in broad daylight, was a shock to everyone. Naturally, everyone wondered where the hell was the RFC. There was not one fast, equipped ship in England to go up after the German boys. All RFC fighters were at the front in France. Every flyer on leave and all the old pilots in England would have given their eye-teeth to have a ship to go after the Gothas, but owing to lack of communication and surprise, all Gothas made it home safe with no interference. The next day, two of the RFC's fast fighter squadrons were ordered back for home defense, so there were no more day raids. The Hun changed their tactics, and sent a Gotha on the hour by the hour most every night. Score one for the Hun with a surprise attack, which the British took in their stride. It was part of the war.

For me, the train will leave for Folkestone on time. The damn Hun didn't even slow my train up, so to the Savoy for a short visit with Jimmy. In the lobby of the Savoy, I see three characters standing in the center, deep in conversation. They are in some kind of uniform. I inquire who and what they are. I am told they are three American officers, one of them a general and the other two lieutenant colonels. The general had a tight fitting jacket which was too short, buttoned up to the top, with the back covering just enough of his rear to leave a baggy seat of pants sticking out. He had shoes and leather puttees, with a round Stetson stiff rimmed hat completing the rest of the gentleman's uniform. The other officers were a little better dressed, as the seat of their pants was not so baggy. These gentlemen wore caps with a short bill, said caps sticking up on top like a lump on a log. What branch of the American Army these gentlemen represented, I didn't know, not being familiar enough with American insignias to tell their unit, but of one thing I was sure: If these were our first official representatives, they were the saddest looking officers I have seen since September of 1914.

Sure, clothes don't make the man. You can fight without any clothes. There are gals who do that every night of their lives, but high ranking officers representing America should look like officers, not something out of a bad dream. Any similarity to Captain Chapman of our embassy? There isn't. He is snappy, not only in uniform, but in his appearance in general. I hope the Americans send Teddy Roosevelt over. He is the only man we have that the British ever talk about or seem to know, and for him they have a lot of respect.

I arrived back at my squadron before any of our fellows knew anything about the raid in London. They were just as much surprised as the civilians of London. What happens now, our RFC headquarters in London will take care of. It isn't often the enemy catch these boys asleep.

I report to Cathey how nice his mother, father and sisters were to me and thank him for the use of his clothes. We have many good talks together, and for some reason he doesn't seem quite up to par. I think he needs a leave, though he isn't due for another month. He seems to have something on his mind. The coming battle, I'm afraid, is worrying him, for he has asked me so many times what he has been doing wrong in his last flights. This is hard for me to answer, as we are in different flights and never in the air at the same time, but I try, though don't seem to help much. He finally asks me if I will see Major Dore and have him transferred to our B Flight. This I can't do but promise to talk to Captain Collier tomorrow, our flight commander, which seems to make him feel better.

There is a rumor that Forty-three are to have Camels, the new Sopwith ship that is just out, as Seventy Squadron has already been equipped with them. They were flying the same Sopwith we have. It may be true. They are a single-seater with plenty of speed and maneuverability, which they say can compare with anything the Hun have. God, I would like just once to have an even break with those boys. B Flight has had two fights in the last three days, where we have accounted for three of Richthofen's best. Captain Collier has two and I have one with a couple probables.

Tonight I was going to visit my old unit, when Major Dore asks me to stay in for dinner. An American general is coming to have dinner with us. God, I hope it isn't the boy of the Savoy Hotel. Dinner is delayed until the American general arrives, which is nine o'clock. This fellow looks like a general. His clothes are snappy, and he is everything in appearance and action that a general should be. It is

Billy Mitchell of the American Flying Corps, only there isn't any flying corps. It is the Signal Corps: Washington is still trying to make
up their mind whether a flying corps is necessary. Here is an American to be proud of. So, being I'm an American, my major asks me to
his quarters with General Mitchell, where we talk until very late, so
late in fact that the general stays the rest of the night with our
squadron, where I am sure he had a wonderful time. Early after
breakfast, I ask him about the three birds in the Savoy Hotel. He
thought they were out of the Engineers Corps but wasn't sure.
They could be any branch. Certainly they bore no resemblance to
America's General Mitchell.*

Today, I have a terribly sad duty to perform. My pal Cathey and
his observer were killed this morning in a dogfight over Messines,
and I must write his family, in whose home I had such a wonderful
time just a few short days before. What does a fellow say and how
does he say it? I almost wish I hadn't gone to Ireland. Words are so
useless in times like this, and certainly writing is one of my very
minor accomplishments. The boy was such a gentleman and his
family are such wonderful people. A fellow should never become
too friendly with his fellow officers; then it isn't quite so tough. I
think back and wonder what would have happened to me had I lost
Price in our first year of war. Life is not funny, it's tragic. Today my
sense of humor is completely gone, so I shall write tomorrow. Today
is not possible. I shall go down to where we have our two horses
quartered and take a ride. It's either fly or ride, so down to the
horses. There is nothing else to do. Tomorrow may be different.

---

*Colonel (and later General) William Mitchell was an aviation pioneer in the
American army who correctly predicted that air power would be a decisive factor in
future wars. His outspokenness on the subject earned him a court-martial and in
1927, after proving that aircraft could sink battleships, he was nevertheless ejected
from the military service.

26

Dinner at the Savoy in London to Honor Our Old Commanding Officer — Back to France, Where We Lose Captain Harold Balfour in a Dogfight

My REGULAR OBSERVER, PRITCHARD, IS ON LEAVE, so I have Flamer Jones. This boy is a regular top observer, also an expert with the Lewis and always full of fight. As far as he can see a Hun, he wants to go after the guy. Hell, if I let him have his way, we would be in a scrap all of the time. He's the damnedest blood-thirsty observer in our squadron. It's good to have this boy; you can always be certain he won't be caught dreaming. On our recent trip over the lines, he knocked off a Halberstadt scout. Stout fellow.

Our Thirteenth Wing is acquiring new squadrons, with new and better ships. Even closer to the lines than we are is a squadron of Sopwith Triplanes with a real group of pilots. These ships are going to give the Hun hell. Wish I could be on one for at least a week. Fifty-six has the improved S.E.5, while Sixty Squadron with Bishop has the new Sopwith Camel. It is still rumored we are also to have Camels. If it only comes off, I will be happy.

Our wing is supposed to have a new squadron with the latest Airco D.H.4. This baby has a three-hundred-seventy-five Eagle Rolls Royce engine with a greater ceiling than any ship on our front, and is faster than any of our enemy planes, especially above ten thousand.

It is certain I'm going to be transferred to some other squadron as a flight commander. My promotion to captain came through today and I have been acting flight commander of C Flight for the past two weeks. I would like the Sopwith Triplane or the D.H.4, although I hate like hell to leave the Forty-third with fellows like our Major Dore, Captain Balfour and my friend Captain Collier of B Flight.

Every day in the RFC, all active combat squadrons receive a communiqué giving a resumé of the previous day's action. We have one pilot in our wing who writes a wicked report. He must be good, but not quite as good as his last report, which I have just read. I will try and recall the report as near as possible.

It seems early in the morning, before anyone else was up, he has his plane wheeled out, goes over to a German air field and routs the Hun out of their beds, strafes the hangars and waits for Mr. Hun to come up. The first two off the ground he knocks off, then gets two more trying to get off. The next two, he chases into a tree and leaves them there like Santa Claus, then destroys two more, so home to breakfast.

God Almighty! Excuse me while I vomit. I have been in this man's flying corps for almost two years. We have waited over the Hun's air field for him to come up and he always does, but it is not that easy. And besides, this particular air field doesn't have a tree anywhere near — of that I am sure. I have been there and have photographs to prove it. It could be the boy was having a nightmare, but nevertheless it came through in a communiqué. This and other reports by the same pilot are the only ones in almost two years that have ever upset me, because all the RFC boys bend over backwards in reporting their victories. They never make this kind of a claim, where there is no chance to confirm. Oh yes, he was in his pajamas and flying coat no less! Quite a stunt. I am still sick at my stomach. If my major will give me permission, I am going to look this air field over and if the damned Hun have grown a tree anywhere within five miles of their field since yesterday, I am going to consider the Hun very unsportsmanlike. Anyway, this guy isn't an Englishman. An Englishman would never write this kind of nonsense, and when I think of Albert Ball and his conservative reports, the kid must be amused or disgusted if he knows about this. Likewise our enemy the good Baron von Richthofen. One thing about the British I shall always like — they never glorify the pilots or observers. They take the attitude that everyone is trying, and they have their own way of showing that you are appreciated.

Mr. Hun is no longer supreme in the air. Our RFC has new ships, and we are giving the Kaiser's boys a going-over they won't forget. For the first time since my joining the RFC, we are flying over the lines when the odds are not all on the enemy's side. Old man Richthofen even has a hard time getting to our poor artillery ships. Sure as hell, when he dives on one of them, some of our scouts are there for protection. So the foxy old baron is having trouble shooting sitting ducks. His party is about over. One of our boys is sure to catch him away and alone. Then we will see how good he really is. God, if Ball was alive with this new triplane, which is a little beauty. I have a leave before transferring to my new squadron and am told that when I return I will at last go on D.H.4s, the finest and latest plane on our front.

Tonight at the Savoy, members of the Forty-third who are in London are giving a dinner to our old commanding officer, Major Sholto-Douglas, who was hurt in the accident with my ship and in-valided home. He is one of the finest gentlemen and commanding officers in the RFC, and it is good to know his recovery is assured. It is a fact that I have never met a commanding officer in this man's army that hasn't been tops. Someone certainly knows how to pick them, which was equally true with my old Canadian motor unit. To find a finer kind of commanding officers than we had — Major Red Harris, Captain Parmalee, Captain McKinnon and Lieutenant El-lard — just couldn't be done. They are all tops for my money.

I haven't enjoyed leave this time as usual, although I have done the same things and visited my old friends. Stayed out to Captain Price's home for a weekend. Am restless and anxious to get back to my new squadron, where we will see what I can do with my new ship. For once I will have an even break with the enemy.

Back to Forty-third Squadron where I am to fly with C Flight until Twenty-fifth Squadron arrives on our air field, which they are to share with Forty-third. This is good news, for I won't be far away from my old crowd — what there is left of them, as today in a low strafing flight on the roads over Hun lines and back of Messines we lost one of our best and finest flyers, Captain Harold Balfour, commander of A Flight. We were busy with a low flying enemy, and I didn't see what happened. God, I hope he was able to land back away from the infantry. It's hell if you don't. If Boelcke was alive, we would hear soon. With this crowd of Richthofen's, I don't know. Balfour is the son of Lord Balfour, former prime minister of England and also our former commanding officer just as Sholto-Douglas is son of Lord Douglas. Both are awfully stout fellows, which I have found is characteristic of this type of Englishman. They ask no favors, but take the war in their stride regardless of who they may be in civilian life.*

I have been given credit for two Huns in the last two days, both confirmed, nothing to compare with a certain pilot in our wing. He is still raising hell on paper. No one seems to see him do it, but if his arm holds out he will pass Ball's record, which seems to be the general idea. My new squadron arrived today under command of Major Guest, and I am moving across the field to my new quarters. Twenty-fifth will have an officers' mess, but our sleeping quarters will be billeted with the town folks of Auchel. Our hangars are practically in the town. I am flight commander of B Flight, and my new ship is a beauty. It has the Eagle Rolls Royce three-hundred-seventy-five-horse engine and is a much longer and heavier plane than my Sopwith. Also, much more speed and climb. It has only one serious drawback: the pilot and observer are too far apart to communicate when in action.

In command of A Flight is an old friend of mine, Captain James

*Libby's prayers were ultimately answered. Balfour, whose father, Arthur, Lord Balfour, drew up the declaration guaranteeing Jews a homeland in Palestine, survived his crash but was made a prisoner by the Germans. Harold Balfour entered politics after the war and won a seat in Parliament. He was later given a lordship himself, and died in 1988.

Fitz-Morris. He is a top pilot with plenty of guts and a fine record and has been decorated with the Military Cross. Through this excellent pilot I have a complete run-down on the D.H.4. As I have never flown one, I take to the air for a test and to get the feel of this baby, also to try a landing or two. While the Sopwith could be landed anywhere, this ship will be different. It is heavier and has a stationary motor, so will land faster, and with our small field there will be no room to spare.

I found the D.H. easy to handle. The Rolls gave all the power needed, was terrific in a climb and to my surprise landed nicely, much better than I anticipated. Everything considered, it was a vast improvement over any ship that I had ever flown. Its performance gives a fellow a world of confidence, and I was very anxious to try it out on any of Mr. Richthofen's boys. Things would be real good if I had Pritchard or Jones, my old observers, but I'll have to train one, as the crop Twenty-fifth have are all new, so here we go again. Good ship with a green observer, but with the Vickers machine gun operating under my control I felt we wouldn't do too bad.

It is real swell being on the same air field with my old squadron. I can go over to dinner anytime and have my good friends Major Dore and Captain Collier to consult with. It is a real fine arrangement.

To remedy the problem of the D.H.'s pilot and observer being so far apart, we have rigged up a phone connection through a rubber hose. If both pilot and observer just sit still and talk, everything works, but in action the observer always pulls his connection loose, which gives the pilot no way of talking to him in an emergency. I have found one other very bad thing about my new ship. In the observer's cockpit is a rudder and a place to insert a stick control, which is fastened on the side with clips. The theory is that if the pilot is done in, the observer, from his position, can insert the stick control and with the rudder fly the ship home or at least land. This is a dream that won't work in reality, for the observers we have are all green and have one tough time just observing. They are all good boys but haven't had experience. The thing I object to is the open rudder, where anything could fall in front of the rudder bar and prevent the pilot from controlling the ship from his front position.

My feeling about the open rudder is proven right, and that defect almost costs me my life as well as my observer. Forty-third has asked me over to dinner. After dinner Captain Collier, who is the only one of the old timers left except our major, tells me they are going on a nine o'clock show of road strafing well back of the German lines. He asks me on my way back from Hun Land, where my flight is going on a photographic mission, if I will drop down and give them some cover, if there are any Huns over them. This I agree to do, so next morning I give my other five pilots orders that on our way back, when I fire a red light, we will all dive down and stay just above my old flight and escort them home.

We make our trip over at fifteen thousand feet with no fight or excitement. When we are back in the place I have agreed to join my old flight, I see Huns everywhere. Firing the red light, I drop down on a Hun's tail. I am giving him the works with my front gun when a Hun dives on us from the rear. My observer empties his Lewis drum and registers a beautiful miss. So I flip the D.H. over to take a crack at Mr. Hun, when my rudder sticks. All I can do is turn one way, while the air is alive with Huns. . . . I continue to fight the big ship, sideslipping toward our line at every available opportunity. I try everything I can to attract my observer's attention, with no success. Throttling back as far as possible, I release my body belt, turn loose of all controls, climb up in my seat and reach back, hitting my observer a hell of a crack on the head. I yell "rudder" and point. The surprised expression which passes over his face is enough. He reaches down and pulls from in front of the rudder bar the empty drum he had removed from the Lewis to change for a full drum. We are now in a turn at about three hundred feet and well back of the German lines. With my rudder free, I make no attempt to climb but start for home, more angry than I have ever been since joining the RFC. We cross the trenches at about two hundred feet, going like hell until I reach our squadron.

The thing that almost did us both in was so unnecessary, so useless and only took up space in the ship. From this experience, three-ply was fastened over every rudder bar in all of our ships so absolutely nothing could interfere with the control of the rudder in the observer's seat. In all new ships afterward I understand this control was left out of the observer's department.

What happened to my Hun, I didn't know. I had been too busy trying to get out of my trouble and I suppose the Huns thought I was gone for keeps. All I was doing was going around and around, sideslipping and losing altitude, so they evidently gave me up as a victim. Nothing but my guardian angel and my luck saved our bacon. Captain Collier, who saw the whole affair, confirmed my one Hun, which doesn't mean a damn. I am so glad we were able to get home all in one piece. Good old Collier, he sees everything.

I have for the past two days had the D.H. up to twenty-two thousand five hundred with a full war load, which includes machine guns, observer, petrol and ammunition. This is higher than the S.E.5, Sopwith or any of our ships go. The D.H. has more altitude and is faster above fifteen thousand than any of our ships, or our enemy's. We have been up for the purpose of catching the one ship the Germans send over on reconnaissance for a fast circle at about twenty thousand feet. The first day we missed him entirely. The second day we caught him on his way coming out of our territory. I was very anxious to get at least one Hun on our side of the lines. We could locate him as our anti-aircraft was throwing up some stuff in his general direction. When his observer evidently spotted us, the old boy began to lose altitude toward a bunch of clouds in the direction of his own lines. Doing our best, we were only able to take a poke at him with a burst from the front gun just as he hit the cloud. Hopping over and past the clouds, hoping to get a real chance when he came out, we lost him completely. All that effort wasted. Such a wonderful chance and I have to miss. Maybe he will choke to death in the clouds. Anyway, we don't get him, so home to our adjutant who gives us each a shot of oxygen, which together with a couple of scotch and sodas clears up the old head. We are as good as new. Tomorrow we try again.

My friend Captain Morris caught a couple of Mr. Richthofen's circus and nailed them both quick. Mr. Richthofen will have a great deal of respect for our D.H.4 before very long, as our boys are just beginning to learn how good a ship we have. If our boys in Forty-third could only have Camels, this Thirteenth Wing would be something to write home about.

I have just landed from an early show when I am met by General Shephard from our wing and given orders to report to RFC General Headquarters, London, for transportation to America. This is a big surprise and something I have not asked for or expected, for I am quite happy where I am and have no desire to go to the American service, although I would like to see my family. I ask the general if it is imperative if I don't want to go. He says certainly not, but I will have to report to London, where I can then decide. Going over to see Major Dore to bid him goodbye and get his advice, I find it was General Mitchell who had the adjutant's office apply for my transfer to the Americans through military channels. I ask him what he thinks about my going. He says General Mitchell told him that America had no pilots with experience, nor did they have any planes that were worth a damn, that they had to start from scratch, also that Mitchell told him that I would be back with one of the first squadrons and we would fly some of the RFC's best planes. "After all, Libby, this will be a big help to us and to America, because one of the things they need the most is experience and this you have, both as observer and pilot. You have had a lot of war. The change might be good for you. I would like to see you back in command of a squadron of fresh pilots. You know our boys are tired, especially the old timers. Some new fresh pilots would be a big help."

Thanking my friend for his kind advice and saying goodbye to all my other friends in Forty-third, I prepare to depart for Boulogne, when I am stopped by my good friend Captain Morris and several of the sergeants and mechanics, who present me with three propeller canes and a new flying coat with a beaver collar. Where they got the coat in so short a time, I don't know. It must have been one Captain Morris had in reserve and donated. With the cheers and good wishes, I head for Boulogne in a blue and unhappy mood, when I should have been gay and glad just to be out of the war for at least a while. Still, when you live with fellows through some of the shows we had been through, you become attached to the men who go with you, to the end of time.

For the first time in my days at the front, I am in no hurry to reach London. The train to Boulogne is plenty fast, though, as is the boat to Folkestone, likewise the train from Folkestone to London. If I missed any connections, it would be okay by me. I have plenty of time. There is no rush to make a decision before I learn all of the facts. To have lived with and fought with four combat squadrons on our Western Front for the past two years has made an impression which will go with me always, not only the officers, but the grand crews of every squadron. Without these boys, there would be no flying. It is these fellows, the sergeants, corporals, enlisted men, every member of the ground crew that work to see that every plane leaves the ground in perfect condition and ready for battle. They carry a great responsibility. One little slip or mistake by your ground crew would be curtains for a ship, the pilot and observer. While they don't fly, these boys feel and suffer when their ship and crew "go west." I have seen them standing out on the edge of our landing field, scanning the skies, hoping against hope that by some chance they will see their ship returning long after the time has passed when their pilot should be home. I shall never forget the day, September 17, 1916, in Eleven Squadron, when all the ground crew of C Flight were standing in front of their empty hangars, knowing that their entire flight had "gone west." The expression on the faces of these chaps was grief without tears, and was one of the saddest sights during my many months with Eleven. One sergeant said, "Sir, it don't seem possible. We had such fine officers with perfect ships, and they only left four hours ago. To lose them all in one flight is hell." All the ground crew of Eleven's C Flight could do was to wait for six new planes and twelve new officers. To the men of our ground crews of the RFC, who gave so much and receive so little recognition, were it in my power I would create a medal for them similar to the Distinguished Service Order (DSO) for officers. To these fellows, every combat pilot owes his life — period.

For the first time, the boat trip across the channel was a pip. The old boat rocked and heaved, and many people heaved with it. Whether this was a bad omen I don't know, but if this short seventeen miles should prove a sample of what's in store for me if I decide to return to America, it won't be fun. While I was not ill, I was damned pleased when this short trip was over. The little old Channel could be real rough, so I had been told. Now I know.

My first night in my apartment on Jermyn Street I survey my loot. I have canes presented me by my ground crew of Twenty-fifth

Squadron, plus a beautiful new flying coat. My old flying coat, which has been with me in every flight since joining Eleven Squadron, is so saturated with castor oil from my rotary engine it can stand alone. My old coat I shall always keep; my new one is something for the future. I have the American flag streamers, along with Lee White's "Old Bill," which has been constantly with me as my mascot. Both Old Bill and the streamers show much oil and exposure to the elements, but both are priceless to me. I have several uniforms, almost new, which I suppose will have to go if I expect an officer's commission in the American Army. While I am doing this, my phone rings and I have Norman H. Read on the wire. He has been trying to reach me every day for a week. He, too, has been reassigned to America and is waiting to see what my decision is before making up his mind. Read has been up to our old RFC headquarters, where he found out I was coming back from the front, so he waited for me. We agree to meet the next day at RFC headquarters, then make our decision for better or worse.

27

Two Americans Who Lost Their Citizenship Return to America at General Mitchell's Recommendation

I<small>T IS</small> S<small>EPTEMBER</small> 14, 1917. America has supposedly been in the war since April. Up to now we haven't seen or heard anything, except that in place of Teddy Roosevelt they have a guy in Paris who I understand has the proper political influence to head the American Army and is likewise a West Pointer, which is mandatory for any appointment of this magnitude. I wonder what happened to the guy who was going to rescue the British from the trenches by Christmas? I'm afraid the British didn't give him a hearing. I don't know what he had — it might have been boots with magic springs, as I understand he was an inventor. It might have been well to give the fellow a hearing. We might not have needed the Paris contingent. What the hell they are doing, I don't know. They haven't made any impression on the British Western Front in five months, of this I am sure.

Read and I have talked with the senior commanding officer of the RFC and find that, in applying to the American adjutant general for our transfer, General Mitchell requested an increase of one rank over our British rating, which means that if we agree, we are scheduled to be majors as of September fifteenth by sending a cable of acceptance to the Adjutant General Office, Washington, D.C. Read is of the opinion that we should stay where we are, that if we accept we'll be sorry. But it just doesn't seem right when your own country requests your services, not responding. This we argue about and finally decide to send the cable, which has been prepared for us at headquarters. As Read says, we can take the trip over and if we don't like it, have a vacation. We can come back home to our old RFC anytime. Having sent our cable, we arrange our transportation to New York on the *Adriatic*, which will be leaving Liverpool in about thirty days. The more time passes, the more I'm sure we've made a big mistake. The fighting is over here. To go over and come back don't make sense unless they have a job of training flyers, which I don't want any part of. We are better here. The only Americans that are in force is the navy. They are snappy in their appearance and look like fighting men should, with none of the drab or dejected appearance of the three army officers of the Savoy Hotel.

Going to the embassy to see my friends and to secure a passport, I am told, in no uncertain terms, what a mistake I have made. They tell me the army is mired so deep in politics that I will be sick at my stomach my first day. Here I learn for sure that what General Mitchell told Major Dore was correct — America had no flying corps, just an outfit known as the Signal Corps — and that General Mitchell was the only outstanding officer who knew anything about flying. Unfortunately, he would be so handicapped by politics and jealousy that Read and I would find Washington impossible. Ambassador Page recommends that we go instead to the Navy Flying Corps and will write a letter to Undersecretary of the Navy Franklin Roosevelt if we will agree to join that service. I explain we have cabled our acceptance of a commission, which he laughs off, saying it means nothing. When we get over, they will ask us to repatriate, swearing allegiance to our own country before we can draw pay as an American officer, so we will be at liberty to do as we please. His recommendation is join the Navy Flying Corps. As Admiral Simms is to be at the embassy with some of his staff for lunch, I receive an invitation to lunch, where I meet a real sharp crowd, some fellows in uniform a fellow American can be proud of.

I find old Read at our favorite spot, the Savoy, and give him all the information which Ambassador Page has told me, together with his recommendation. With all this, we decide to take the boat as per schedule and take our chances. We are two dumb Americans who just can't believe that our country is so badly controlled by a political few.

We have two weeks before the boat sails. I am fed up with inactivity, so go to RFC headquarters and request an assignment to some home defense squadron while waiting. Our senior officer explains that if he gives me such an assignment and I get bumped off, he is in trouble, because I am now supposedly an American officer, regardless of my British uniform, which I am not going to give up until the last minute. The old boy finally breaks down after much phoning and delay, giving me orders to report to a night-flying Camel squadron. The Hun Gotha is now coming over at night, one at a time, four or five times a night. Wishing me good luck, he sends me on my way with the warning "Don't get bumped off, just for my sake, or we're all in trouble." I report to a squadron under the command of Major Green, one of the really stout pilots of the D.H.2 pushers of 1916, with some forty enemies to his credit.

With five exciting nights on Camels, I am transferred to Northolt, where some Americans have reported to Thirty-fifth Bristol fighter squadron for training as mechanics, not flyers. I found the Bristol fighter the best ship I had ever flown. This was the improved plane soon to go to France. It was powered by the famous Rolls Royce, was short like a Spad scout, with observer and pilot close together and with the usual Vickers and Lewis machine guns. It was a deadly ship in the hands of two good flyers. If I could have this ship in action, just once, it would be a treat. Especially with one of my old observers, Pritchard or Flamer Jones.

Every day I take some of the Americans up for a ride and to see London from the skies, including my old pal Coapman. No difference where I may be, Old Coap shows up sooner or later, whenever it suits his fancy. He located me through the RFC, as he is in England to take his training as a pilot. No observing for him. Somehow he bypassed the observer's period and is going direct for his pilot's wings. He is one of the many from my old motor unit for whom I signed papers requesting they be given a commission in the RFC. Meeting Coap in London, I invite him out to Northolt for a ride and squadron dinner. The guy is still a private. I take him up over London and give him the works with a few rolls, loops and a spin, which he takes in his stride like I knew he would.

After landing, we go to my quarters, where I doll the guy up in one of my best captain's uniforms, with pilot's wings and Military Cross ribbon complete, then to the mess where I introduce him as my brother. To the amazement of no one, they all believe it, except the commanding officer from who I had asked permission to do the stunt, otherwise the going might have become rough if he had started to question us too much.

I am spending my last two days in London visiting friends before leaving for America. I should be awfully bucked up and happy, which isn't the way I feel. I meet my old friend Bogart from Eleven Squadron, who tries to cheer me up, but I have a feeling that is difficult to describe. It seems like I am leaving my best friends, which I am, as there is no one in America as close to me as the fellows in France and the folks in London, except my own family. The American embassy is like home, thanks to Ambassador Page and Captain Chapman. Lee White and Clay Smith have a new show at the Strand. There is a new girls show at the Gaiety. Beatrice Lillie is all the rage, George Robie is going strong. I wonder if I shall ever see them again? I shall have dinner tonight with my favorite tailor and Jimmy, where we shall just spend a quiet evening like good friends should, and tomorrow I shall say goodbye to my old pal Captain Price, where we will have a quiet lunch. All these friends I am leaving, for what I don't know. Only time will tell, but for better or worse Read and I are on our way tomorrow evening for Liverpool where the *Adriatic* will be waiting. It will be goodbye to London and all my friends who have been so kind to me. I hope fate is good and I return soon.

Catching our train for Liverpool, we climb in a compartment, where we meet one of the fellows that joined my old Canadian unit in Calgary, Alberta, September 2, 1914 — Lieutenant Bob Roberts. He had joined the RFC after I did and got his observer's wing, then he was hurt. Was on his way back to Canada, having been discharged and returning home. We traveled to Liverpool together, where he left for Canada while Read and I sailed for New York.

Our trip back was restful and delightful. The big boat only had forty-five first class passengers. We were loaded and waited twenty-four hours for a clearance from the navy. On the thirteenth of October, 1917, we sailed for New York, without escort but with the big ship running a zigzag course the first forty-eight hours. Read and I were seated at the purser's table where we had every attention possible. We both wore mufti the entire trip until our last night, when everyone dressed for dinner and a swell time was enjoyed by all. And on the twenty-second of October we landed in New York, the home of the free and the brave. That's what they taught me in school. The customs people boarded the boat before we landed, and we were given clearance without the usual customs inspection, as Read and I were the only officers on the ship. Upon landing, we took a taxi for the Waldorf Astoria, where I immediately phoned one of my relatives who I had not seen since my boyhood days in Massachusetts. From this cousin I learn that I have lost Father. He passed away in his sleep a few days before I left England. This is my number one blow upon landing back in America. Others may follow, but they can't compare with this jolt.

I had high hopes of going home for a couple of weeks. Now, I can't. It wouldn't be the same, even to see my brother and all our wonderful friends in the little town in the valley of the Platte River where, when a friend returns home, he is welcomed like royalty and a stranger is made to feel he has found a home for life.

Read goes to the Yale Club for lunch and I join my cousin for the Bankers' Club, where I promise to spend the weekend at his home on Long Island. So Read and I split for the weekend, agreeing to leave for Washington early Monday morning. All my relatives are thrilled about helping win the war, although none of them are in uniform. Everyone is sure that America can win the war single-handed. The fact that France and England have been fighting like hell for three years hasn't made any impression on the people I have met. Ninety-nine out of every hundred don't know the uniform I am wearing. If anyone does recognize that I have been overseas, immediately you are supposed to go into a song and dance about the great German atrocities, where women have been crucified and their breast cut off and all this kind of rot. If you explain there has been no such thing, that someone has been giving them a lot of bull, you are at once considered a person who has seen no action, or a little loose upstairs. They all want to hear horrible things. Certainly, the war is no picnic, but who the hell wants to talk about war all of the time, just to satisfy curious people? No one seems to know or care that you would like to be left alone to relax. The small-town talk gives me a pain in my rear. I am wondering where I will go after Washington and how soon will I be able to go back to the front. If they have no pilots, the powers who are might let me take a squadron over to train in England, where everyone knows the ropes. This would be faster and better. Monday will tell.

Have arrived in Washington, which has the appearance of a convention. All the hotels are full to the hilt. Read and I have just been turned down at the Mayflower, when I think of my friend Raymond Price. Not expecting any results, I ask the clerk if Mr. Raymond Price means anything to him. The results are amazing: "Certainly, sir." Instead of being cold as a stepmother's breast, the fellow warms up with the information that if Mr. Price would vouch for us, he might find a room in the great village. This is a good start. Finding out from our very new friend, the clerk, where to reach Mr. Price, we are immediately out of trouble with a fine double room and twin beds and a very courteous and changed clerk. In less than an hour Mr. Price puts in his appearance at our hotel. He gives us a grand greeting, something we appreciate as this is the kind of welcome we were used to overseas. Unhappily, we learn from Mr. Price the same things Ambassador Page told us in London. It seems there is no air corps, just a signal corps, because the big boys in power think a flying corps is not too necessary. Price is very upset with the situation here and is one of the dollar-a-year men, spending his own money trying to help his country. To him, we have a great feeling of gratitude. At least we have one man on our side.

Tuesday morning we report to three different places before we find anyone who knows anything about us. So we are finally in front of the great man. He is very much at ease when we appear. He has his feet on the desk, with his hands clasped back of his head, evidently perfectly satisfied with his own greatness. He is undoubtedly delighted to see us, for he never moves out of his chair or gives us a handshake or any kind of pleasant greeting such as was always the custom with any major or squadron commanding officer of the RFC. Here we are, both captains reporting to our own country at the request of the adjutant general's office to a major who hasn't the decency to get off his dead behind and, whether he likes it or not, show some courtesy. We didn't expect him to kiss our bottom, just a small welcome, which we sure as hell rated.

This important individual jumped into his act. No mention of General Mitchell, who was in France. No questions about what ship we had been flying. He began first by telling us we would have to take the oath of allegiance to America, then to get out of our British uniforms and into American uniforms like he was wearing. This was a tight fitting tunic, buttoned to the top, with riding pants, boots and spurs. The wings he wore, we could not wear. In fact, we could not wear any wings until we took an old Jenny, a Curtiss JN-4, up to five thousand and made a dead-stick landing. He explained there were only three senior military aviators in America. To be a senior military aviator, you had to be granted this great honor by Congress. The best we could hope for would be junior military aviator, which was the lowest. They had a military aviator above the junior, but certainly this was not for us.

All this without Read or me saying a word. Why we didn't kill the gentleman, I'll never know, except I was too stunned. It just didn't seem possible. But Read comes to life with a bang and, in a language this bird can understand, tells him to shove the wings, the Jenny and his damn commission where it will do the most good. He is going to Massachusetts for a rest, and to Maine for a hunting trip, then back to the RFC, "and I am going to try to take Libby with me." Read also tells him, "Your treatment of us today is unbelievable. Libby has had two years of RFC in four fighting squadrons, has more hours in the air and more enemy ships to his credit than any American. All of this you must know. He is the only American with a real record and recommended by Billy Mitchell." At the name of Billy Mitchell there is a look in this fellow's eyes which doesn't speak well for General Mitchell, who we both like and respect. As we start out, the great man asks in a somewhat less pompous voice, "What about you, Libby?" I reply that I will make up my mind later. With this, the great man tells me where to report for orders and to become a citizen again, with the information if we don't we will be court-martialed.

I am sick all over. Read doesn't give a damn, but I do. My old friends in the RFC are expecting much of me, and surely the American military can't all be like this major. And there is my New York and Boston family, to say nothing of my brother. Also there is General Mitchell, who outranks this bird. And my good friend, Raymond Price, who I shall see at lunch. The jealousy and greed are all that I was told in London, only more so. I would be ashamed to go back to the RFC and let them know how lousy we have been treated by our own country. We lunch with Mr. Price, who is deeply hurt over our reception, although he knows what it's all about. When we tell him who our man is, Price explains that this fellow is a West Pointer and General Mitchell isn't. Only Mitchell is a keen flyer who has the desire to have a real flying corps, but jealousy from many sources is slowing up all progress, as they are assigning all West Pointers to command the flying branch of the Signal Corps wherever they can. While these fellows can't fly — they are out of infantry, cavalry and artillery — they're in command of what few flyers are available. That we should have to take a test before wearing wings, after flying everything the British had, is, as he indignantly expresses it, the act of an overly ambitious egotist.

What to do and how is my problem. Certainly I want to get out of Washington, which should be easy after our reception this morning. The sourpuss major will see to that. Just what an aviator does with spurs is one for the books. I was raised with a pair of spurs, but wouldn't the RFC boys laugh to see me with boots and spurs? Climbing into a plane, I'll bet old sourpuss can't fly a good British plane even with spurs and a saddle. What a hell of a ragtag outfit I got myself into — after all the good advice I had in London. God, I'm dumb! And this repatriation is a royal pain in the tail. You would think that with America in the war, this kind of bunk wouldn't be necessary, especially where a fellow's family was over here with the Indians where my great-great-great-grandfather chased Pocahontas' great-great-great-grandma over the hill every night. Now, with America in the war, I must swear allegiance to my own country.

The major isn't the only one that's nuts. I have made the big decision. After talking to some of my family, I have again become an American citizen and have my orders to report to Toronto, Canada, to Twenty-second Squadron, which is supposed to be in training with the Canadians. It has been a long circle. I left Toronto in 1915 for England, via Halifax, and here I am receiving orders to report to some American squadron in Toronto. Read is leaving for his home in Massachusetts tonight. He has been waiting, hoping I would go with him. God knows I would like to, but it doesn't seem the thing to do, so I shall try to make the best of a big mistake.

Bid farewell to my two real friends, Mr. Price and Read, and I am off for Toronto, which to say the least is away from Washington where a politician will give you anything the hen laid, except the egg. These politicians are worse than a pimp. A pimp only takes a gal's dough. These boys will take everybody's dough. They damned near own our country. My guess is, no politician will get hurt in this or any other war. Speaking of taking your dough, when Read and I asked for our bill at the Hotel Mayflower, we were told no statement. This place where we had difficulty being admitted was very gracious as long as there was a man like Raymond B. Price to pay the check. Life is funny. There is certainly a difference between people. Any resemblance between Mr . Price and our beloved major? There ain't.

The trip to Toronto is slow and uncomfortable. The government has taken over all railroads and is operating them, so naturally every train in America is running late and the service is getting worse. Even the hobos won't ride them. Walking is safer.

Here in Toronto, I feel very different than in Washington. There are RFC boys everywhere, many back on leave, who know what war is all about. I am still wearing my RFC uniform and am in no hurry to take it off, even if it did seem to upset the senior military aviator (with nothing to aviate). The only difference, I am now an American, by the act of oath, in a British uniform, and it's a cinch they don't care if I remain in their uniform for the rest of the war. Tonight I am going on an old fashioned binge with some of the RFC crowd, as tomorrow is soon enough to look over my new American squadron. Three years ago I was stationed in Toronto's Exposition

Park as a full fledged private, without a care in the world. I still don't have any worry, except the change from something to nothing.

For the past two months I have been having a great deal of pain in my back and find it very difficult after three or four hours of flying to get circulation back to normal. Our good squadron doctor in France said I was not playing enough tennis and horseback riding. Both of these are my favorite pastimes but only succeed in causing a great deal more pain, so I am convinced it isn't exercise that I need. Today the pain is worse, and I have trouble getting out of bed. Maybe I am just getting old. I have just passed my twenty-fifth birthday. Crippled old man that I am, I call a cab to take me out to the air field and report my presence to whoever is the colonel commanding. Washington didn't seem to know. I am expecting the worst. True, I'm not disappointed. When we reach the Canadian headquarters and make my mission known, the Canadian colonel patiently explains that the squadron which I have traveled from Washington to Toronto to join has been in Texas for the past two weeks. I am shown a letter to Washington addressed to the Signal Corps, advising of their departure. I inquire about the personnel of Twenty-second, to see if there are any trained pilots. I am assured there are no pilots, just a few men for training, and that the squadron is supposed to be completed and trained in Texas where America has built a new air field close to Fort Worth.

Back to my hotel. After a few highballs to relieve my disposition and back, I wire Washington, telling them where their lost squadron is and requesting orders and two weeks leave to visit my darling Aunt Jo in Boston. Next day, I receive my orders to report to Hicks Field in Texas after my two weeks leave, which makes for a long train ride across the U.S.A. With the trains as they are, time means nothing. Arriving in New York, I have decided to order two American uniforms, as I have seven beautiful RFC outfits complete. I don't intend to throw them away, even if I just keep them with the hope that the American uniform may be made more comfortable and my British uniforms may be useful.

28

Two Weeks with My Family in Boston — Then Texas, Where Space Began — A Hospital That Was a Morgue

REMEMBERING MY EXPERIENCE WITH MY FIRST UNIFORMS in London, I make no mistake here. I inquire if any money is available from the government for the first uniforms. There is not only no money for uniforms, there is no money to drink to anyone's health either. Here a fellow is strictly on his own. This is possibly the reason for the three motley looking officers in the Savoy Hotel lobby in London.

Finding a tailor to make the two uniforms, which I shall pick up on my return en route to Texas, I am measured and on my way. Or I think that I'm on my way. The gentleman informs me very firmly no money, no cuttie, just like London only so different. This fellow wouldn't trust his own mother. So, if I want the uniforms, I have to fork over the cash. Boy, I now know that this is home sweet home, and my honeymoon in this man's outfit is going to be a pip. To get any money out of the army, you have to fill out a voucher with a lot of red tape and find an American paymaster someplace to cash it, on or after the first of the month. So different from my past three years, where everything on the ground they made easy for you. All that is required is your devotion to your job, and the world was yours. Paying my newfound tailor, I am off for Boston to spend two weeks with the grandest female I have ever known. With her, I knew there would be no pressure. If I wanted to talk, swell, if I didn't — that would be good too. So, I am in higher spirit than any time since the boat landed in New York.

Catching the early morning train out of Boston for Marshfield Center, I'm expecting no one to meet me at the station, so I am greatly surprised by a very attractive young lady with a sports car who informs me that she is my cousin. Aunt Jo has insisted I would be on the morning train, although she received no word from me or anyone. My cousin Maud, who I was meeting for the first time, was sure I must have wired, or otherwise how would she know? When I explain to my new cousin that our dear aunt is clairvoyant, she very spiritedly says to hell with that — tell me about the war.

Here we go again! I have just met the gal. How I wish that I could paint her a real horror picture about women and children hanging by their heels, but for this I'm a total loss. No one is going to believe I have been in the war. I can talk specific enough, but they all want the gory kind. My war wasn't for them. We only were killed, not butchered. I can tell about the Gurkhas, only there were no women in the trenches. There must be women or no dice, it just wasn't war. This is due to the damn lecture agencies, who are getting financially fat sending out lecturers with a tailor-made story to the women's clubs, all at a fancy price. They give the girls a picture of rape and mayhem that thrills them to the quick. An honest soldier doesn't have a chance with these birds. They are the biggest bunch of liars alive and getting real dough, food and drink for one hour of bunk. Home with my charming aunt, I am protected from our mutual relatives and curiosity seekers where I can lounge around in mufti and just rest and give the old back a chance to improve. Tonight, Cousin Maud is entertaining. There will be many young people, and I am supposed to be the honored guest. So Aunt Jo and I shall attend in all our glory.

At this dinner, I outdid myself socially. Surrounded by the elite of young socialites, I was going strong, on about my sixth cocktail before dinner, when some young thing asked if I knew Guy Empey. Her inquiry fell on deaf ears — it just didn't register. I had never heard of the guy. It seems he was in the British Army somewhere, someplace, and was discharged, so returned to America where some fast promoter grabs the boy and they write and publish a book called

Over the Top. This book made Empey the greatest hero since Paul Revere. He was the answer to a maiden's dream, and I, poor sap, had never heard of him. It was impossible; evidently I hadn't been in a fighting unit or I was a rank four-flusher. My prestige, my standing at the small gathering, especially with the girls, took a decided tumble.

It was after dinner and how many drinks later that they asked me to tell of some of my experiences overseas. They have me on the spot. When I inquire whether they have ever heard of the great Baron von Richthofen, the boys have, the girls slightly, so I launch forth and give the great baron his biggest buildup, how he is the hero of all Germany with a castle in every village. But best of all, he and I are close personal friends, that every other Wednesday I land near a woods by Arras, where we have lunch with three of his pet ladies, then he escorts me back across my lines toward home. In fact, his sister and I rendezvous every other night in a woods close by and are considering naming our first child Rick, after the great man.

My girl audience are eating it up. What the hell? the males are thinking. I don't give a damn, when Aunt Jo takes me home. Home sweet home, where I have breakfast in bed with fresh custard pie for dessert and my darling aunt laughs until tears run down her cheeks. When she inquires if I know Guy Empey, I don't think that my beautiful cousin has quite forgiven me, although she did inquire of our aunt if she thought it was true. The baron has my apologies. I don't know if the old boy has a sister, but hell, she wouldn't mind. It was all in clean fun and an overdose of scotch. My prestige must have hit a new high, for we have been invited every day to a lunch or dinner, which Aunt Jo has declined with one exception. My darling has been worried about my back, which is constantly paining me, so we only go out once to an old friend of the family, where I am not asked to perform. It is sufficient that we are all together. This is friendship, which few appreciate or understand.

Two weeks of the happiest time of my life since my schooldays with Aunt Jo have passed, and it's back to the war for me, or at least away to Texas. What happens there is for the future. Saying goodbye is always tough for me, so we agree to say goodbye or farewell, which Aunt Jo prefers, at home.

My cousin drives me to the station, whispering in my ear, "Darling, write a book and tell them about Empey and Richthofen." I am away and back in circulation. Damn the war, Empey and the baron included. I have just begun to rest. Now it is over.

My good tailor has completed one uniform and it looks like something the cat drug in, after my RFC uniforms. The other uniform he wants to send to Texas. This boy is a real one. He has had two weeks to play with my money and make one uniform, so I give him twenty-four hours to complete the other. It will make me twenty-four hours late reporting to Texas. The train is sure to be twenty-four hours later, so with luck the war may be over before I reach the great state, and it is a safe bet whoever is in command in Texas doesn't know I am alive. Both my predictions are correct. After a miserable trip made up of mostly stops and starts, the old train pulls into Fort Worth twenty-six hours late, and Colonel David Roscoe, commanding the aviation section of the Signal Corps, who is a cavalry colonel with no air experience, doesn't know anything about me. At least he is a gentleman. He gives me a decent welcome and is anxious to know how long it will take me to teach him to fly. This colonel is in no hurry about my status, tells me to report to his office tomorrow and he will have someone drive me out to the new field where I understand they have one Curtiss Jenny with a Curtiss engine of uncertain ability.

Hicks Field, later to be known as Taliaferro Field, was approximately seventeen miles out of Fort Worth. It was a flat piece of land, like all of Texas, the difference being there were a few small buildings for officers' quarters, with four large structures for hangars if planes were available. At one end was a large tent, like those used in a circus, for a cook place and dining hall. Everything was completely new, even down to the personnel. The only flyers with any experience were the Canadian instructors, and four former RFC officers who were brought back via Canada by request of General Mitchell. All were in American uniforms with the rank of major, which was the rank promised all officers who were transferred with the rank of captain from the RFC. So I naturally expected my commission, when it did come through, would be as a major. I reported to Twenty-second Squadron, which was commanded by Lieutenant

Garland Powell, with Lieutenant Frederick Clapp as adjutant, two wonderful chaps with several cadets and one plane to train said cadets and complete a squadron.

A hell of a bleak looking future, which looked like a loss of time, a loss of training when flyers are so badly needed at the front. This same bunch, with one month on an RFC training field in England, could be whipped into a combat squadron. I had a lousy dinner at the public trough, and spent the night in my bed roll on the floor of my newly assigned quarters. Sleep was impossible as my back was really giving me hell, so in the morning I had difficulty getting into my uniform. After some coffee about ten o'clock, I decided to take the Curtiss Jenny up for a look at Texas from the air. Having the boys wheel the old Jenny out, I climb in and the tin cans in the engine go off. This is a motor? Taxiing out, I yank the old crate in the air. It is a pain in the neck. Its performance is equally bad or worse than my first training ship. It just flies, with no ratio of safety, but there is all of Texas to land in, so I try a loop, a roll and a spin and all are bad, but I am having some fun trying. Why it didn't fall apart, I don't know. It didn't, so I land and have to be helped out of the ship. I am so lame and the pain in my back is terrible. Trying the floor in my quarters, I send for the doctor, who, when he arrives, is a very decent sort. He is new in service, though evidently a very efficient doctor in civilian life. He gives me something for my pain with instructions to remain quiet. This advice was unnecessary as, the way I felt, they would have to carry me out. One hour later, this kind person was back, with the news he had cleared me with the command and he personally was going to drive me to a hospital, as there was no equipment where we were to treat anyone in my condition. What my condition was, he didn't know, but I certainly needed some care. My doctor was a kindly soul and a wonderful person. What happened was no fault of his. It was the fault of too much hurry and lack of experience.

Our journey took us back to Fort Worth, out to a place called Camp Bowie, about three miles out from Fort Worth. My first glimpse of this place was a perfect picture of a prison camp. It was surrounded by barbed wire and contained many low-built frame structures, all mounted on some kind of wood so there was a clearance of about two feet between the ground and the floor of the building, where the wind could howl through and under with a vengeance. Taking me to the CO office, my good doctor finally finds someone to direct him to the officers' quarters, which is a building like all the others, only it is vacant and I am the first customer. It is beginning to get dark and cold. We find the lights, but no heat. The doctor tells me the hospital has just been completed and to climb into one of the beds, which he makes up with some blanket folded on one end, then he goes to find a nurse or a doctor. My poor doctor. He is the most unhappy man in Texas. He finds we are in a place built under contract. It has no heat in any of the buildings, there are no toilets, just the big JC galvanized can which has to be emptied every day. There is no hot water and, worst of all, there are only five doctors for over two thousand sick soldiers and only four nurses with just a few trained orderlies. All other orderlies are just newly enlisted men. Any food which I am to receive has to be carried across an open space, through the wind and weather, so it will be well cooled by the time it hits our quarters. "Damn it, Libby, I can't leave you like this. I'm a doctor, not a military man." By now, my sense of humor is coming through. At least I am inside, out of that cold wind I can hear, so I tell Doc to put a sign on the door and leave the light on and someone will find me. "Just give me a couple more blankets, and say, Doc, if you have a pint of good bourbon in your satchel, leave me that. This is a hell of a lot better than the trenches."

Covering me up with a couple more blankets, he finds an oil stove which he is afraid to light, but promises to find a nurse somewhere. He ducks out to his car and comes back with a smile on his face. "You know, this is highly unethical, but I'm going to prescribe this pint of Old Crow for you." The guy won't even take a drink with me and won't accept any money. It is a pint he had in reserve for his own needs.

For once, I open my mouth at the right time. Leaving me with the promise he will be back tomorrow, my friend heads for the cookhouse to register me in. He has no faith in the head office, as he puts it. Before they show any interest, I'll possibly be well and gone, especially if I have a little to eat. What a doctor! After the shot he had given me for my pain, and the shots I had administered for my stomach's sake thanks to him, I am not uncomfortable when two characters from the kitchen enter my quarters. True to the doctor's promise to register me in for food, these two boys have pushed through the rain at the late hour of nine o'clock with food, carried in two dish pans, one over the other in an attempt to keep my dinner warm. They have stew, coffee, bread and butter with some kind of dessert. From these boys I learn the history of my new home, which is very new but loaded with sick people and completely under-staffed. There are sick men with influenza, measles, spinal menin-gitis and pneumonia all herded together, with an average death rate of ten per day. This isn't the fault of the doctors and nurses, it is too many damned sick men with not enough help to care for or to min-ister to their needs. Included in all these patients are five cadets from the flying field, all of whom are bed patients with broken arms or legs resulting from a crash while making their solo flight. It seems the status of these cadets is not known. They're in training for their officer's commission, but how to treat them while in training is a puzzle to the officers commanding, so they throw the boys in with the enlisted men for fear of giving them a break, which might upset all army regulations. This I decide to do something about in the morning, so have my boys from the kitchen help me get the old uni-form off. I go to bed, like a fellow should, with plenty of blankets and the lights on. I resolve to help the cadets and have them moved over to the officers' ward, which may not be much of an improve-ment, for up to now I haven't seen a post doctor or nurse, and with the rain like it is, I am sure I won't until morning.

Morning didn't dawn. It just arrived with rain and wind, but my own doctor made his first call. It seems his quarters were in Fort Worth, which made it easy to see me first before going to Hicks Field. He knew all about the cadets being over in one corner of a ward, and they were under the care of a bone specialist in private practice in Fort Worth as the doctors in our hospital are medics, not bone specialists. His opinion was that if we could have them re-moved to our officers' ward, it might do wonders for their morale and they might have better attention. At least we could help each other. It would take an act of God and the CO's permission to have these fellows moved, but Doc was game. He starts for the CO's office with my assurance that these fellows are officers. They just haven't received their commissions as yet. Evidently, the cadets have been raising hell on their own, for the CO is glad to wash up the whole affair. If the doctor and I will assure him that everything is all right, he will have them moved immediately. As the doctor explained when he gave me the good news, the CO was relieved to transfer the responsibility to someone else. He had been on the hot seat ever since the boys arrived. With all his other troubles, relief from any source was welcomed.

With new life in our quarters came a doctor and nurse. When seeing me for the first time, they inquired how long I had been a patient. They showed no surprise when I informed then I was there when they built the joint; I was just waiting for the rain to stop. The two who were hurt real bad were Biddle and Read of Philadelphia. Both were badly broken up and needed real care in the nursing department, which they had not been getting. All were extremely grateful to be moved into officers' quarters, although to me it was doubtful if the change was such a vast improvement.

Read had a tube in his throat from the outside, which had to be cleared every so often to keep him breathing. As both his arms were broken, this little matter of life and death had to be performed by someone other than himself. We worked up to where we were assigned an orderly, who was supposed to be constantly on the job, and a nurse supposedly to visit us twice a day. This schedule was never made. With me the only one in our group having two good hands and feet, although also a weak back and an unquestionable weak head, I took on both duties. The only way Read could attract attention when he was choking to death was to kick on the wall with his one good foot. I would then struggle like hell to get out of bed and over to him to remove the tube so the poor devil could breathe. My cadets were five good game boys who had been pushed too fast in training on some bum ship. They were the kind of Americans I would have liked to have taken to the front under the RFC command and flying RFC ships. Here were five young potential pilots cracked up, without a decent chance, and no one appears to give a damn. It is my fifth day. The dead are being hauled out one by one,

with the parents of the boys raising hell continually. Parents are trying to take their boys out to private hospitals, only the army won't
release them while they are alive. Only when a boy is dead can a
parent claim the body. It is a horrible thing to see happen. Fellows
dying like flies. Thousands of miles from the front, just dying through
carelessness and inefficiency. Were their sons dying of wounds or
exposure in battle, no parent would feel quite so bad, but dying this
way isn't any part of a war. It's murder!

Today my doctor brought a specialist with him, with the hope
he can do something to relieve my pain and help me to get in condition so I can go back to the front. To get out of this mess and back
to France is all I ask. Back with my friends. Anywhere but here. The
specialist is an ear, eye and nose doctor from Kansas and is newly
commissioned a captain. He is very sincere, with a desire to help,
which is what I need — help!

After a long examination, he promises me nothing, except that
he feels taking my tonsils out may be the answer as my neck is now
completely stiff. There is a chance that by removing my tonsils, it
may improve my condition. God, I am willing to try anything if I can
relieve the pain. So, I ask when he wants to operate and we agree on
the next day. He is going to make arrangements at a private hospital
in Fort Worth where there are real accommodations, all at the government's expense. How he is going to wangle this little deal, I
don't know, but it is okay with me. I hope for results. Picking me up
in his car, he drives me to the hospital about four P.M., where the
doctor has arranged a private room and is going to operate at eight
o'clock in the morning. I have insisted on gas as an anesthesia, having a past experience with ether, which made me deathly ill, but
there is no gas, so ether it is — anything to get the job done. My final instructions are to eat a light dinner, get a good night's rest, operation at eight, then back to the officers' ward at four in the
afternoon.

Following my instructions, I have a light dinner and retire early
in a decent bed, hoping for a decent rest. Possibly because of my
comfortable bed or change from usual routine, I fall asleep with no
difficulty. Then the door facing my bed opens slowly and wide, and
in walks death in the proverbial long black robe with the hood over

the skull and the ghastly appearance which we have seen in many horror pictures. This apparition walks across the room to the side of my bed and falls across my legs. It is so real that I jump in my sleep, causing great pain in my back. I let out a yell which brings a nurse to my room quick. This dream or vision or what-have-you was so ghastly, so frightening, that I don't tell the nurse, just allow her to think the pain caused me to wake up. It is six-thirty and my operation is listed for eight, so I have time to shave and think. Was that just a bad dream or a warning not to have the operation? This is something to think about. I have been assured that the removal of my tonsils may help. It seems like the only thing that might get me well quick, so I can go back to the front. To hell with my ghost, only I won't tell my doctor.

There is nothing to the wild dream, for I am still alive and on my way back to our officers' ward. I tell my doctor all about my affair with Mr. Ghost. It is well I didn't tell him before he operated, for he very firmly says there would have been no operation. So it is over. All I have to do is improve. The only joker: he is disappointed that the tonsils were firm and sound with no imperfections. The guy is honest. He is afraid my tonsils were not the answer. Anyway, they're gone. All I can do is hope. At least my doctor tried. He was also hoping.

After one night in a real hospital, our quarters are more than miserable. More sick soldiers are brought in every day until there are well over two thousand real sick boys. With the worst conditions for doctors and nurses to work in. With the rain and mud increasing along with the death rate.

On my ninth day, the CO office sends for me. An investigator is here from Washington in response to all the complaints filed by the parents of dead sons. His first question to me is: How does this hospital compare with hospitals overseas? It seems I am the only person in said hospital who has been out of the country, so he decides on me to answer his question. I assure the gentleman that, when a big push was on in France, the casualty clearing stations near the lines were better than Camp Bowie even on a rainy day. I am taken back to quarters expecting to be shot and perfectly willing, only it doesn't happen that way. By twelve o'clock the following day, I am given orders for transfer to Army and Navy Hospital, Hot Springs, Arkansas, by order of Washington. They want me out of Bowie and I'm glad. No one knows what kind of a place the Army and Navy Hospital is, only that it is old and that the waters have a curative power. This may be my answer, especially the hot water, as our present death trap doesn't have hot water, along with the other things they don't have.

I find the town of Hot Springs strictly a resort town, where the boys and girls from New York and other large cities that can afford the traffic come to play and bathe for two or three months from January through March. My future home is on top of a hill, almost in the center of town, with a climb of ninety steps to reach the entrance. It is a large old fashioned frame structure, which looks very comfortable in comparison with my recent hospital. It is commanded by a regular army colonel of the Medical Corps and is well staffed with nurses and orderlies and has a very exclusive officers' quarters. Here, each officer has a large separate room, with a joint mess together, with colored cook and waiter. In fact, this is the first real officers' mess I have seen since leaving the RFC. The officers' quarters have twenty rooms, with one nurse and orderly on duty twenty-four hours. On my arrival, I made the seventh officer in quarters that could easily care for forty with only two in a room, so different from Camp Bowie. Certainly someone in Washington did me a favor. It must have been the surgeon general's office. Here at one of the finest military hospitals in the world, I am given every known treatment by a fine staff, with no favorable results. The news from the Western Front where my old squadrons were, and where I had spent most of two years, was all bad. The RFC boys were getting some better ships, but their losses were terrible. Practically all of my old friends had gone west or were out of service, either wounded or prisoners of war.

One bright spot: on Christmas Eve, I received a wire from my old home town, signed by our mayor, together with signatures of twenty-five of my best friends, wishing me a speedy recovery and a quick trip home. Among them was my old friend Guy Galbrieth, who got me the job with Tom Aikens at Flagstaff, Arizona. It was a great boost to be remembered by this bunch of fellows whom I had known the greater part of my life. But my condition is becoming slowly worse, which does away with any trip home. As I can't go home, my big brother comes to visit me, which is wonderful, only I am limited in the time I can spend with him. Despite this he sticks around for a week and we do as much visiting as possible. What a pal he is to a crazy young brother.

This Christmas, my fourth in uniform, I shall have Christmas dinner with six fellow American officers. Last Christmas I had dinner at the Savoy Hotel with Bill Thaw and Bert Hall. The year before dinner in France with my old motor unit, and my first Christmas in uniform was in Toronto Exposition Park with my motor unit. Where I shall spend my fifth, I wonder. To be crippled and alive is better than average. Only time will tell how much better.

Christmas dinner, 1917, has been wonderful. Cooked by a typical Southern mammy, the food is plentiful and excellent. You wish it could be shared by some of the boys in the trenches. While the food was wonderful, the liquid refreshments were dry, very dry. Milk, tea or coffee, which is supposedly going to be America's favorite drink for the future. As of January first, anything containing alcohol is taboo for servicemen. Not even the elite who come to eat may partake of alcoholic beverage. Swell country we took from the Indians.

29

New York to See a Great Specialist —
The Auctioning of the First American
Colors to Cross the German Lines

Here, at the start of America entering the war, they take alcohol as no good for the boys or girls. Wait until a few of them get their feet wet in France — if they ever do. It wouldn't surprise me to see the entire outfit desert to the British Army where rum is a steady diet to a fighting man. And what a diet. If I had any brains, I would quit trying to return to France, desert and start a still of white mule in the Ozarks or the Blue Ridge Mountains of Virginia and let the revenuers hunt me. Washington won't be able to fight the war and keep the stills all shut down at the same time. My guess is that the war will be won by our politicians, drinking the product from the still they voted to shut down. Life will go on the same, only worse.

It is March and news from the front is bad, especially from my old hunting ground, Arras, Cambrai, Douai, the Somme front, where my old squadrons are catching hell from the Heinie while I am worse than ever, only hoping for a miracle. I want a miracle but have a break in the monotony when a first lieutenant by the name of William Hoffman Miller is assigned to our hospital as a patient. I have been enjoying a room by myself when I am asked if I would object to a roommate. I am quick to insist that he be placed in my room as this boy is from the flying corps. We at least have something in common. When he is deposited in my room, he is a sight to behold. He had recently landed with ship afire, and in place of saving his own skin he pulls the observer out of the flames, which causes him to lose a couple of fingers from one hand and to have his features all messed up with burns but nevertheless saves his observer's life. For all of this, he is ignored by Washington. The best he winds up with is a hospital room and a chance to live. No word of congratulation, or citation well deserved, just a chance to get well. You bum, you shouldn't have gotten afire in the first place. These commanding officers are sure students of human nature, I don't think. I have finally met one of my countrymen I can talk to. The boy has guts and understanding with a suave air that says do your worst, I can take it. He is my kind of folks. We are friends from the start and will always remain friends without a lot of promises or conversation.

Through my friendship with this boy, my stay in the hospital was made much easier, as with him I could talk about the front and my old crowd with a perfect understanding. He was always interested. I would have liked to have Bill with me in a fighter squadron. He would have been one hell of a fighter pilot, a fellow one could depend on when the going became rough.

August has arrived and my pain is no better. This wonderful hospital staff of Army and Navy have tried everything they know. The waters have only soothed my stiff back temporarily, so I have been given six months sick leave to go to New York at my own expense to see the great specialist, Dr. Joseph Frankel, who my cousin Frank Dame feels can help or at least diagnose my trouble. Thanks to my cousin, an appointment is made and I see the great man. Here I learn I am through, that I have spondylitis deformens of the spine, which will cause me agony for years and then become ankylosed for the rest of my life. My days of flying are over. It is just a question of time what happens and how fast. My dream of going back to the front is only a dream. I am finished, washed up — that is his opinion, not mine. I may fool the doctor. At least I shall try.

New York is a madhouse, people going everywhere in a hurry. The theaters are full, and during intermission there is a Liberty Loan drive to raise money for the war effort, which is quite true of every gathering. Financially, the war has come to New York. My friend Bob Roberts, who went overseas in my old outfit, the motor transport, has turned hero, has a promoter and has published a book called *The Flying Fighter*. I think the promoter got most of the money, because Bob has a rich dame on the hook, which shows what a uniform can do. One real bright spot: my good friend Getz Rice has returned from the front and is in a show with Blanch Bates and real good. He is a fellow who deserves the best.

I have turned my streamers of the American flag over to the Aero Club of America to auction off on a Liberty Loan Drive at Carnegie Hall. This auction wasn't intended by me as a stunt for publicity. In fact, I had a feeling of embarrassment, as these streamers had been part of my plane for many, many hours of combat service. Along with and in the same formation with these streamers had flown many of the RFC's best, both in Forty-third and Twenty-fifth Squadrons. They had become a part of me. They were with me in many a battle, some of which we lost, some of which we won, but we always came back together. All of this caused me to hesitate when I was asked to allow the streamers to be auctioned. Only the assurance of the Aero Club president, Mr. Alan R. Hawley, that it was the thing to do to help the Liberty Loan drive and was for the good of humanity convinced me of its merit. My feelings were best described by a *New York Tribune* writer, his name I don't know. To this writer I have always been grateful. In a story published in the *Tribune*, he wrote: "A timid young officer with a tattered thing in his hand mounted the Liberty Theater platform yesterday afternoon, and while he stood there, cheeks burning with embarrassed red, and eyes looking straight down his nose, a crowd that the moment before had gaped and grinned and jostled, after one slow stare with a sudden passion, stormed toward him. They rolled forward in a tumult of noise, men and women with welcome in their voices and tears in their eyes. Not Fifth Avenue sightseers cheering a show, but a people greeting their own hero. Then a girl reached out and over the crowd, caught hold of the tattered thing, held it hard and with swimming eyes raised it to her lips. The voices stopped and the air was silent as a prayer. The first American flag to fly over the German lines, in the hands of the aviator who carried it there, had come back to New York to be baptized with tears and kisses of a motley New York throng. Those hundreds sought to grasp the precious stripes of red and white and to shake the hand of Captain Frederick Libby. This torn old thing amid all the bright flags of Fifth Avenue was a holy banner. And so the procession passed along, touching its rags as though becoming a sacrament. Some touched it lightly, some shook it as if it were a paw. The women kissed it, the soldiers saluted it. While Captain Libby still tried to hide behind it with the shame that every real hero seems to have for his own valor."

The auction is October seventeenth and raises $3,250,000. On the twentieth, I'm leaving New York for one of my very favorite spots, Imperial Valley, California. The weather in New York is turning cold and my doctor advises a warm climate, so I am away to California. Bob Roberts wants to go with me. He is fed up with the big city. I think the promoters have made a sucker out of him, which is par for the course in this town. With anyone in uniform, these parasites do real well. I shall never forget Guy Empey and my family in Boston. I have often wondered how much the promoter let Mr. Empey have out of his book *Over the Top*. It was one of the first war books published, but my guess is that Brother Empey probably finished owing the promoter.

Our trip to California was the usual slow and miserable journey, thanks to government supervision. Time means nothing to first class trains. The only ones that seem to go through are the troop trains and even they are doubtful. We finally arrived at San Diego, where everyone is wearing a flu mask. It seems there is an epidemic of influenza, so waitresses and all public servants are wearing masks to protect themselves as well as the public. I'm feeling worse than ever. I feel like hell, so to a hotel for a night's rest before taking the stage to Imperial Valley.

I hit the bed real sick with a chill, so Bob goes looking for the only remedy we know, a pint of bourbon. The guy finds a doctor who gives him a prescription for a pint of Four Roses, which helps some, but in the morning I know that Old Flu has caught up with me. The hospitals are not taking flu patients. They are either nursed at home or sent to a "pest house" on the outskirts of the city. This is not for me, so we call a cab. I dress and am driven to the St. Joseph Hospital, where I walk in and demand a room and a doctor at once. Being in uniform, I get away with it. I am put to bed in a private room and a doctor is called. It's a cinch. I'm a beautiful flu patient and the hospital wants me to leave. Here my doctor goes to bat, saying that I am too sick to be moved and must have a special nurse immediately, and the fight for my life begins. On the night of the crisis where I either go over the hill or remain around, with a nurse fighting a strong battle to pull me through, I am conscious of a lot of whistles blowing, cans rattling and a continuous noise like a New Year's celebration. I am too sick to mind, but my nurse goes to the front office to see what is happening. In a voice filled with emotion, she tells me it's the Armistice. What an awful way to end the war, flat on my back, after more than four years of service, with the big show ended. I am in a room far away from all of my comrades. I have overheard whispers, which indicate that they expect to carry me out — feet first. It seems I'm the only one who doesn't believe their whispers. I just couldn't die in this bed this way. True, it might be better than going down in flames on the last day of war, so I pass out or go to sleep. In the morning I am very weak, with no fever and not quite sure about the noises, but my nurse assures me there is an Armistice and that I am out of danger. The war is over! I am damned weak, but with tomorrow will start to get up. All I need, my doctor says, is rest and quiet where it is warm and sunny.

My first move, when out of the hospital, is to wire my resignation to Washington, D.C. I want out of this man's army fast as possible. With the wire off of my mind, I catch a stage for Imperial Valley, to the town of Calexico, where before the war I had many friends, sincere friends like the Wylie family, my old buddy Chuck Stanton, the Andersons, the Litzenberg boys and others too numerous to mention. Surely some of these kindly people will be there to welcome me. My stage is the same big Packard, with the same driver who brought me from Imperial Valley over three years ago, when I started my trip to someplace, anyplace, Tahiti preferred, and ended up in a war. The driver remembers me and, possibly because of the uniform, I have the seat in front with him where one is more comfortable and can enjoy the luxury of a delightful ride through the mountains to Imperial Valley. With a stop for lunch and a chance to relax, the trip is most enjoyable.

The day I landed in the hospital, Bob Roberts left for Imperial

Valley to meet my friends, as there was no reason for him to wait in San Diego for my demise or recovery. So, when we pull into the stage depot in El Centro, Bob with a crowd of my old friends is on hand to welcome me home. How they found out I was coming on this particular stage, I don't inquire. It is sufficient they are there. The war is over and everyone is in high glee. I am weak but happy. Climbing into a new Packard owned by Paul Datto, one of the famous family of Dattos, we go to Calexico and to the mayor's house which Bob has been calling home. I find one of the Anderson girls married to the mayor of Calexico, Casey Abbott, a real swell person in any country. Here at Casey's home we are welcomed in a fashion only possible in a valley of the nicest and most friendly people on earth. I have returned to the right spot, warmth, beautiful sunshine and, most of all, real friendship. Why I went in search of something other than this, I will never know. Here I settle down to freedom and rest, mentally and physically, with no plans for the future. All this could wait. I am still a young man in years, but really old in experience from my constant association with older people in my very young days.

While waiting for an answer to my wire of resignation to the War Department, I have nothing to do except visit with my old friends and enjoy the beautiful climate. I found my old pal Chuck Stanton and his lovely wife, together with Mother and Dad Stanton, who were like my own folks. The Lyons boys were back from service. My Chinese friend, Big Foot, was in China on a trip. My old pal Clint Wylie and family had moved to Los Angeles, as had Sam and Bonnie Jones. The Litzenberg boys were still around, as were most of my old friends, and with the help of good sunshine I was feeling better each day. With no results from the War Department, I decided to shoot another wire of resignation. The first one they evidently threw in the waste basket. What I am going to do, I don't know, but I want to be free to do it, if only selling pencils on the corner.

30

A Free Man, Lucky Beyond Belief

M Y FRIEND NORMAN READ WAS TRUE TO HIS PROMISE, took himself a hunting trip, then to Alaska and a mining expedition. Our mutual friend the great major couldn't do anything, as we were both men without a country. Even if we did cable our acceptance of a commission from London, one had to swear allegiance before becoming a qualified officer. This my friend did not do, so he was a free man.

Today I am also a free man, for my order for a discharge came through. I received the sixty dollars for a suit of clothes and could have had transportation back to London from whence I came, but this would have been quite a touch. I felt sorry to hit the exchequer in Washington too hard after a great war, so I settled for the sixty and freedom. The battle to kill is over. The great war is ended. Democracy, the thing we were told would be preserved by victory, is safe. What our enemies were fighting about, I don't know, but they put up a hell of a battle over something.

This war to end all wars is over. Everyone shall live in peace and love each other, even our recent enemies. I was never mad at them anyway. A fellow had to fight to survive. Like myself, hundreds of flyers will be turned loose from the Signal Corps with the usual sixty bucks and become Mr. So-and-So. Whatever their rank, they will never be given the courtesy of the honorary rank which they acquired through service and poor training. They are through as far as the War Department is concerned, unless they are badly needed again. There will be no recognition of a job well done unless some individual flyer has a politician under his obligation. Then he may be given some cross not made of wood.

The brass hats of our War Department have no time for the multitudes who by their service and loyalty keep the great men secure in their jobs. For instance, I had occasion to write the American War Department to try and ascertain the address of a fellow officer, Captain Chapman, military attaché to Ambassador Page. I received my letter and envelope back — they were too tired to throw it in the waste basket — together with a mimeographed piece of cheap paper containing several paragraphs, one of which they checked, stating if I would give them the officer's address and serial number, and one dollar in a money order or cashier's check, they would take a look.

The same day, I wrote the British Air Ministry for the name and address of a fellow officer of the old Royal Flying Corps. From them, I received a beautiful letter on Air Ministry stationery, with a reference number in the event I needed any other information, with the name of my officer and, in addition, my complete service record with the RFC for the two years. Most surprising of all came the information (and I am quoting the exact words) I am "permitted to retain the honorary rank of Captain in the RFC on joining the American Flying Corps." And the letter was addressed "Captain F. Libby, M.C." Quite a difference in protocol. The letter was signed "Your obedient servant. . . ."

True, I have been lucky beyond belief. On what started out to be a pleasure trip to see the world, I finished up in a shooting war from September 2, 1914, to September 30, 1917. Now that the war is past history, I shall recall some of the things of which I am the proudest. To have been a participant with the Canadians for my first year of service and the Royal Flying Corps through 1916 and 1917 on active duty is a memory in itself. One thing of which I am extremely proud and that gave me the greatest satisfaction happened in Eleven Squadron in 1916 under the command of Major Hubbard, when I came up with the original idea of a buttstock for the Lewis machine gun. It was with Major Hubbard's permission that the buttstock was carved out of a piece of wood by Number Eleven's gunnery sergeant and was first tried out by Captain Price and me on our

F.E.2b. With the buttstock as an addition to the Lewis, I could hold the gun steady with my shoulder, leaving the left hand free, where before it required both hands. There was no publicity or hot air about this improvement, as it was done on active service in the line of self-preservation for myself and my pilot. The absolute need for the buttstock was proven by the fact that in a very short time it was standard equipment in our squadron, as well as other squadrons of the RFC. I can safely say that the buttstock was the greatest improvement that happened to the Lewis gun from a gunner's standpoint except the increase of the ammunition drum from forty-seven rounds to ninety-seven. This was done by the Lewis factory and made it a deadly weapon in the hands of a trained man. I am naturally proud of my Military Cross, awarded me by His Majesty King George the Fifth in the late summer of 1916, the citation reading "For conspicuous gallantry while engaging and destroying enemy aircraft." The actual decoration I did not receive until December 13, 1916, at Buckingham Palace, where I was personally decorated by His Majesty. I was unquestionably the first American during the year 1916 to be so honored and to be credited with more enemy planes destroyed than any American in any service on the Western Front.

It was in August of 1916 that I was qualified and awarded the observer's wing. Of this wing I am prouder than of the pilot's wings, which I qualified for on March 4, 1917, in England before returning to active service in France on March 7, 1917. My observer's wing was earned the hard way, on active service in France through a probation service, where the observer was the pilot's only protection in the F.E.2b. He also did the photography, bomb dropping and reconnaissance.

On March 7, 1917, when I returned to France as a full fledged pilot after ten hours solo, I had the good luck to be assigned to Forty-third Squadron, under the command of Major Sholto-Douglas. Here I served under both Major Douglas and Major Dore, two of the RFC's finest. And in the summer of 1917 I was promoted to flight commander with the rank of captain and transferred to Twenty-fifth Squadron. It was during the spring of 1917, shortly after America entered the war, that I was given an American flag by a fellow officer of Forty-third Squadron, which, at the suggestion of Major Dore, I used as streamers, designating leadership of my flight. This I did with no thought of a stunt or being first with anything. While America had declared war, there were no signs of action by it. So my major thought the American streamers going over the line would show the Hun some Americans were there and actively joined in war against them. For months before I returned to the United States, before leaving the front on September 13, 1917, these American streamers crossed the German lines every day, weather permitting. They were the first American colors to cross the German line or see action, long before any American flyers were near the front.

During those months, the streamers took an awful beating from the wind, the castor oil from my rotary engine and weather in general, but the colors still remained visible. It is nice to think that these streamers and Lee White's gift of Bairnsfather's Old Bill for mascot might have contributed to my good luck, because they started together and were always transferred to every plane I flew during a period of several months.

As a pilot, I went through the Somme, Arras and Messines battles, having my share of dogfighting, sometimes winning, sometimes losing, but always returning to go back another day. We were in constant action, always back of the German lines. I had my share of victories but always tried to reserve enough petrol and ammunition to see me back across our line, and there were many times this would not have been possible were it not for some one of our scouts coming to my assistance. A stiff head wind and a group of enemies between a fellow and his own trench would upset the best calculated plan.

The Hun was always tough, with a natural advantage of fighting always on his own side of the line. He was never a pushover. Consequently, our casualties were terrible. Out of the original members of the four fighting squadrons with whom I served during 1916 and 1917, only a few survived. To glorify oneself as a killer of your enemy, especially when it is a matter of self-preservation, isn't exactly my dish. A fellow must be a hero to do that, and I am not a hero. They are a dime a dozen and can be found selling papers or apples on most any corner. To take one's place with a group of stout fellows, to fight and carry on and have the respect of your fellow officers, is more gratifying than words can describe.

Of my record, I am very proud. It was made under tough conditions where the going was rough, with a flying group of real sportsmen, who were always on the offensive, many times with inferior ships. The consolidation of the Royal Naval Air Service and the Royal Flying Corps into the Royal Air Force on April 1, 1918, gave the RAF a wonderful group of fighting men, the like of which the world has never known. The new RAF command didn't only inherit the living personnel but also a tradition handed over by these two great flying groups, a record of courage, accomplishment and leadership not equaled by any country in the world. It is a priceless heritage. Men whose experience and leadership were responsible for the great success of the RFC in World War I included: Major Sholto-Douglas, Major Stanley Dore, Captain Harold Balfour, Captain Stephen Price, Captain Frank Courtney, Major Hubbard, Captain Sam Collier, Major Ross Hume, Major Guest and many, many others, all great leaders and top pilots.

May the war which was fought to end all wars stay ended, and their service never again be necessary. The war is over, the adjustment period is on, everyone loves everyone, so they say.

What will happen to me is immaterial, irrelevant and nonconsequential, as the attorneys say, but they don't always know, no more than do the doctors who say I'm through. Whatever it is, it will involve action of some type. Just to sit still and wait for the axe to fall is not for me. Yet what the future holds won't frighten me much, as, many a time on my way over to engage the enemy in do or die, I used to think that if the day ever came and I am a civilian again, the world will be my oyster.

As the French have been saying for years, it is now "après la guerre."

AU REVOIR

Acknowledgments

I OWE MANY A DEBT OF GRATITUDE. There is Sergeant Chapman of Twenty-third Squadron. He was an inspiration at all times. My old major Red Harris of my motor unit, whose advice and counsel were always helpful. Lieutenant Hicks of Twenty-third, my first pilot in combat. Had it not been for his skill we would never have survived.

Then my good friend and pilot, Captain Price, to whom I owe so much. His friendship, his grin and courage in and under all conditions are things I shall always remember. In Eleven Squadron, Major Hubbard gave Captain Price and me all the support and help necessary in introducing the buttstock for the Lewis machine gun. It was under his command that I received my observer wing and my Military Cross. Also, the sergeant of Eleven Squadron who made the buttstock helped save many lives many times.

Then there is Albert Ball, the little fellow with the little Nieuport to whom I and many others owe our lives. His ability to be at the right spot at the right time when most needed will never be forgotten.

At Forty-third Squadron I am grateful to majors Sholto-Douglas and Stanley Dore, two outstanding commanding officers and aviators whose understanding of what makes a flyer tick was responsible for our success. To have served under their command was an honor and a privilege. Also there are Captain Collier and Captain Balfour, two of Forty-third's stoutest pilots, and good friend Babe Cattell, who gave me my American flag streamers and a beautiful pair of officer's boots. The courage of this boy was an inspiration to all of us. Him, I shall always admire.

Our adjutant at Forty-third, Perdie, made our life brighter just with the knowledge that he was our friend — "Good old Perdie."

At Twenty-fifth Squadron my pal Captain James Fitz-Morris,

flight commander and pilot, was always with a fellow when the chips were down. This boy's ability in a dogfight was something to see and remember. And then there are the men who receive no great recognition, the ground crews that keep the planes flying. Never did they let any of us down. Anything that happened after leaving the ground was never the fault or due to the neglect of our ground crews but always something over which they had no control.

The sincerity and loyalty of this group of fellows will remain strong in my memory, and I'm sure all flyers of the RFC echo my sentiment.

Afterword

My grandfather was quite a man, whom I adored and admired for his courage and love of life. I have never met anyone who so truly embraced life and all its experiences. Not much interfered with his appetite for adventure. Living on different coasts, we did not see each other often, but when we did he completely charmed me. My first memory of him was of his visit to New York. As I watched him hobble down the airfield toward us, it was love at first sight. Here was my hero, of whom I had heard so much. I remember sitting on his lap and him calling me "princess." If I was his princess, then he was my prince. When I was born, he changed the celebration of his birthday to mine.

My family and all who loved him called my grandfather Cap. Growing up, I heard many wonderful family stories about him, and I had the pleasure of living with my grandparents for a short time in 1962 when I first came to California. Of my many memories, these are but a few:

Cap spoke of the devastation of World War I and his experiences in the war. I remember him telling, with sadness, of returning to the officers' mess after a day's sorties to find it nearly empty of the familiar faces that had been there in the morning, with new men filing in to replace the missing. Many of those absent faces belonged to dear friends who would never return. When he began flying for the Royal Flying Corps, most of his comrades were in their early twenties. Before he left the front, the British were bringing in boys in their teens. I've read that, at the time when Cap logged his three hundred fifty combat hours, the average lifespan of a flier was about ten hours. The young men putting their lives on the line had to be truly courageous.

I remember Cap's immense respect for the British. He spoke of

World War I as a war of honor, one that was very personal, as the combatants in the air seemed to know many of their enemy intimately and held some in great respect. Cap recounted how, when the German ace Oswald Boelcke was shot down, pilots from the RFC flew over enemy lines and, to honor him, dropped a wreath over his home squadron.

Back in the United States and out of the air service, my grandfather met my grandmother, Caroline Von Stein, whom he called Peg. Cap was such a romantic that I wouldn't be surprised if he nicknamed her Peg after the song "Peg o' My Heart." Yes, she was of German heritage. They met in a train station. At the time, she was on her way to Chicago to marry a famous cardiac surgeon whom she had met while in the Red Cross. But once Peg and Cap crossed paths, prior plans went awry. Three weeks later they were married, a union that lasted, with mutual adoration, until their deaths. This was in the Gay Twenties, and Peg was no stranger to gaiety. Granddad had given her a thousand dollars to buy herself an engagement ring. She spent sixty dollars on the ring and the remainder she spent on their engagement party.

To me, they seemed destined to marry each other. Caroline was born in El Paso, Texas, to a well-to-do family. At sixteen she wed an American who owned a ranch in Chihuahua, Mexico. While living there she had many encounters with the notorious bandit and revolutionary Pancho Villa, who would occasionally stop by their ranch to borrow livestock and supplies. Of course, no replacement or return was ever expected. After her divorce from her first husband she returned to the States, and during World War I she was active in the American Red Cross. Before meeting Granddad, she adopted her brother's two daughters, her nieces Madeline and Merle, whose mother had died of influenza during the infamous "Spanish flu" epidemic that was responsible both for my grandmother joining the Red Cross and for the overflow of patients in the army hospitals in Texas. Madeline was my mother.

Two years after their marriage, Peg confessed to Fred that she had failed to mention her two adopted girls, aged twelve and ten, who were living in a convent in Texas. Though astonished, my grandfather declared without hesitation, "Well, what the hell are they doing in a convent? Bring them here!" From then on, Madeline and Merle lived with Peg and Granddad.

My mother told me how my grandfather would soak in a bathtub of iodine to relieve the pain from his war injuries. Those injuries, combined with a crippling arthritis, made my grandfather's spine fuse and left him hunched over. He was not yet thirty years old when his doctors predicted he wouldn't live past forty, owing to the compression of his lungs and other internal organs. However, not for one minute did this stop Captain Libby in his pursuit of life.

My mother had stories of an alternative use for that bathtub when Cap was not soaking in it, which was to brew gin and beer. My grandparents would store the contraband in the basement. One time someone had not properly corked the beer and, on a very hot summer day, one bottle after another exploded, flooding the basement and giving the house the odor of a speakeasy. Doubtless this memory was all the stronger for my mother because she and her sister were responsible for cleaning up the mess.

Curiously, I never saw my granddad drive a car and never heard of him owning one. He went everywhere in a taxicab. For years he would rely on the same driver, who would come at his every call. Whether his spinal injuries played a part in this my parents couldn't say, but to their knowledge Cap had never driven a car, much less a truck, since the war. As for me, I wonder whether this was a delayed reaction to his first driving experience, the Canadian adventure with the Ford and the pillars, or whether he just decided that breaking horses and flying planes were less risky than driving a car.

Following the war, Cap worked in the oil industry as a wildcatter. Oil, as you may recall, was what brought him into the war in the first place. Afterward, he still wanted to be a millionaire. He became well known as an oil engineer and traveled the world consulting for companies, including Richfield and Union Oil, and prospectors desirous of tapping his knowledge and ability to locate oil. He founded the Eastern Oil Company and struck it rich with his own wells. He made his millions, but retire young he did not. He founded Western Air Express, which began as a cargo airline and became a commercial carrier. It was later sold to Western Airlines. Later in his life he drilled wells in Playa del Rey, near the Hughes Aircraft Company, and lost everything. As it turned out, the oil was there, but deeper than his capital could take his drill. He spent the remainder of his life writing his memoirs, short stories, and screenplays and endeavoring to set up another wildcat oil operation. He was completing the editing of his memoirs when he passed away.

When he was sixty-five, to his delight, the Air Force presented him with the honor of flying in a supersonic jet with a top test pilot in celebration of their fiftieth anniversary. The pilot, Captain Ivan Kincheloe, turned over the controls to granddad while in flight and Cap flew his first jet. Captain Kinchelow had flown 101 combat missions in Korea and set the world's altitude record in the X2, the forerunner of the X15. Kincheloe, who was thirty at the time, had just been selected to fly into outer space the following year, but unfortunately, before he could accomplish that feat, he was killed soon after takeoff on a test run at Edwards Air Force Base.

My grandfather died on January 9, 1970, at the ripe old age of 78. Despite the prognostications of doctors, he lived a long and active life that spanned aeronautical history from what he humorously calls in his memoir the jet-propelled flight of an antelope to the age of jet planes and space travel. This cowboy turned World War I ace lived to witness the American landing on the moon. My grandfather was a romantic and a character. He stepped into the living of life with little forethought other than to enjoy and test the adventure of it, much the way he roped that antelope as a young boy. But true to his cowboy heritage, where a man's word and handshake were all there was and his honor was never to be forfeit, he lived with the consequences of his actions honorably and most admirably.

Sally Ann Marsh